$34.50

Shop floor bargaining and the state

Shop floor bargaining and the state

Historical and comparative perspectives

edited by
STEVEN TOLLIDAY
and
JONATHAN ZEITLIN

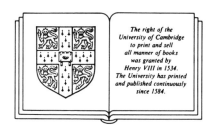

The right of the
University of Cambridge
to print and sell
all manner of books
was granted by
Henry VIII in 1534.
The University has printed
and published continuously
since 1584.

CAMBRIDGE UNIVERSITY PRESS

Cambridge
London   New York   New Rochelle
Melbourne   Sydney

Published by the Press Syndicate of the University of Cambridge
The Pitt Building, Trumpington Street, Cambridge CB2 IRP
32 East 57th Street, New York, NY 10022, USA
10 Stamford Road, Oakleigh, Melbourne 3166, Australia

First published 1985

Printed in Great Britain at the University Press, Cambridge

Library of Congress catalogue card number: 84–22943

British Library cataloguing in publication data

Tolliday, Steven
Shop floor bargaining and the state : historical
and comparative perspectives.
1. Shop stewards   2. Industrial relations
I. Title   II. Zeitlin, Jonathan
331.87'33   HD6490.S5

ISBN 0 521 26711 0

WV

Contents

List of contributors

STEVEN TOLLIDAY is a Fellow in the Research Centre, King's College, Cambridge

JONATHAN ZEITLIN is a Fellow in the Research Centre, King's College, Cambridge

ALASTAIR REID is a Fellow of Girton College, Cambridge

NOEL WHITESIDE is a Lecturer in the Department of Social Administration, University of Bristol

HOWELL HARRIS is a Lecturer in the Department of History, University of Durham

GIOVANNI CONTINI is a Fellow in the Research Centre, King's College, Cambridge

BRYN JONES is a Lecturer in the School of Humanities and Social Sciences, University of Bath

Acknowledgments

This book is based on the proceedings of a conference held by the Research Centre project on 'Shop Floor Bargaining, Job Control and National Economic Performance' at King's College, Cambridge in September 1982. The editors are grateful to the managers of the King's College Research Centre for funding this project; to the Nuffield Foundation for help with conference expenses; to the other participants and paper-givers for stimulating discussions; and to Joseph Melling, Paul Worm and Hazel Clark for valuable advice and organisational assistance.

1

Shop floor bargaining and the state: a contradictory relationship*

JONATHAN ZEITLIN

I

There are few aspects of modern politics whose interpretation is so hotly contested as the uneasy relationship between trade unions and the state. Disagreement among the major theoretical paradigms extends well beyond the assessment of past trends and future prospects to surround with controversy the definition of the interests, goals, and even identities of the contending parties. Where some observers discern the growing involvement of trade unions and employers' associations in macro-economic policy formation, others emphasise instead recurrent and intractable clashes over incomes policy, public expenditure, labour law and other crucial issues. At a deeper level, where liberals see a neutral state's defence of the public weal against the selfish pressures of sectional interests, Marxists see efforts to shore up the crumbling foundations of a capitalist society whose ultimate beneficiary is the dominant class. Similarly, liberals and Marxists alike are divided among themselves as to how far trade unions should be seen as representative of working-class interests rather than as bureaucratic organisations involved in unequal compromises with employers and the state which bring them into periodic conflict with a more militant rank and file.

But whatever their views on the class nature of the liberal-democratic state or on the representative character of trade unions, a surprising consensus appears to exist among analysts from widely different theoretical and ideological perspectives on the existence of an underlying antagonism between the state as economic manager and shop floor bargaining in defence of workers' material interests. Thus both liberals and Marxists have identified a deep and pervasive conflict between the job controls exercised by workers on the shop floor and the imperatives of managing a capitalist economy, especially one experiencing the difficulties of the United Kingdom. Assumptions of this kind have underlain most proposals since the mid-1960s for the reform of labour law and of the broader framework of industrial relations in Britain; and they play an important part even in current debates about the left's alternative economic strategy.[1]

The sources of such a consensus are not difficult to identify. In nearly every Western country, the end of the postwar boom has undermined fragile settlements between capital and labour and reopened long-standing controversies about the legal and political status of trade unions and collective bargaining. To confine ourselves to postwar Britain, the striking parallels and continuities in disputes over pay policy and labour law reform under Labour and Conservative governments, from the miners' strikes to the winter of discontent, from *In Place of Strife* to the Industrial Relations Act, have done much to diffuse the idea of an underlying opposition between trade unions and the state irrespective of the party in power. And, at this moment, another Conservative government has embarked on a far-reaching attempt to revise the legal framework of industrial relations in ways that call into question key rights and immunities acquired by the unions in repeated skirmishes between parliaments and the judiciary since the late-nineteenth century.[2]

Such clashes between the state and the labour movement undoubtedly constitute a central feature of modern politics. But a growing body of empirical studies of industrial relations in Britain and elsewhere – including the essays collected in this volume – point to a countervailing dimension to this relationship: they suggest that at certain moments the state has played a key role not only in overcoming employer opposition to trade unionism, but also in eroding managerial prerogatives at the workplace. Thus, recent work on the development of collective bargaining in late-nineteenth- and early-twentieth-century Britain has stressed the role of public policy in diffusing procedures of conciliation and arbitration which in certain cases diluted the individual employer's unilateral control over the utilisation of labour and capital equipment.[3] Similarly, studies of industrial relations during the two world wars – such as those presented by Alastair Reid and Steven Tolliday – have highlighted the gains, some transitory and others more durable, won by unions through bilateral bargaining with wartime government ministries. Even in so crucial an export sector as the postwar motor industry,

Tolliday's work suggests that the extension of shop floor bargaining and job control in the late 1950s and 1960s was the product not only of tight labour markets, but also of the continuing pressure on employers from both Conservative and Labour governments to avoid serious outbreaks of industrial conflict. More recently, policy makers' faith in the conflict-reducing powers of a revised 'British model of industrial relations' led them to favour the introduction of shop steward organisation to new sectors such as the docks and the public services, while state initiatives over productivity bargaining – together with the unintended consequences of incomes policies and new industrial legislation – have been seen as a major contributor to the spread of plant and company bargaining in the 1960s and 1970s.[4]

Analogous processes can be observed in the history of industrial relations in other Western countries. As Giovanni Contini shows, a quiet process of legal and political change played a key role in the revival of shop floor bargaining in Italy after the employers' crushing victory at the beginning of the 1950s; these developments bore fruit during the strike wave of 1969–70, whose challenge to managerial authority in the workplace appears to have run deeper than any other in postwar Europe, as the centre–left government restrained employer resistance, while a radical reform of labour law aided the unions to consolidate their gains. A more conscious attempt to tilt the balance of shop floor power in favour of the labour movement can be seen in the sweeping changes in labour law enacted by Swedish Social Democratic governments in the early 1970s which gave workers' representatives far reaching powers over work organisation in the factory.[5] Even in the United States, where the courts had historically opposed collective bargaining, Howell Harris shows that state support was indispensable in overcoming employer resistance to the unionisation of the mass production industries in the 1930s and 1940s. While debate continues about the constraints which the resulting system of administrative regulation ultimately imposed on union activity, Bryn Jones' comparative study of the aerospace industry in this volume suggests that, at least in certain cases, American unions are able to manipulate the complex provisions for seniority, job classification, and arbitration contained in their legally enforceable contracts to win control over manning on new technology analogous to that secured through open bargaining by their British counterparts.

This ambivalent and contradictory relationship between shop floor bargaining and the state finds little space in existing theories. Instances of government support for the extension of workplace bargaining pose evident difficulties for those who postulate an immanent conflict between trade unions and the state. To be sure, one strand of thought among both Marxists and liberals emphasises collaborative relations between trade unions and the state, and so might accord the latter a positive role in establishing the conditions for the emergence of responsible collective bargaining. But since these theorists generally see such arrangements as aimed at forestalling more radical challenges to the capitalist order, they tend to view the resulting compromises as producing new conflicts between 'incorporated' trade union officials and a rank and file more deeply committed to the defence of shop floor earnings and conditions. Hence, these theories provide little guide to situations in which state policies have enhanced the autonomy of workers' organisations and undermined managerial prerogatives in the workplace. And since their explanations are normally pitched at an abstract and general level, such theories are no more helpful in accounting for the real constraints that specific systems of legal and administrative regulation may impose on union activity under particular circumstances.

The inability of existing theories to account for the contradictory relationship between shop floor bargaining and the state revealed by empirical research arises from deep-rooted weaknesses in their basic systems of assumptions. As we shall see in greater detail, both liberalism and Marxism in their many variants regard the interests served by institutions such as collective bargaining and the state as fundamentally determined by the underlying logic of a modern market society. It is their conviction that the operation of the market and the power relations associated with it places inexorable limits on the outcomes produced by social and political institutions that leads these theories to reject in advance the possibility that state actions might result in a genuine erosion of managerial prerogatives in the workplace. The aims of this essay are first to show that it is only by abandoning these underlying assumptions that we can properly interpret the findings of empirical studies such as those contained in this volume; and second to set out some preliminary suggestions towards an alternative understanding of the relationship between shop floor bargaining and the state which they reveal.

The argument which follows takes up the problem first from the

side of shop floor bargaining and then from that of the state. Section
II examines theories of collective bargaining as the institutionalisation of industrial conflict, arguing that the contradictions of any
possible managerial strategy make some degree of job control for
workers on the shop floor inevitable despite the competitive pressures of the market. Section III considers theories of the state as a
passive respondent to social interests and pressures, arguing a
parallel case for the potential autonomy of state officials. Sections IV
and V develop an alternative approach which treats states as historically formed institutions whose autonomy and coherence vary
considerably from case to case, while the final section draws some
tentative conclusions about the implications of this approach for our
understanding of the relationship between shop floor bargaining and
the state.

II

Empirical studies of the relationship between shop floor bargaining
and the state confound existing theories by their persistent discovery
that state actions have often contributed significantly to the growth
of workplace organisation and the erosion of managerial authority
on the shop floor. But, striking as their findings may be, case studies
such as those collected in this volume are always open to divergent
interpretations, and many partisans of the existing theories would
doubtless reject the one advanced here. For, as we have already
observed, these theories tend to view state support for trade unionism as evidence of a more sophisticated strategy of 'incorporation'
aimed at drawing workers' representatives into a set of bargaining
procedures which systematically limit their freedom of action and
their incursions into managerial prerogatives. Originally applied to
national union officials engaged in regular negotiations with
employers and the state, this argument has increasingly been
extended to cover shop steward organisation itself. But whatever the
locus of incorporation, the argument continues, if the 'rank and file'
repudiate the official structures and overstep the boundaries of
'responsible' behaviour, they will ultimately run up against the
power of the state, thereby confirming the claims of the original
theories.[6]
   This argument rests on a widespread but misleading analysis of the
nature of trade unions and collective bargaining shared by compet-

ing theories of industrial relations despite their political differences. As Hugh Clegg observes, 'The pluralist can accept every word of . . . the Marxist theory of economism, or incorporation, or institution-alisation. . . . The terminology may differ. . . . But translation is easy'.[7] As this quotation suggests, liberals and Marxists alike have generally concurred that official trade union organisation and formal collective bargaining procedures inherently tend to institu-tionalise conflict and contain industrial disorder, while attaching opposed valuations to this outcome. Thus in the well-known debates of the 1960s and 1970s over the reform of British industrial rela-tions, both the 'Oxford School' pluralists and their radical critics substantially agreed that the principal threat to industrial peace was located outside the established institutions themselves, in 'unofficial' action and 'informal' bargaining which failed to respect the rules of the game. For the pluralists, of course, these rules were the legitimate product of joint regulation between management and unions, while for the radicals they were a hollow sham imposed by a mixture of superior force and ideological domination which left managerial prerogatives and the capitalist ownership of industry substantially intact.[8]

Abstracting from its many variants, the logic of the argument can be presented schematically as follows. Marxists and liberals both take as their point of departure the idea that trade unions in a capitalist society must engage in regular bargaining with employers to survive as organisations. The bargaining process depends, by its nature, on the possibility of compromise, which presupposes in turn an underlying willingness to concede a legitimate sphere of interests to one's bargaining partner: at the bare minimum, to recognise his right to exist (the right to bargain collectively over terms and conditions of employment for trade unions, the right to do business for employers). This process of mutual recognition then comes to define the scope of the bargaining process so as automatically to exclude demands which threaten the basic existence of the other side. As Richard Hyman, a leading British radical, puts it, 'What unions demand in collective bargaining is necessarily constrained by what is considered realistic, and what is considered realistic is defined in terms of what the employer can be persuaded to concede in a negotiated settlement. This clearly does not extend to any radical alteration in the balance of power in industry.' Conflict therefore comes to focus on issues which are amenable to compromise, and however bitter disputes may become, they no longer represent a fundamental threat to the social order, because they no longer revolve around fundamental issues.[9]

While sharing this general analysis of the bargaining process, liberals' and Marxists' conflicting evaluations of the interests it serves lead them to divergent assessments of its long-term stability. While liberals freely admit that particular grievances may give rise to bitter disputes between workers and employers, they normally go on to argue, in Alan Fox's words, that the 'mutual dependency' of the two groups ultimately gives them a more basic 'common interest in the survival of the whole of which they are a part'.[10] The bargaining system, on this view, represents a genuine method of conflict resolution which corresponds to the underlying interests of both workers and employers and can therefore be regarded as intrinsically stable and self-reproducing. The principal source of disruption thus lies in exogenous developments – such as rapid economic and technological change – which may require appropriate adjustments to the institutional framework of collective bargaining.[11]

Conversely, while most Marxists accept that particular groups of workers may share specific concerns with their employers – concerns which also divide them from other workers – they nonetheless insist, in Hyman's words, that 'between these two classes there exists a radical conflict of interests, which underlies everything that occurs in industrial relations'.[12] On this view, the narrowing of the scope of the bargaining process excludes workers' deeper interests in demands which can only be satisfied by the supersession of capitalism itself, and must therefore be regarded as a means of suppressing rather than resolving conflicts which may be expected to resurface in new forms. As Hyman concludes, 'The process of institutionalisation is itself beset by contradictions. . . . The institutionalisation of industrial conflict does indeed achieve a *provisional* containment of disorder; but where workers' grievances and discontents are not resolved, they give rise eventually to new forms of conflict. . . .'[13] For Marxists, therefore, the bargaining system is fundamentally unstable and given to periodic explosions of discontent generated from within.

But beneath these differences, both liberals and Marxists fundamentally agree that the interests served by collective bargaining are predetermined by its place in the wider society, so that its outcomes cannot be expected to encroach significantly on managerial prerogatives or to undermine the competitiveness of a capitalist economy in the longer term. This surprising convergence between liberal and Marxist analyses of industrial relations derives in turn from a pair of shared assumptions, one reductionist and the other determinist. The first, reductionist, assumption holds that objective interests can be imputed to social actors without reference either to their conscious interpretations or to any specific context; the second, determinist, one, that institutions such as collective bargaining necessarily stand in a fixed relationship to these objective interests, so that the results of their operation can be predicted in advance of any empirical investigation. The most sophisticated liberal and Marxist analysts of industrial relations, such as Hugh Clegg and Richard Hyman, hedge these assumptions round with innumerable qualifications and relax them substantially in the course of empirical research; but as we have seen, in framing more general claims, they invariably return to their original positions.

These underlying assumptions of liberal and Marxist theories of industrial relations are open to serious challenge on a combination of theoretical and empirical grounds. Thus there is no self-evident reason to assume that social actors' own assessment of their interests should necessarily correspond – even in the long-run – to an abstract definition of their essential interests put forward by an external observer.[14] Much recent work on the methodology of the social sciences suggests instead that interests should be regarded as inherently ambiguous and context-dependent. From this perspective, interests emerge from an interaction between social actors' prior interpretative framework – understood as a vision of the world which is at once descriptive and prescriptive – and the specific situation in which they find themselves.[15] From these reflections it follows that whatever the objective bases for conflict and cooperation between workers and employers, there can be no way to determine in advance which tendency will prove more fundamental. Indeed, recent studies of industrial conflict confirm that workers' behaviour depends not merely on their objective position in the division of labour, but equally on the expectations they bring with them to the factory, on the behaviour of other groups, and on the wider historical and political context.[16]

Similar objections can be raised against the claim that institutions necessarily favour particular interests – however defined – irrespective of the context. Without a specific mechanism to ensure otherwise, the operation of any institution over the longer term will normally be *indeterminate*: the outcomes it produces will depend, at least in part, on factors external to the institution itself; on the movement of the business cycle or the political complexion of the government in power, to choose examples of obvious relevance to industrial relations. Hence for such arguments to hold, a mechanism must be specified in every case to explain why that particular institution should necessarily generate a predetermined outcome.

The arguments put forward in support of determinist claims characteristically take one of the following forms: intentional, functional or structural. *Intentional* arguments deduce the operation of an institution from its original design: created to serve a particular set of interests, an institution may be expected to do so in practice. *Functional* arguments depend instead on institutions' unintended consequences: whatever its origins, on this view, an institution survives because it benefits a particular set of interests; or, put the other way round, the needs of those interests perpetuate the institution. Finally, *structural* arguments deduce the operation of an institution from some causal feature of its internal structure or external environment: an institution serves a particular set of interests because it is constrained to do so.

On closer inspection, however, both intentional and functional arguments for determinism collapse without further specification. This is most obvious in the case of intentional arguments: unless one can point to some fixed feature of the institution which faithfully reflects the original design, there is no reason to assume that it will produce the desired results. But recent writing on functional explanation in the social sciences points to a similar problem in this case as well: it has become increasingly recognised that it is illegitimate to explain the survival of an institution by reference to its unintended and unrecognised benefits for a particular set of interests (or even by the absence of negative effects on those interests); a 'feedback mechanism' must also be specified to account for the reproduction of this outcome in the absence of any conscious efforts to sustain it.[17]

Each of the first two arguments can therefore be reduced to the third, since each depends on the identification of a specific structural feature of either an institution or its environment which ensures that its operation always favours a particular set of interests irrespective of the conscious intentions of the participants or the weight of changing circumstances. While structural mechanisms are methodologically unexceptionable, however, their existence is exceedingly difficult to demonstrate in practice, since there are few constraints so powerful that they permit only a single response; and the identification of even a single significant exception fatally weakens the argument by suggesting that the outcome depends on some unspecified background condition not contained within the institution itself.

Each of these three types of determinist argument – intentional, functional and structural – has been deployed in support of the analysis of trade unions and collective bargaining, shared in different ways by liberals and Marxists. Intentional arguments have figured most prominently in accounts of liberal reform or incorporation as conscious strategies adopted by management and the state to forestall an actual or potential challenge from shop floor militancy. As we have seen, the emphasis in these accounts falls on the deliberate efforts of managers and state officials to construct a system of bargaining procedures which permit the resolution of specific worker grievances without threatening the basic principles of a market economy. Recent Marxist writers such as Friedman and Burawoy have carried this line of argument one step further by suggesting that under certain circumstances management may consciously cede a limited sphere of job control to particular work groups in order to secure their active participation in the production process and their broader consent to managerial priorities.[18] But whether the concessions in question are procedural or substantive, the implicit assumption is that their consequences will be compatible with the long-term profitability of the enterprise and the national economy, or else they will soon be withdrawn.[19]

Whatever the plausibility of this analysis as an account of the motivations of managers or state officials – and it is fair to say that these ideas in their pluralist form have often influenced proposals for the reform of industrial relations – it provides little guide to the results of the bargaining system once in operation, as a number of the essays in this volume demonstrate. Thus, as Howell Harris observes, the politicians and administrators who revamped American industrial relations in the 1930s and 1940s appear to have aimed at developing a stable framework for collective bargaining which did not infringe basic managerial prerogatives, and the Italian lawyers who drafted the *Statuto dei Lavoratori* at the end of the 1960s consciously set out to emulate what they took to be the American achievement. But as Bryn Jones and Giovanni Contini argue in this volume, once in place the new bargaining systems have allowed workers to acquire powers on the shop floor in ways their founders never anticipated. In Britain, too, Noel Whiteside shows that policymakers' assumption that decasualisation would promote efficiency and industrial peace on the waterfront foundered in practice on ordinary dockers' ability to take advantage of the schemes' benefits without abandoning their deep-rooted attachment to casual working practices.

The underlying problem, of course, is that neither state officials nor corporate managers have any secure means of knowing in advance the long-term costs of any particular concession. Economic environments may change and established rules give rise to new interpretations in unpredictable ways that make existing agreements far more onerous for management than either party expected at the outset. The widespread disgruntlement of managers in postwar Britain, and, more recently, the United States, with collective bargaining systems that were hailed in their heyday as pluralist showpieces, offers a conspicuous case in point.[20] And the greater the original emphasis on pressure from below as a source of concessions, the less plausible it seems that their boundaries may be redrawn at will. Hence some impersonal mechanism working behind the backs of the actors themselves must be adduced to explain how the outcomes of the bargaining process can be confined within predetermined limits.

Both liberal and Marxists theorists of industrial relations have often sought to short-circuit this problem by postulating a functional relationship between the collective bargaining system and the institutional requirements of a capitalist economy. Whether conflicts of interest between workers and employers are held to be contingent or fundamental, some means for their resolution is necessary to maintain the social order and protect the economy from constant disruption, and the function of channelling workers' discontent in this direction is then attributed to trade unions. As a leading American pluralist, Frederick Harbison, put it in the 1950s, collective bargaining is an essential bulwark of 'democratic capitalism' because it 'provides a drainage channel for the specific dissatisfactions and frustrations which workers experience on the job'.[21] Similarly, as Richard Hyman argues: 'The union official . . .

experiences a natural commitment to the existing bargaining arrangements. This commitment is attributable less to any personal characteristics of the official than to his *function*: the negotiation and renegotiation of order within the constraints set by a capitalist economy and a capitalist state.'[22]

The difficulty with functionalist arguments of this kind is two-fold. On the one hand, they ignore the *dysfunctional* consequences of particular bargaining arrangements for individual employers or even the national economy, provided that these do not themselves result in the abolition of capitalism as a whole. On the other hand, no precise mechanism is adduced to explain why the actors in question should always perform the roles assigned to them by the theorist. Without further elaboration, functionalist analyses of trade unions and collective bargaining represent little more than unsubstantiated assertions that the systemic needs of capitalism generate the means of their own satisfaction; or tautological claims that *any* development which retrospectively appears advantageous for or even compatible with the survival of capitalism can be explained by reference to the latter's functional requirements.

A structural mechanism is therefore required to explain why the bargaining process should necessarily give rise to outcomes which are functional for the reproduction of a capitalist economy, irrespective of the conscious strategies of workers and employers or the details of particular bargaining arrangements. Marxists have histori-cally been more sensitive to this consideration than liberals, since unlike the latter they do not assume that the bargaining system itself tends to produce an enduring resolution of industrial conflict. As the quotation from Hyman suggests, two principal mechanisms have been proposed for this purpose: the constraints placed on collective bargaining by the market and the state. While the latter will be considered more fully in the next section, the former can be taken up here. The central idea is that competition imposes uniformity: excessive concessions to labour, whether in the form of high wages or job control, place firms at a disadvantage in the market; when this disadvantage becomes serious, management will be forced to win back its freedom of manoeuvre or perish. Workers, for their part, remain dependent on their employers for income and employment and their representatives will be faced with a similar choice between accepting the necessary changes or allowing the firm to go under, setting a grim example to its neighbours. But either way, it is claimed, and here the neo-classical economist would agree, the market ensures that the outcomes of the bargaining process are kept compatible with the demands of profitability.[23]

This notion of market discipline has considerable appeal, particularly in the current economic climate, but it is vulnerable to a number of serious objections. The first is that real-world markets rarely conform to this abstract model, as Marxists themselves often point out. Segmented demand, administrative regulation and imperfect competition are instead the rule, so that firms seldom face a clear-cut choice between radical changes in industrial relations and competitive failure.[24] Where major firms are on the verge of bankruptcy, by contrast, it is often too late for collective bargaining concessions to save them.[25] A second objection is that there is no single appropriate response to competitive pressure, however severe. Thus a comparative study of industrial relations in the world automobile industry, in which the pace of competition has dramatically accelerated, shows that the strategies adopted by the major companies vary dramatically from mass redundancies and the reassertion of managerial prerogatives in Britain and Italy to the extension of employment guarantees and attempts to involve trade unions in plant-level decision-making in West Germany and the United States.[26] Finally and most importantly, recent studies of workplace industrial relations in Britain and the United States suggest that even at the depth of the worst postwar recession management has not recovered a free hand on the shop floor, apart from a few well-publicised cases. Even where shop floor organisation is comparatively weak, management's need for cooperation in risky experiments with new products, processes and working methods appears to have created opportunities for strategically placed work groups to improve their position.[27]

This last point suggests a more positive claim which reaches decisively beyond the limits of market determinism. If we begin our analysis from the bottom up, from the perspective of the enterprise rather than that of society as a whole, it becomes apparent that some degree of job control is an inevitable result of the internal contradictions of any possible managerial strategy. Even if we assume, therefore, that managers always seek to control a recalcitrant labour force, the inadequacies of the strategies available to them make this goal unattainable in practice.

There are many typologies of managerial strategy available, and none is entirely satisfactory, but among the more useful is Friedman's distinction between *direct control* and *responsible autonomy* as methods for controlling the labour force.[28] Following the first strategy, management seeks to minimise its dependence on the workforce by reducing as far as possible the skill and initiative required by their jobs; following the second, it accepts the need to grant a significant measure of discretion to at least a part of the workforce, but seeks to channel its use in accordance with the goals of the enterprise. Neither of these strategies, I would argue, can be pursued consistently to the exclusion of the other, and it is from the resulting gap in managerial authority that opportunities for job control emerge.

Direct control represents the main line of management thinking since Taylor and Ford: separate conception from execution, invest in specialised machinery and divide tasks as finely as possible to reduce the demands on the individual worker to a minimum; then use close supervision and harsh discipline to ensure that the worker does what he or she is supposed to do. These methods have gone a long way towards reducing skill levels in certain types of blue-collar jobs, of which the assembly line is the archetypal example. But they have failed to emancipate management from the need to obtain the cooperation of its workers for two opposed but interrelated reasons: the impracticability of preplanning every aspect of production on the one hand; and the enhanced vulnerability to breakdown and disruption arising from the increasing complexity of the productive system on the other. The more bureaucratic the administration of production, the more dependent management becomes on ordinary workers' initiatives to avoid costly breakdowns and on small groups of highly skilled craftsmen to repair them; and the more interdependent the production process, the more vulnerable it becomes to disruption at the hands of strategically placed work groups. Conversely, as most detailed studies of factory life testify, a variety of unforeseen factors – fluctuations in the quality of raw materials, the demand for the final product, and the particular set of employees who show up for work on any given day – all combine to demand much more know-how and discretion from even 'unskilled' workers than their formal job descriptions require.[29]

These dilemmas are, of course, symmetrically related to one another: the more management attempts to control every aspect of the working environment, the more its vulnerability to disruption increases; but if instead it attempts to streamline the apparatus of control, management must then rely openly on the initiatives of the workforce.

Hence even the most determined protagonist of direct-control strategy must ultimately come to depend in some measure on the voluntary cooperation of shop floor workers and must therefore allow them some margin of discretion. But from discretion flows bargaining power, and management is thus forced to acknowledge, if only tacitly, some limits on its arbitrary authority in the workplace.

In the responsible-autonomy strategy, by contrast, management explicitly incorporates its dependence on workers' initiatives into the organisation of production. This strategy has many advantages, but the underlying problem it raises for management is that of directing workers' initiatives in line with the firm's priorities: of ensuring, in short, that autonomy remains 'responsible'. No reliable means, however, can be found for achieving this end: positive inducements such as high wages and privileged status merely enhance workers' independence and bargaining power, hence their unpredictability, while negative sanctions provoke resistance. This dilemma becomes most evident when shifts in market conditions or technology tempt management to reorganise production in ways that infringe the autonomy and prerogatives of strategic work groups. In such situations, however, managers often discover that their prior reliance on responsible autonomy has so compromised their freedom of manoeuvre that a shift to greater control has become difficult if not impossible.

Other typologies of managerial strategy are of course possible, such as Richard Edwards' distinction between 'simple', 'technical' and 'bureaucratic' structures of control. On closer inspection, however, as Edwards himself acknowledges, each of these strategies also has its own contradictions and tends to break down in practice, and the notion of an ideal managerial strategy becomes accordingly illusory.[30] Over the long-term, therefore, management must bargain for the voluntary cooperation of its workers; and as a result, it is forced to accept some formal or informal limitations on its authority in the workplace. The resulting proliferation of work rules and bargaining procedures in turn defines the contours of that antagonistic cooperation which is the normal relationship between workers and employers in capitalist societies.[31]

These compromises have, to be sure, stark limits from the workers' perspective. Only rarely do trade unions secure a significant voice in key managerial decisions about investment, product design or pricing policy; and workers therefore remain dependent on capital for the continuing security of their earnings and employment. Cherished rights, moreover, may prove vulnerable to renegotiation when economic or political circumstances give management the upper hand. But, for all that, work rules and bargaining practices often represent significant incursions on management's prerogatives in the enterprise, and there can be no theoretical guarantee that they will not circumscribe the responses of individual firms or whole national economies to changing competitive conditions.

If the impersonal operation of the market cannot predetermine the outcomes produced by the bargaining system, what of the conscious intervention of the state? It is to this question we turn in the next section.

III

Just as liberals and Marxists converge on an analysis of collective bargaining as the institutionalisation of industrial conflict, so too they share a common vision of the state as a passive respondent to pressures and imperatives generated within civil society. In each of these theories – and in their corporatist variants – we can find two basic conceptions of the state, in part competitive and in part complementary. Either the state appears as an *arena* within which contending social groups strive to impose their wills, or as a *functional entity* performing necessary tasks of coordination and conflict resolution which are beyond the capacity of the individual social actors, whether to the advantage of a dominant class or of a broader public interest. It will be evident that these conceptions of the state correspond respectively to the intentional and functional arguments for institutional determinism encountered in our discussion of theories of industrial relations; and as we shall see, some theorists have sought to develop a structural account of the constraints on state action as well.

In putting forward this broad-brush characterisation of these theories, my aim is not, of course, to provide a detailed or comprehensive inventory of approaches to the state in contemporary political thought. Indeed, any such summary treatment is bound to do violence to the subtlety and diversity of individual positions. Rather, my aim is to identify what I take to be the main lines of debate, and to pinpoint the underlying assumptions which I believe need to be overcome if we are to develop a more satisfactory understanding of the problems raised at the outset.

There is widespread agreement on the absence of any elaborated theory of the state in pluralism, still probably the most influential account of the political process in liberal democracies. Closely linked to liberalism as a normative theory, pluralism sees legitimacy and consent as the foundations of the political order, and accordingly treats the political system rather than the state as the principal force in policy formation. At the descriptive level, of course, pluralism is best known for its emphasis on the unending struggles among a multitude of contending interest groups, none of which is strong enough completely to dominate the others, as the central influence on government decisions. Insofar as pluralists *do* focus directly on the state, they tend to adopt some combination of the two basic approaches outlined above. On the one hand, they treat state agencies such as the military or government departments as simply a special type of interest group, competing for resources and influence with the rest. On the other, they see the state as an agency responsible for the provision of public goods necessary for the operation of the economy but unprofitable for private entrepreneurs to supply themselves; or, more broadly, following functionalist theories of political development, they interpret the growth of specialised governmental bureaucracies as an adaptive response to the increasing complexity of modern industrial societies.[32]

Corporatism, as many commentators have observed, does not constitute a unified or coherent body of theory in its own right. Contemporary corporatist theorists rarely propose a normative political theory of the type popularised under this aegis in interwar Europe and Latin America, and so share mainly a common emphasis on the growing importance of functionally organised interest groups – particularly those representing capital and labour – in the political life of liberal democracies, interpreting this trend through diverse theoretical optics.[33] Thus, a central theoretical divide in corporatist thought concerns the identification of the dominant partner in the emerging set of tripartite arrangements: the interest groups or the state. Where the emphasis falls on the capture of public functions by powerful private groups – as in neo-liberal critiques of corporate structures as a threat to parliamentary democracy and the rule of law – the result is an oligarchic interpretation of the conventional pluralist account of the state as an arena for competing interests in which some well-organised groups are favoured over the rest.[34] Most corporatist theorists stress instead the state's ability to coopt and subordinate the interest groups to its own policy goals.[35] But, as Pierre Birnbaum among others has observed, this does not lead them to devote much more attention to the state itself than is usual in pluralist accounts.[36] Rather, the expansion of state activity in liberal democracies normally appears in these theories to be a functional response to the changing requirements of modern capitalism for the global exercise of coordination and conflict resolution. Within this general framework, of course, controversy rages among liberal and *Marxisant* exponents of the theory as to whether this expansion of state power systematically favours capital over labour or, rather, promotes a neutral public interest. Similarly, corporatist theorists diverge as to whether tripartite arrangements are geared more to meeting the economic or the political needs of advanced capitalism: thus, for Leo Panitch, the fundamental purpose of corporatist structures is the maintenance of wage restraint and profit levels during periods of full employment; while, for Keith Middlemas, their aim is rather to avert a potential revolutionary challenge to the political order on the part of the working class, even at the cost of a marked deterioration in relative economic performance.[37]

Among the main theoretical paradigms, it is Marxism which has addressed the problem of the state most explicitly, and we will therefore need to examine this literature more closely. It is perhaps appropriate to reiterate at this juncture that these remarks are not intended to be comprehensive, but merely to identify the most salient features of the debate. Nonetheless, I would assert that they do apply *pari passu* to the vast majority of Marxist treatments of the state; moreover, the very multiplicity of individual positions can be seen as a result of the difficulties in overcoming the antinomies generated by the underlying assumptions of this theoretical tradition.[38]

Historically, the most common and currently the most discredited approach to the state within the Marxist tradition is *instrumentalism*, the claim that the state systematically pursues capitalist priorities because it is controlled (or at least heavily influenced) by powerful capitalists who shape policy to suit their own interests. Where the state pursues policies opposed by particular sections of capital, instrumentalists view these as the product of initiatives by the dominant fraction of the capitalist class, whose size and strategic position enables them to look beyond the myopic pursuit of day-today interests in safeguarding the long-term needs of the class as a whole. Formulated in this way, an instrumentalist account of the state is simply a Marxist version of the conventional pluralist model, calling attention to a variety of economic and social reasons why business is normally the best organised and most powerful interest group in liberal democracies, with an attendantly disproportionate influence over government policies.[39]

This perspective has been almost universally rejected in recent years, both by Marxists and by their opponents, for a combination of theoretical and empirical reasons. Theoretically, an instrumentalist account of the state is unsatisfactory to Marxists because it provides no deep reason why the state in a capitalist society should necessarily favour capitalist interests: there is an irretrievably contingent cast to its stress on the political power of organised business and on the social ties which bind government officials to the dominant class. Moreover, this approach leaves the internal structure of the state very much in the background, and puts forward no compelling reasons why it could not be captured wholesale by a well organised labour movement and turned to quite different ends.[40] Empirically, the instrumentalist view has been confounded by two key discoveries which undermined the notion of far-seeing capitalists directing state policies: first, historians demonstrated that key reforms which Marxists believed had enhanced the long-term stability of capitalism – such as the unionisation of mass-production industry in the United States or the nationalisation of the steel industry in Britain – were bitterly opposed at the time by the most important sections of capital itself; secondly, and relatedly, a variety of studies suggested that capitalists – particularly in Britain but even in the US – were so deeply divided amongst themselves by competition and divergent short-term interests that they seemed incapable of formulating any coherent definition of their class interests as a positive guide for state policies.[41]

Hence, Marxist theorists in the 1960s and 1970s began increasingly to look for a structurally grounded approach which could establish the inherently capitalist character of the state irrespective of the shifting balance of forces between organised business and labour as direct influences on government policies. In the process, however, they turned principally towards explicitly functionalist theories which deduce the nature of the state and its activities from the changing systemic requirements of capitalism as a mode of production. As with the functionalist versions of corporatism which we have already discussed, this approach comes in two complementary variants: one which stresses primarily the *economic* functions which the state performs for capitalism, and another which emphasises instead its *political* functions. Ultimately, of course, each emphasis presupposes the other, since the reproduction of a capitalist economy depends on the maintenance of a political order at the same time as it constitutes the purpose for which that order is maintained.

The most influential political functionalist approach to the state in contemporary Marxism can be found in the early work of Poulantzas, who defines the state from the outset as 'the factor of cohesion of a social formation and the factor of reproduction of the conditions of production of a system'.[42] On this view, regardless of who controls it or what pressures it faces, 'the state automatically functions to stabilize and reproduce the capitalist system'.[43] Since capitalism as a system 'itself determines the domination of one class over another . . . the participation of this class in government in no way changes things'; indeed, Poulantzas contends that 'the capitalist state best serves the interests of the capitalist class only when the members of this class do not participate directly in the state apparatus, that is to say, when the *ruling* class is not the politically *governing* class'.[44] Given this overtly functionalist point of departure, it is hardly surprising that Poulantzas devotes little attention to identifying any precise mechanisms whereby the convergence of this 'relatively autonomous' state's actions with the long-term interests of capital is secured.

While Poulantzas' definition assigns the state both the economic role of securing the conditions for the reproduction of capitalist relations of production and the political one of protecting the capitalist order against potential challenges from the subordinate classes, the overwhelming burden of his argument falls in practice on the latter. Thus, Poulantzas sees the state as responsible for maintaining political stability in capitalist societies by disorganising the working class, while simultaneously building cohesion within the capitalist class; most centrally, it forestalls any possible revolutionary threat from below by a judicious mixture of concessions and repression. As even sympathetic critics have observed, Poulantzas gives little weight to any economic constraints on the concessions which the state can at a particular moment offer the working class; apparently any state action short of the abolition of capitalism itself could be interpreted as a functional contribution to its reproduction in the longer term.[45]

A second strand within contemporary Marxism – particularly developed in West Germany – focusses less on the political role of the state in containing class struggle than on the economic functions it performs in the reproduction of capitalism.[46] The characteristic point of departure for this approach in its many variations is a derivation of the necessary functions of the state from an abstract analysis of capitalism as a mode of production. In these theories, the smooth operation and reproduction of a capitalist economy is held to require the performance of certain general functions which it would be impossible or unprofitable for individual capitalists to provide for themselves – such as the establishment of a secure legal and monetary framework for capitalist relations of production and exchange, investment in infrastructure and welfare, and provision for the reproduction of the labour force – and the existence of a state institutionally separate from the economy which can act as an 'ideal collective capitalist' is deduced from these requirements.

Like Poulantzas, this 'state derivation' school asserts that the state must be relatively autonomous from direct capitalist control in order to perform its system-regulating functions; and they therefore postulate the existence of 'structural selectivity' mechanisms in the internal organisation of the state and its relation to the economy which ensure that it operates according to the logic of capital in the long run. More specifically, the state's exclusion from the organisation of capitalist production and from the allocation of private capital is held to make it dependent on capitalists' investment decisions for the economic growth necessary both for the achievement of its policy goals and the maintenance of its revenues; and this dependence on the healthy functioning of a capitalist economy in turn compels the state to tailor its activities to the long-term needs of capital.

In more sophisticated versions of these ideas, such as those developed by Claus Offe (who is not directly connected with this school), the state's dependence on private investment decisions is seen as creating serious obstacles for its ability to steer the economy in line with the changing systemic requirements of capitalism; and, in a reversal of Middlemas' approach, the pressures on the state to provide favourable conditions for accumulation are seen as subversive of the appearance of class neutrality which enables the state to fulfil the equally essential *political* task of maintaining its own popular legitimacy. In this case, functionalist premises produce dysfunctional consequences, and the state is compelled to oscillate between contradictory objectives, so that its course of action in any particular situation becomes fundamentally indeterminate.[47]

The predominance of functionalist assumptions in Marxist theories of the state has aroused widespread dissatisfaction among Marxists as well as their critics. As in the case of collective bargaining, functionalist accounts of the state – whether Marxist, liberal or corporatist – normally represent little more than unsubstantiated assertions that the systemic needs of capitalism generate the means of their own satisfaction; or tautological claims that *any* development which retrospectively appears to be advantageous for or even simply compatible with the survival of capitalism can be explained by reference to the latter's functional requirements. Thus, as many critics have observed, the simple identification of external requirements or conditions for the reproduction of capitalism offers no assurance that these will be met in practice, nor does it provide any guide to the precise mechanisms which might work to this end in specific historical situations. Despite the apparent autonomy assigned to the state in these theories, moreover, the assumption that it would nonetheless be compelled to act in the long-term interests of capitalism as a system deprives its internal structure and policies of any real importance in their own right; at the same time, it gives little effective weight to popular movements or pressure from below as a substantive influence on state policies in any context short of revolution

Insofar as Marxists have not reverted towards the older instrumentalist and pluralist accounts of state policies as the outcome of competing social pressures (as can be seen in much of the recent literature which stresses the centrality of class struggle), they have tended to search for structural mechanisms which could explain how a state which is independent of direct capitalist control could both be able to implement reforms essential for the long-term stability of capitalism even in the face of determined resistance from capitalists themselves, and yet be constrained to act in the general interests of the capitalist class.

The most ambitious attempt to overcome these difficulties by developing a non-functionalist theory of the capitalist state which assigns a central role to state autonomy and class struggle, and is sufficiently specific to be applied to real historical situations, can be found in the work of the American Marxist, Fred Block.[48] Like Offe, Block takes as his point of departure an empirically observable split between capitalists maximising their short-run economic interests who do not control the state, and state managers (high-ranking civil servants and politicians) maximising their individual and institutional power and influence who do not control private production and investment.

Since state managers are dependent on the healthy performance of the economy for the maintenance of their revenue base and electoral popularity, they find it necessary under normal circumstances to maintain business confidence by pursuing policies acceptable to capitalist interests.[49] But in periods of crisis, such as war and depression, the withdrawal of business confidence becomes a less effective constraint on the state's autonomy, and state managers are therefore able to undertake more ambitious policies directed at overcoming the crisis. At such moments, as well, the state's autonomy is often enhanced by the emergence of powerful popular movements which challenge the hegemony of the dominant class, and which necessitate concessions orchestrated by state managers, normally in the form of greater state intervention in the economy. But since state managers are still ultimately dependent on private investment for the revival of the economy, they therefore take care to structure and adjust these concessions so as to maintain their compatibility with the requirements of a capitalist economy.

Block's argument, which is extensively illustrated with examples from twentieth-century American history, comes closer than any other to creating a plausible structural foundation for a theory of the capitalist state. But on closer inspection it turns out to be vulnerable to a number of major objections, which cast profound doubt on the viability of the project itself. The core of these objections is that by approaching the state primarily in terms of its potential ability to play a functional role for capital, Block at once overestimates and underestimates its autonomy and coherence in specific historical contexts.

On the one hand, the ability of state managers to stabilise and rationalise capitalism presupposes the existence of a state apparatus endowed with sufficient autonomy, coherence, resources and administrative capacities. But as Theda Skocpol has demonstrated in a penetrating critique based on the empirical case of the New Deal on which Block relies heavily, the existence of such a state apparatus – which was absent in the US of the 1930s – cannot be taken for granted, but is rather the product of specific processes of political development which vary greatly from country to country and which can in no sense be deduced from the needs of an industrial capitalism which they often predate.[50] One might add that the state managers' abilities to promote the prosperity of a capitalist economy may also depend on the availability of an intellectually convincing programme of action which cannot be presumed to be present at all historical moments: thus, it is far from apparent that any of the main prescriptions currently available for economic policy formulation – whether monetarist, Keynesian, or socialist – would be likely to provide a secure exit from the current difficulties of Western capitalist economies whatever the intentions of state managers who applied them.

On the other hand, where a sufficiently autonomous, coherent and self-confident state apparatus does exist, Block's claim that in the long run it will always be constrained to pursue capitalist priorities seems unconvincing. The forces he cites as the bases for the state's ability to override capitalist opposition to its policies in times of crisis also operate, albeit to a lesser degree, during 'normal' periods. Thus, Block rightly treats war as a central source of state autonomy, but military pressures are far from absent in peacetime; indeed, to anticipate the argument of the next section, military and political competition between states is both one of the most conspicuous features of the modern world and historically one of the most important means by which state managers have enhanced their independence from civil society. Similarly, as most Marxists would agree, pressures from subordinate classes which promote the mediatory role of the state are by no means confined to exceptional periods such as depressions; and alliances between state officials and popular movements through the medium of mass political parties have served as one of the most powerful levers for the extension of government intervention in many Western economies. Hence, it is always possible to discover forces at work promoting the state's autonomy which in some measure (though not completely) offset the constraints imposed by business confidence. Finally, as Block himself acknowledges in his most recent writings, the extension of state leverage over the dominant class can reach a 'tipping point' beyond which it is no longer constrained by capitalist interests, adducing the example of Nazi Germany as a concrete if profoundly negative case in point.[51]

These difficulties with Block's argument suggest that the underlying project of developing a structuralist theory of the capitalist state is fundamentally unviable. As critical and sophisticated writers in the Marxist tradition such as Jessop and Hindess and Hirst have recently argued, the formula of the state's 'relative autonomy' is a mirage: either the state is subordinate to the imperatives of capitalism, whether because it is directly controlled by capitalists or because it is defined *a priori* in functional terms; or the state really is autonomous, in which case there can be no theoretical guarantees that it will pursue capitalist interests, whatever the constraints imposed by business confidence.[52]

These problems highlight the intrinsic limits of all theories – whether Marxist, corporatist or pluralist – which approach the state primarily from the perspective of interests and needs generated within civil society. Whether they conceive of the state as an arena for contending social groups or as a functional entity performing tasks which civil society cannot perform for itself, these theories are unable to grant any real autonomy to the state as such without undermining their basic premises. For once it is acknowledged that states pursue goals which can be derived neither from the play of interest groups nor from the needs of the economy or the class structure, and that their autonomy and coherence vary greatly over time and space, a theoretical focus on states as distinctive structures with their own specific histories becomes unavoidable.

The inability of the existing theories to account for the complex and contradictory relationship between shop floor bargaining and the state is a direct outgrowth of these weaknesses in their basic assumptions. For the evidence we have adduced that at certain moments states have played a positive role in the extension of shop floor bargaining and job control are simply particularly graphic examples of the fact that neither in the short run nor in the long run do they necessarily act in the interests of the dominant classes – nor even in the public interest, however defined. A more adequate understanding of this relationship requires an alternative approach to the state which goes beyond the assumptions on which these theories are founded. This is not to say that the existing theories should be rejected root and branch: while their functionalist components are indefensible, other central emphases, such as the roles of interest-group pressures, business confidence, and debates about the public interest as influences on state policy formation, would certainly occupy a prominent place in any revised account. But a more satisfactory treatment of the relationship between shop floor bargaining and the state will also require a much more direct theoretical focus on states as separate entities with a distinctive internal logic and particular individual histories; and it is to this task that we turn in the next section.

IV

Discourses about the state, like states themselves, bear the marks of the historical context within which they were constructed. Thus, theories which analyse the state from the perspective of civil society are characteristic of countries such as Britain and the United States in which states have been most thoroughly subordinated to social and institutional constraints; and their underlying assumptions reflect this trajectory of political development. If we want to place the state at the centre of our analysis, we will need to supplement these society-centred approaches with ideas drawn from an alternative theoretical tradition – which for want of a better term can be called statist – developed in those societies, mainly on the European continent, which experienced the rise of much stronger and more intrusive states than those of the Anglo-Saxon world.[53]

More recently, as growing concern with the active role of the state has spread dissatisfaction with the dominant society-centred paradigms of political analysis, elements of the statist tradition have been taken up and re-elaborated by a variety of contemporary political scientists, sociologists, and historians in the English-speaking world as well as in its more established strongholds. The discussion which follows attempts to draw together some of the principal strands of this emerging body of work, linking it where appropriate with insights from the society-centred theories already examined. In so doing, my aim is not to put forward a new general theory of the state, but rather to set out an alternative analytic framework which should be of heuristic value in untangling the contradictory relationship between shop floor bargaining and the state with which this volume is centrally concerned.

The core of the statist tradition is its vision of the state as an autonomous sphere whose distinctive goals and institutional structure set it off from the contending interests of civil society. As in the case of society-centred theories, these ideas can be found in many competing variants, of which the most useful for our purposes are those associated with such nineteenth-century German historians as Ranke, Treitschke, Meinecke and Hintze. These writers called themselves 'realists' because, in contrast to the idealist and legalist theories which had dominated German political thought since Hegel, they concerned themselves not with what the state ought to be but with what particular states actually did.[54] Where their opponents saw pacific entities striving to reconcile the multitude of antagonisms within civil society into a higher common good, the realists, whose gaze was fixed firmly on the history of European nation–states, saw instead bellicose machines which fought wars, suppressed rebellions, collected taxes, and built up vast civil and military bureaucracies. Underlying these various activities they discerned a simple if brutal rationale: the pursuit of power backed up by force. As Treitschke put it in a famous epigram, 'In the first place, in the second place and in the third place, the essence of the state is power'; and as he elaborated elsewhere, 'the state is the public force for offence and defence'.[55] A particularly radical version of these ideas was put forward in the 1920s and 1930s by the right-wing German jurist, Carl Schmitt, for whom war and the potential 'existential negation' of the enemy constituted the basic foundations of political life.[56]

More modern social scientific practitioners of a realist approach (who rarely share the militarist and nationalist values of its originators) view the state primarily as a historically constructed organisational complex which seeks to control a given body of territory and its inhabitants. As Theda Skocpol puts it in her study of the French, Russian and Chinese revolutions: 'The state properly conceived . . . is a set of administrative, policing, and military organizations headed, and more or less well coordinated, by an executive authority. Any state first and foremost extracts resources from society and deploys these to create coercive and administrative organizations.'[57] Put in the opposite way, 'an organization which controls the population occupying a defined territory is a state *in so far as*: (1) it is differentiated from other organizations operating in the same territory; (2) it is autonomous; (3) it is centralized; and (4) its divisions are coordinated with one another'.[58]

From this perspective, two major implications follow. The first is that states pursue interests distinct from, and potentially opposed to, those of *all* the contending groups which make up civil society; the second is that particular states differ greatly in their institutional structures and their ability to realise their interests at a particular moment. Both the character of state interests and the obstacles to their realisation are in turn linked to what realists regard as the central influence on the historical development of individual states: their janus-faced position at the intersection between conflict-riven societies and an international system of competing states. As the realist historian Otto Hintze put it in a classic formulation: 'two phenomena conditioned the real organization of the state. These are, first, the structure of social classes, and second, the external ordering of the states – their position relative to each other, and their overall position in the world'.[59]

Foremost among the state's interests in the realist conception are those which directly affect its external and internal security: the defence of its territory against other states abroad; and the maintenance of public order and political stability against potential challenges to its rule at home.[60] These overriding concerns in turn impose others: and state officials are continually preoccupied with the supply of financial and human resources needed to sustain their coercive and administrative apparatus, and with subordinating the latter more effectively to central direction and control. In any particular situation, realists characteristically see states' interests as powerfully shaped, if not determined, by objective features of their social, economic, and geo-political environments which define the constellation of threats and opportunities facing their rulers. The latter may respond to these objective pressures in various ways, but as Robert Gilpin observes of the geographical, military and power-political forces which bear most heavily on states' external security: 'A ruling elite which fails to take these factors into account does so at its peril.'[61]

There follows from the existence of objective challenges posed by states' foreign and domestic environments no presumption that their leaders may at any moment be in a position to meet them. Since, as realists emphasise, states are historically constructed organisations, they vary enormously in their autonomy, coherence, and ability to impose their will on their subjects. These variations in institutional structure – which can from a certain perspective be viewed as the crystallisation of states' past responses to tasks presented by their environments – in turn shape the organisational and political resources available to their leaders in confronting new challenges.

This logic of challenge and response has long figured prominently in comparative studies of political development. Thus, for example, in explaining the classic contrast between the relative statelessness of Britain and the more pronounced *étatisation* of French society, historians and political scientists generally place great weight on the cumulative impact of long-standing differences in the two countries' domestic and geo-political environments. In this vein, the weakness of the British state can be attributed to its early and relatively painless unification, coupled with its geographically-based insulation until the twentieth century from the endemic land warfare which proved so potent a stimulus to state-building on the continent; while in France, the exigencies of integrating a variety of heterogeneous territories into a cohesive national unit and defending its many exposed borders against foreign invasion are held to have resulted in the construction of a far more centralised and intrusive state apparatus. And these differences in the autonomy and coherence of the two states are in turn adduced as central determinants of their divergent modes of dealing with such contemporary problems as economic planning, movements for territorial autonomy, and industrial conflict.[62]

Presented in this way, the attractions of a realist perspective on the state are readily apparent. In contrast to theories which reduce the state to a passive respondent to social pressures, or deduce its behaviour from a static functional analysis of social needs, a realist approach enables us to treat state leaders as independent actors with their own goals and priorities, and states themselves as historically formed institutional complexes with widely different structures and capacities. At the same time, it identifies the central influences on the determination of state interests and the development of state structures in the interaction between domestic social conflict and international military competition.

But the limitations of a realist perspective are equally important. Its insights do not themselves constitute a full-blown alternative theory of the state, but rather a set of more or less persuasive generalisations derived inductively from the historical experience of particular states. If we press these ideas forward in the direction of a meta-historical theory (as certain realists have done), the result turns out to resemble closely the society-centred theories whose deficiencies we have been at pains to point out. Thus, if we inquire more deeply into the meaning of state power, a realist approach would lead us to conclude either that states are essentially instruments in the hands of a politically defined ruling elite, or that they are functional products of the need for domestic order and political authority created by the impossibility of escaping a Hobbesian state of nature in the international arena.[63] In the latter case, we are not far from an explicitly functionalist theory modelled on the biological theory of evolution, in which state structures are seen as adaptive responses to the pressures of a competitive state system, in much the same way as neo-classical economists believe that the market forces individual firms to adopt profit-maximising criteria for decision-making.[64]

The problems with this type of argument can be seen most clearly in its treatment of state interests. As we have noted, realists characteristically regard state interests as strongly conditioned if not determined by objective circumstances, particularly those of a geopolitical kind. Now it is certainly true that one can find states whose failure to adjust their internal structure to the demands of their external position resulted in their disappearance as independent entities – the political equivalent of bankruptcy – of which eighteenth-century Poland with its aristocratic *liberum veto* is perhaps the most notorious example. But in most cases, the pressures of the international state system, like those of the market, are seldom so intense and the criteria for distinguishing success from failure are rarely so apparent. Indeed, the interpretation of what is usually referred to as the 'national interest' is normally the subject of intense debate within the state apparatus itself as well as outside; the resulting decisions will be as much the product of ideological controversy as the pragmatic calculus of political advantage.[65]

A second limitation of the realist perspective – understood as an alternative general theory of the state – flows naturally from its own assumption that states are historical structures which vary greatly in their autonomy and coherence. Since states are not 'real historical subjects' or unitary, rational actors, but complex associations of many individual agents, there can be no presumption that they will produce coherent, decisive policies without some definite institutional mechanism for resolving conflicts between competing decision-centres. The forms and effectiveness of such mechanisms are a product of each state's individual history and therefore differ considerably from case to case. And just as their historical development conditions states' internal decision-making process, so too does it shape their relationship with civil society. Some of the constraints on state autonomy flow from the resistance of organised interest groups or from the effects of economic and military forces outside their control. But others flow from the coexistence of most states' executive authorities with a set of legal and political institutions which regulate their activities to varying degrees and provide some form of representation for their citizens in policy formulation and implementation, most notably in liberal democracies. To the extent that the state's top executive and legislative personnel are themselves selected through such representative procedures, they will find themselves torn between the competing demands of their roles as state officials and as leaders of political organisations responsible at least in theory to constituencies outside the state apparatus. Whether this blurring of the line between state and society results from formal constitutional structures or the informal realities of power – as in clientilist political systems – it then becomes essential to supplement a realist approach with insights drawn from society-centred theories which draw attention to the limits of executive authority and the penetration of social forces into the state machinery itself.

V

Bearing in mind the strengths and weaknesses of a realist perspective, we can now go on to consider briefly some of its implications for the state's orientation towards two problems that by all accounts form the central framework for its relationship to shop floor bargaining: social conflict on the one hand and economic management on the other. The state's distinctive interests in domestic order, external security and the extraction of resources place it in a highly ambivalent relation to the cleavages and antagonisms of civil society. Its desire to maintain public order and to assure a steady flow of revenue often leads the state, as Marxists have always insisted, to support the existing structure of social and economic relations against potentially disruptive challenges from subordinate groups. Similarly, when their own resources are constrained, states will naturally resist any demands from below which appear to threaten their own financial solvency, as workers employed in the public sector have frequently discovered. Where states do not themselves control economic activity, they will often need to reach accommodations with the possessors of key economic resources in order to achieve their own political and military ends, as Block's account of the dynamic of business confidence suggests. And where they have not already built up an independent bureaucratic apparatus of their own, states may be forced to compromise their autonomy still further by recruiting members of powerful social elites into their service and devolving to them the local exercise of their fiscal, administrative, and judicial powers.

But the state's broader interest in the preservation of domestic order may also prompt it to strike bargains with subordinate groups which restore social peace at the expense of propertied elites; and many British employers viewed the concessions made to striking workers by politicians and civil servants during the First World War in precisely this light.[66] Since a large portion of its tax revenues is drawn from the coffers of the propertied classes, the state will always in some measure appear to the latter as a competitor for scarce resources: and this notion clearly underlies the widespread contemporary claim that excessive public borrowing crowds private investors out of the capital market. Similarly, international conflicts may interfere with foreign trade and disrupt the domestic economy; while as students of 'late development' have argued, military competition with industrially more-advanced rivals may spur states to pursue far-reaching projects of economic transformation which cut across the interests of established entrepreneurs.[67] For all these reasons, dominant classes from seventeenth-century Prussian Junkers to twentieth-century American corporate executives have characteristically preferred to limit as far as possible the state's autonomy and access to resources, provided that they can fend off challenges from below independently and are not threatened by imminent foreign invasion.[68]

The state's efforts to preserve its tax base and its supply of military recruits can at certain moments lead it beyond occasional encroachments on the interests of the dominant classes into a more active championship of the people against their exploiters. Thus, in the seventeenth and eighteenth centuries many European absolutist states adopted conscious policies aimed, with varying degrees of success, at preventing enclosures and protecting peasant property against seigneurial exactions. Echoes of these preoccupations can be seen in the welfare policies pursued by states in modern capitalist economies: thus, the low physical quality of army recruits for the Boer War figured prominently in the political debates leading up to the 1906–11 Liberal welfare reforms; and the British state's concern with the health of the civilian population during the First World War appears to have resulted in nutritional advances which markedly increased the life expectancy of the poorest sections of the working class.[69]

The burden of state exactions may provoke contending social groups to bury their differences in a common struggle against governmental authority, as tax revolts from seventeenth-century France to twentieth-century California testify. But the state's efforts to win support against its enemies at home and abroad may likewise pave the way for an explicit alliance between state leaders and subordinate classes, which often yield substantial benefits for the latter. In democratic political systems – themselves often the result of previous accommodations with subordinate groups – the state's need to mobilise active popular support for its policies is correspondingly increased, particularly in wartime, and with it the scale of potential concessions. Thus, in most combatant nations, the two world wars were the occasion for a wide array of measures designed to satisfy working-class demands, some temporary and others more permanent; in Britain these ranged from controls on rents, food prices and profits to the extension of the franchise, trade union recognition and welfare benefits.[70] This potential alliance between state officials and popular classes may be articulated through the medium of mass political parties which bring together intellectuals and sections of the working class on a common platform of increased state intervention in economy and society; examples include the social democratic parties of Western Europe, the Labour Party (and on some interpretations the prewar Liberals) in Britain, and the New Deal Democratic coalition in the United States.[71]

Similar ambivalences arise when we examine the state's orientation towards economic management. As we have already observed, both Marxists and liberals often share a common image of the modern state as an economic manager, whatever their disagreements about the ultimate beneficiaries of its activities. But viewed from a realist perspective, it becomes apparent that states rarely pursue economic growth for its own sake, but rather as a means to their own political and military ends. Thus, state managers can be seen as natural mercantilists, whatever their economic programme, because they characteristically regard wealth as a source of power – of international influence, of government revenues, and of popular legitimacy and support – rather than as an end in itself. Hence, as statesmen and historians have both observed, free trade as much as protectionism may be deployed as an instrument of empire.[72]

Thus, when states deliberately set out to promote economic growth, their priorities will normally be different than those of all the major economic actors – whether industrialists, bankers, landowners, or workers. In this sense, the overlap between the aims of state policy and the interests of any of these groups will be both partial and contingent: thus, depending on the circumstance, governments may favour capital-goods producers over consumer-goods producers, as in Imperial Germany; finance over industry, as in twentieth-century Britain; or more exceptionally, labour over capital, as in the case of the Wagner Act, whose framers believed that the establishment of strong trade unions would promote economic recovery by redistributing income to workers and increasing effective demand.

Many examples could be cited of the ways in which states' distinctive priorities lead them to pursue economic policies which can be assimilated neither to the maximisation of general economic welfare nor to the promotion of the collective interest of the capitalist class. But let us confine ourselves to one case whose relevance to shop floor bargaining should be readily apparent: the primacy of financial objectives in twentieth-century British economic policy. Among the most widespread criticisms of British economic policy is that at crucial moments – notably the 1920s and the 1950s to 1960s – it sacrificed the interests of the domestic economy to financial goals connected with the stability and international role of sterling. This bias has in turn been seen as a central precipitating factor in the many clashes between government and trade unions during this century: thus, the return to the gold standard set the stage for the general strike; and it was above all the preoccupation of successive postwar administrations with the balance of payments which led them into highly contentious experiments with incomes policy and with the reform of industrial relations. One might add on the other side that short-term financial considerations have also repeatedly undermined more ambitious state strategies for shifting power away from workers on the shop floor: thus, in the mid-1950s, Conservatives' concern with the balance of payments led them to pull the rug out from under the engineering and shipbuilding employers whose resistance to trade union demands they had hitherto encouraged; and Labour's efforts to remove restrictive practices through productivity bargaining collapsed in the late 1960s when their efforts to hold together an incomes policy led them to sanction many deals which were animated by rather different aims.[73]

This peculiarity of British economic policy has given rise to two competing interpretations: one which emphasises the vulnerability of government to financial pressures; and the other which emphasises a historically determined convergence between policy makers' perceptions of Britain's economic interests and those of the financial community. The first view argues that British governments have prioritised financial objectives because the City is the most influential pressure group in the policy-making arena; or, to use Marxist language, that finance is the dominant fraction of capital, exercising hegemony over industry within the framework of a national power bloc. Exponents of this view emphasise the City's close links with crucial policy-making institutions such as the Treasury and the Bank of England; the willingness of industrialists to defer to the bankers' judgement on key financial issues; and the ability of the financial community to cripple government policy initiatives and undermine its credit by withdrawing their confidence.[74]

The second view points out that these arguments, however well founded, do not fully account for the willingness of successive governments to accept the priorities set by the City and its bureaucratic allies; on closer inspection, most of the central policy battles were settled not by financial *force majeure* but rather by the evident commitment of the Prime Minister of the day and a majority of his cabinet to financial objectives such as the defence of sterling. In this second interpretation, therefore, the primacy of financial concerns in British economic policy appears instead as a product of what Gilpin calls 'a natural harmony between Whitehall and the City' rooted in a convergence between the state's international interests and those of the financial community during the nineteenth century. There is no space to examine this process in any detail here, but the key steps date back to the City's emergence as an essential source of cheap public finance during the Napoleonic Wars, and its subsequent evolution through its guardianship of the gold standard and its role in capital exports into the hub of the liberal international economy which in turn made possible the symbiosis of British commercial and naval supremacy during the nineteenth-century *pax britannica*. The restoration of the financial system on which British international hegemony had rested thus became the central preoccupation of policy makers during the 1920s, despite the costs to the domestic economy; and the postwar preoccupation with the stability and international role of the pound was likewise tightly bound up with foreign policy considerations such as the preservation of the Commonwealth, the maintenance of Britain's special relationship with the United States, and a more general ambition to retain a major role on the world stage.[75]

VI

Returning to our point of departure, what implications can we draw from this analysis for an understanding of the contradictory relationship between shop floor bargaining and the state with which we began? Though no new general theory appears possible, some tentative conclusions can nonetheless be sketched out.

The first is that the very real contradictions observable in the relations between states and trade unions are paradoxical only in the light of those theories which fail to recognise that states are potentially autonomous entities with their own interests and historically specific capacities for action. In the simplest sense, the relationship between shop floor bargaining and the state is contradictory because the overlap between the state's interests and those of social groups is necessarily partial and contingent. Since few states are all-powerful, they will normally need to collaborate with a variety of social groups in achieving their policy objectives – among them, of course, employers and workers. But since the state's priorities are fundamentally distinct from those of any of these groups, the potential for conflict is always present. At certain moments, some social interests of course carry more weight than others: and therein lies the force of claims that the dynamic of business confidence gives employers special leverage in a capitalist economy, but also of those which stress the leverage which full employment confers on workers. In democratic political systems which allow workers to form unions and participate in electoral politics, few governments will long be able to ignore their interests entirely; but even under authoritarian regimes, the state may find it necessary to place limits on management's freedom of action in the workplace, as in the case of Italian fascism.[76] Secondly, since states are historically formed structures, they differ greatly in their institutional coherence and interventionary capacities. The weaker its executive authority, the more likely that the state's individual branches will pursue competing policies flowing from the particular tasks with which they are entrusted – whether the control of public expenditure, weapons procurement, or the maintenance of industrial peace – and that no long-term set of planning priorities will emerge. Certainly, the prevalence of short-term decision-making and conflicting objectives appears to be one of the defining features of the twentieth-century British state, and goes a long way towards accounting for the contradictory impact of its policies on the development of shop floor bargaining.

Finally, state interests are always in part ambiguous and open to competing interpretations in which ideological considerations play an important role. Since state managers, like the rest of us, must make do with partial and incomplete economic and social theories, there can be no guarantee that their policies, even if effectively implemented, will produce the intended results. Thus policy makers in Britain, Italy and the United States all set out at various moments to create bargaining systems which would reconcile workers' collective rights with management prerogatives; but as we shall see in the essays which follow, once in place these systems have often allowed workers to acquire powers on the shop floor in ways their originators never anticipated.

NOTES

* In addition to my co-editor and the participants in the conference to which this essay was originally presented, I would like to thank the following friends and colleagues for helpful comments and advice: Giovanni Contini, John Dunn, Diego Gambetta, Istvan Hont, Janos Kis, Joe Melling, Alastair Reid, Charles Sabel and Fred Smoler.
1 See, for example, S. J. Prais, *Productivity and Industrial Structure* (Cambridge, 1982); O. Kahn-Freund, *Labour Relations: Heritage and Adjustment* (Oxford, 1979); A Kilpatrick and T. Lawson, 'On the Nature of Economic Decline in the UK', *Cambridge Journal of Economics* 4 (1980); and R. Hyman and T. Elger, 'Job Controls, the

Employers' Offensive and Alternative Strategies', *Capital and Class* 15 (1981).

2 See Lord Wedderburn, J. Clark and R. Lewis, *Labour Law and Industrial Relations* (Oxford, 1983), especially ch. 6.

3 For a review of the literature, see R. Tarling and F. Wilkinson, 'The Movement of Real Wages and the Development of Collective Bargaining in the U.K. 1855–1920', *Contributions to Political Economy* 1 (1982).

4 H. Clegg, *The Changing System of Industrial Relations in Great Britain* (Oxford, 1979), pp. 35–7, 214–15, 217–18; W. Brown (ed.), *The Changing Contours of British Industrial Relations* (Oxford, 1981).

5 A. Martin, 'Sweden: Industrial Democracy and Social Democratic Strategy', in G. D. Garson (ed.), *Worker Self-Management in Western Europe* (New York, 1978); and W. Korpi, *The Working Class in Welfare Capitalism* (London, 1978).

6 For a clear, but qualified, statement of the incorporation thesis, see R. Hyman, *Industrial Relations: A Marxist Introduction* (London, 1975), pp. 67–9, 87–92, 142–5; for its application to shop steward organisation, see R. Hyman, 'The Politics of Workplace Trade Unionism: Recent Tendencies and Some Problems for Theory', *Capital and Class* 8 (1979); M. Terry, 'The Emergence of a Lay Elite: Some Recent Changes in Shop Steward Organisation', translated in *Sociologie du travail* (Oct.–Dec. 1979); and M. Terry, 'Shop Steward Development and Managerial Strategies', in G. Bain (ed.), *Industrial Relations in Britain* (Oxford, 1983). For a powerful empirical critique of this thesis as applied to British industrial relations in the 1970s and 1980s, see J. England, 'Shop Stewards in Transport House: A Comment upon the Incorporation of the Rank and File', *Industrial Relations Journal* 12, 5 (1981); and E. Batstone, 'Shop Steward Organisation in the Depression', paper presented to the colloquium on 'Economic Crisis and the Politics of Industrial Relations', King's College, Cambridge, September 1983.

7 Clegg, *Changing System*, p. 455.

8 For representative views, see the essays collected in A. Flanders, *Management and Unions* (London, 1970), and Hyman, *Industrial Relations*, pp. 151–9. A compelling critique of the distinction between formal and informal bargaining is M. Terry, 'The Inevitability of Informality', *British Journal of Industrial Relations* 15, 1 (1977); and for an acknowledgement of this difficulty by a leading pluralist, see Clegg, *Changing System*, pp. 232–40.

9 From a pluralist perspective, see Clegg, *Changing System*, pp. 228–57 and 452–6; F. H. Harbison, 'Constructive Aspects of Industrial Conflict', and R. Dubin, 'Collective Bargaining and American Capitalism', in A. Kornhauser, R. Dubin and A. M. Ross (eds.), *Industrial Conflict* (New York, 1954). From a Marxist perspective, see Hyman, *Industrial Relations*, pp. 89–91 and 97–9 (the quotation is from p. 99); and M Burawoy, *Manufacturing Consent* (Chicago, 1979), p. 115.

10 'Industrial Sociology and Industrial Relations', Royal Commission on Trade Unions and Employers' Associations, *Research Papers*, 3 (London, 1966), p. 4. Cf. Fox's 'Industrial Relations: A Social Critique

of Pluralist Ideology', in J. Child (ed.), *Man and Organisation* (London, 1973), pp. 195–6. Some pluralists, such as Clegg, deny that they are committed to the view that the procedural consensus involved in collective bargaining must ultimately override all normative divergencies between the parties, but it is difficult in this case to see why they believe that the bargaining system will provide a stable means for resolving conflict in the longer term: see his 'Pluralism in Industrial Relations', *British Journal of Industrial Relations* 13, 3 (1975). A useful, if necessarily partisan, account of the pluralist–radical debate is R. Hyman, 'Pluralism, Procedural Consensus and Collective Bargaining', *British Journal of Industrial Relations* 16, 1 (1977).

11 See, for example, Flanders and Fox's analysis of the breakdown of national bargaining in postwar Britain in 'The Reform of Collective Bargaining: From Donovan to Durkheim', reprinted in Flanders, *Management and Unions*.

12 Hyman, *Industrial Relations*, pp. 22–3. But cf. p. 42 for his acknowledgement that workers' 'overriding concern tends to be with the narrow area of interests and loyalties that lies closest to hand; and hence in many situations they may be more conscious of those interests which divide them from other workers than of those which unite them'.

13 *Ibid.*, p. 199.

14 Some writers who postulate objective interests accept that these might not be recognised by the actors themselves. But as Barry Hindess rightly observes, this position depends on the idea that there might exist some ideal conditions under which the actors in question *would* recognise their true interests (for example, under conditions of democratic participation); and as he goes on to object, not only are such claims intrinsically unsubstantiable, but 'there seems no good reason why interests acknowledged in one situation should be considered any more *real* than those acknowledged in another', 'Power, Interests and the Outcomes of Struggles', *Sociology* 16, 4 (1982) p. 508; cf. also his *Parliamentary Democracy and Socialist Politics* (London, 1983), pp. 73–4.

15 Good statements of this position, which can be traced back to the methodological writings of Max Weber, include C. Geertz, *The Interpretation of Cultures* (New York, 1973), and P. Bourdieu, *Outline of a Theory of Practice* (Cambridge, 1977). The claim here is not that actors define their interests without reference to objective features of their experience, but rather that this experience does not give rise to a single, unambiguous interpretation or course of action.

16 For a comprehensive analysis of the literature, see C. Sabel, *Work and Politics* (Cambridge, 1982) and his 'The Ambiguities of Class and the Possibilities of Politics', in A. Liebich (ed.), *The Future of Socialism in Europe?* (Montreal, 1978).

17 See J. Elster, *Ulysses and the Sirens* (Cambridge, 1979), pp. 28–35; 'Marxism, Functionalism and Game Theory', *Theory and Society* 11, 4 (1982); and *Explaining Technical Change* (Cambridge, 1982), pp. 49–68.

18 A. L. Friedman, *Industry and Labour* (London, 1977) and Burawoy,

Manufacturing Consent. Cf. also Hyman and Elger, 'Job Controls'; and Terry, 'Shop Steward Development'.

19 Cf. Burawoy, *Manufacturing Consent*, pp. 79–81, 176.
20 On the US, see M. J. Piore, 'American Labor and the Industrial Crisis', *Challenge* (Mar.–Apr. 1982).
21 Harbison, 'Constructive Aspects of Industrial Conflict', p. 274; cf. also C. Kerr, J. T. Dunlop, F. H. Harbison and C. A. Myers, *Industrialism and Industrial Man* (Cambridge, Mass., 1960), pp. 234–5; and Flanders, *Management and Unions*, pp. 246–51.
22 Hyman, *Industrial Relations*, p. 91. For an interpretation of British labour history in these terms, see R. Price, *Masters, Unions and Men: Work Control and the Rise of Labour in the Building Industry, 1830–1914* (Cambridge, 1980), and his 'Rethinking Labour History: The Importance of Work', in J. Cronin and J. Schneer (eds.), *Social Conflict and the Political Order in Modern Britain* (London, 1982); for a critique of this approach, see J. Zeitlin, 'Trade Unions and Job Control: A Critique of "Rank-and-Filism",' abstract in the *Bulletin of the Society for the Study of Labour History*, 46 (Spring 1983).
23 See, for example, Hyman and Elger, 'Job Controls', especially p. 119. For a well-known statement of the neo-classical view, see M. Friedman, 'Some Comments on the Significance of Labor Unions for Economic Policy', in D. M. Wright (ed.), *The Impact of the Union* (New York, 1951).
24 For discussions of the indeterminacy of market structures and the role of political factors in their constitution, see S. Berger and M. J. Piore, *Dualism and Discontinuity in Industrial Societies* (Cambridge, 1980); Sabel, *Work and Politics*, pp. 31–77 and 194–231; and B. Elbaum, W. Lazonick, F. Wilkinson and J. Zeitlin, 'The Labour Process, Market Structure, and Marxian Theory: A Symposium', *Cambridge Journal of Economics* 3, 3 (1979). For a particularly striking case in point, see Bryn Jones' discussion of the aerospace industry in this volume.
25 It may be, of course, that industrial relations only constitute a subsidiary component of a company's difficulties in the first place: see, for example, the case study of British Leyland in K. Williams, J. Williams and D. Thomas, *Why are the British Bad at Manufacturing?* (London, 1983).
26 W. Streeck and A. Hoff (eds.), *Workforce Restructuring, Manpower Management and Industrial Relations in the World Automobile Industry: A Report and Seven Case Studies Submitted to the Commission of the European Community* (2 vols., mimeo, International Institute of Management, Berlin, August 1983).
27 M. Rose and B. Jones, 'Managerial Strategy and Trade Union Response Plant-Level in Reorganisation of Work', in D. Knights, H. Wilmott and D. Collinson (eds.), *Job Redesign: Organisation and Control of the Labour Process* (Forthcoming, London, 1984); Batstone, 'Shop Steward Organisation in the Depression'; and H. Katz, 'The US Automobile Collective Bargaining System in Transition', *British Journal of Industrial Relations* 22, 2 (1984).
28 A. L. Friedman, *Industry and Labour.*

29 For a good discussion of the deskilling debate, see S. Wood (ed.), *The Degradation of Work?* *Skill, Deskilling and the Labour Process* (London, 1982); and for an examination of the skills required by different sections of the labour force in modern industry, see Sabel, *Work and Politics*, pp. 57–77; K. Kusterer, *Know-How on the Job: The Important Knowledge of 'Unskilled' Workers* (Boulder, Colorado, 1978); and T. Manwaring and S. Wood, 'The Ghost in the Machine: Tacit Skills in the Labour Process', in Knights, *et al.*, *Job Redesign*.

30 *Contested Terrain* (New York, 1979), pp. 48–57, 126–9, and 152–62. As C. Littler and G. Salaman observe, Edwards is particularly prone to the 'panacea fallacy': the assumption that because particular managerial strategies failed to provide a total solution to the 'labour problem', something else did. 'Bravermania and Beyond: Recent Theories of the Labour Process', *Sociology* 16, 2 (1982).

31 For a demonstration of similar tendencies in state–socialist societies, see C. Sabel and D. Stark, 'Planning, Politics and Shop Floor Power: Hidden Forms of Bargaining in Soviet-Imposed State–Socialist Societies', *Politics and Society* 11, 4 (1982).

32 For a critical review of the treatment of the state in the pluralist literature on public policy formation, see E. A. Nordlinger, *On the Autonomy of the Democratic State* (Cambridge, Mass., 1981). On public goods and the liberal theory of the state, see W. J. Baumol, *Welfare Economics and the Theory of the State* (London, 1952); and M. Olson, *The Logic of Collective Action* (Cambridge, Mass., 1965). For an exposition and critique of the political development literature, see B. Badie and P. Birnbaum, *The Sociology of the State* (Chicago, 1983). C. Lindblom, *Politics and Markets* (New York, 1977), is a sophisticated recent restatement of the pluralist position.

33 See, for example, the survey in L. Panitch, 'Recent Theorisations of Corporatism: Reflections on a Growth Industry', *British Journal of Sociology* 31, 2 (1980). Two collections which encompass the best of the recent debate are P. Schmitter and G. Lembruch (eds.), *Trends Towards Corporatist Intermediation* (London, 1979); and S. Berger (ed.), *Organizing Interests in Western Europe* (Cambridge, 1981).

34 See, for example, M. Crozier, S. Huntington and J. Wanetuki, *The Crisis of Democracy* (Washington, D.C., 1975); and for an analysis which situates these arguments in the context of the underlying antinomies of liberal political thought, see R. M. Unger, *Knowledge and Politics* (Glencoe, Illinois, 1975), ch. 4, and his *Law in Modern Society* (Glencoe, Illinois, 1976), pp. 192–203.

35 For an effective demonstration that the internal politics of corporate groups set sharp limits to the state's ability to coopt their leaders in this way, see C. Sabel, 'The Internal Politics of Trade Unions', in Berger (ed.), *Organizing Interests*.

36 P. Birnbaum, 'The State versus Corporatism', *Politics and Society* 11, 4 (1982); and A. Cox, 'Corporatism as Reductionism: The Analytic Limits of the Corporatist Thesis', *Government and Opposition* 16, 1 (1978).

37 L. Panitch, 'The Development of Corporatism in Liberal Democracies', *Comparative Political Studies* 10, 1 (1977); 'Recent Theorisations of Corporatism'; and 'Trade Unions and the Capitalist State', *New Left Review* 125 (1981). K. Middlemas, *Politics in Industrial Society* (London, 1979).

38 For recent surveys of the Marxist literature, see B. Jessop, *The Capitalist State* (Oxford, 1982); B. Frankel, 'On the State of the State: Marxist Theories of the State after Leninism', *Theory and Society* 7 (1979); D. A. Gold, K. Lo and E. O. Wright, 'Recent Developments in the Marxist Theory of the State', *Monthly Review* 27, 5–6 (1975).

39 For the classic statement of this position, see R. Miliband, *The State in Capitalist Society* (London, 1969); and despite disclaimers, J. O'Connor, *The Fiscal Crisis of the State* (New York, 1973).

40 For an equally classic statement of these objections, see N. Poulantzas, 'The Problem of the Capitalist State', in R. Blackburn (ed.), *Ideology in Social Science* (London, 1973).

41 On the US, see T. Skocpol, 'Political Response to Capitalist Crisis: Neo-Marxist Theories of the State and the Case of the New Deal', *Politics and Society* 10 (1980); S. Vittoz, 'The Economic Foundations of Industrial Politics in the United States and the Emerging Structural Theory of the State in Capitalist Society: The Case of New Deal Labor Policy', *Amerikastudien/American Studies* 27 (1982); W. H. Becker, *The Dynamics of Business–Government Relations: Industry and Exports, 1893–1921* (Chicago, 1982); and the essay by Harris in this volume. On Britain, see D. McEachern, *A Class Against Itself: Power in the Nationalisation of the British Steel Industry* (Cambridge, 1980); S. Tolliday, *Business, Banking and Politics: The Case of British Steel, 1918–1939* (forthcoming, 1985); Elbaum, *et al.*, 'The Labour Process'; and the essays by Reid, Whiteside and Jones in this volume.

42 Poulantzas, 'Capitalist State', p. 246; see also his *Political Power and Social Classes* (London, 1973).

43 Skocpol, 'Political Response to Capitalist Crisis', p. 173.

44 Poulantzas, 'Capitalist State', p. 246.

45 See Jessop, *The Capitalist State*, pp. 181–91.

46 For reviews of this literature, see J. Holloway and S. Picciotto (eds.), *The State and Capital: A Marxist Debate* (London, 1978); and Jessop, *The Capitalist State*, ch. 3.

47 See especially C. Offe, 'Structural Problems of the Capitalist State' in K. von Beyme (ed.), *German Political Studies* 1 (1974); 'The Theory of the Capitalist State and the Problem of Policy Formation', in L. Lindberg, R. Alford, C. Crouch and C. Offe (eds.), *Stress and Contradiction in Modern Capitalism* (Lexington, Mass., 1975); and C. Offe and V. Ronge, 'Theses on the Theory of the State', *New German Critique* 6 (1976). Quite similar claims that 'the form of the state problematises its function' are put forward by more orthodox exponents of the state derivation approach: see the account of J. Hirsch's ideas in Jessop, *The Capitalist State*, pp. 101–6.

48 F. Block, 'The Ruling Class Does Not Rule: Notes on the Marxist Theory of the State', *Socialist Revolution* 33 (1977); and 'Beyond

Relative Autonomy: State Managers as Historical Subjects', *Socialist Register* (1980).
49 For a famous, but more explicitly functionalist version of this argument, see M. Kalecki, 'The Political Implications of Full Employment', reprinted in his *Selected Essays on the Dynamics of Capitalist Economies* (Cambridge, 1971); and for a restatement in pluralist terms, see Lindblom, *Politics and Markets*, pp. 170–200.
50 Skocpol, 'Political Responses to Capitalist Crisis'.
51 Block, 'Beyond Relative Autonomy'.
52 Jessop, *The Capitalist State*, ch. 5; A. Cutler, B. Hindess, P. Hirst and A. Hussain, *Marx's 'Capital' and Capitalism Today* (2 vols., London, 1977).
53 For extended discussions of the complex interaction between state building and ideas about the state in Western Europe, see K. Dyson, *The State Tradition in Western Europe* (Oxford, 1980); and F. Meinecke, *Machiavellism: The Idea of Raison D'Etat and its Place in History* (London, 1957).
54 Marxism, of course, originated as an alternative response to the Hegelian theoretical inheritance.
55 Quoted in Dyson, *State Tradition*, pp. 45 and 103.
56 C. Schmitt, *The Concept of the Political* (New Brunswick, N.J., 1976).
57 T. Skocpol, *States and Social Revolutions* (Cambridge, 1979), p. 29.
58 C. Tilly (ed.), *The Formation of National States in Western Europe* (Princeton, N.J., 1975), p. 70; cf. P. Nettl, 'The State as a Conceptual Variable', *World Politics* 20 (1968).
59 F. Gilbert (ed.), *The Historical Essays of Otto Hintze* (Oxford, 1974), p. 183.
60 For other recent analyses which emphasise the interaction of external and internal forces in state formation, see F. Schurmann, *The Logic of World Power* (New York, 1974); P. Gourevitch, 'The Second Image Reversed: The International Sources of Domestic Politics', *International Organization* 32, 4 (1978); A. Zolberg, 'Strategic Interactions and the Formation of Modern States: France and England', *International Social Science Journal* 32, 4 (1980); and A. Zolberg, 'Origins of the Modern World System: A Missing Link', *World Politics* 33 (1981).
61 R. Gilpin, *Multinational Corporations and US Power* (New York, 1975), p. 39.
62 For historical comparisons of French and British state building, see Tilly, *National States*; Zolberg, 'Strategic Interactions'; and P. Anderson, *Lineages of the Absolutist State* (London, 1974). For arguments which draw out the contemporary significance of these contrasting trajectories, see P. Birnbaum, 'State, Centre and Bureaucracy', *Government and Opposition* 16, 1 (1981); P. Birnbaum, *La Logique de l'état* (Paris, 1982); and P. A. Hall, 'Policy Innovation and the Structure of the State: The Politics–Administration Nexus in France and Britain', *The Annals* 466 (1983).
63 For the oscillation between these poles in the realist conception of power, see Meinecke, *Machiavellism*, especially, pp. 9–10.
64 For the parallel between power and profit maximisation in realist

theories of international relations, see S. D. Krasner, *Defending the National Interest: Raw Materials Investments and US Foreign Policy* (Princeton, N.J., 1978), p. 37; and for the analogy between market processes and natural selection, together with some of its difficulties, see Elster, *Ulysses and the Sirens*, pp. 28–35 and 133–7.

65 Hence the concept of 'national interest' cannot properly be identified, even retrospectively, with the preferences of central decision-makers, as Krasner does in his otherwise stimulating study of raw materials investments and US foreign policy: see *Defending the National Interest*, pp. 13–14 and 42–5.

66 See J. Turner, 'The Politics of "Organized Business" during the First World War', in J. Turner (ed.), *Businessmen and Politics* (London, 1984); J. Melling, 'Scottish Industrialists and the Changing Character of Class Relationships in the Clyde Region, c. 1880–1918', in T. Dickson (ed.), *Capital and Class in Scotland* (Edinburgh, 1982); and the essay by Reid in this volume.

67 A. Gerschenkron, *Economic Backwardness in Historical Perspective* (Cambridge, Mass., 1966).

68 Compare H. Rosenberg, *Bureaucracy, Aristocracy and Autocracy* (Cambridge, Mass., 1958) with D. Vogel, 'Why Businessmen Distrust their State: The Political Consciousness of American Corporate Executives', *British Journal of Political Science* 8, 1 (1978).

69 B. B. Gilbert, *The Evolution of National Insurance in Great Britain* (London, 1966); B. Semmel, *Imperialism and Social Reform* (London, 1960); G. R. Searle, *The Quest for National Efficiency* (Oxford, 1971); J. Winter, 'The Impact of the First World War on Civilian Health in Britain', *Economic History Review*, 2nd series, 30 (1977).

70 On Britain, see the essay by Reid in this volume; P. Addison, *The Road to 1945* (London, 1975); and J. Harris, *William Beveridge* (Oxford, 1977). On the US, see M. Dubofsky, 'Abortive Reform: The Wilson Administration and Organized Labor', in J. Cronin and C. Sirianni (eds.), *Work, Community and Power* (Phila., Pa., 1983); and on Germany, see. G. Feldman, *Army, Industry and Labor in Germany, 1914–1918* (Princeton, N.J., 1966).

71 For an interpretation of the New Deal in these terms, see Schurmann, *The Logic of World Power*; and for a comparative study which emphasises the positive impact of social democratic governments on welfare provisions and income distribution, see J. Stephens, *The Transition from Capitalism to Socialism* (London, 1978).

72 For recent reviews of the literature on the 'imperialism of free trade', see W. R. Louis (ed.), *Imperialism* (New York, 1976); and P. J. Cain, *The Economic Foundations of British Overseas Expansion, 1815–1914* (London, 1981).

73 See the essay by Tolliday in this volume; H. Clegg and R. Adams, *The Employers' Challenge* (Oxford, 1957); and R. McKersie and L. Hunter, *Pay, Productivity and Collective Bargaining* (London, 1973).

74 F. Longstreth, 'The City, Industry and the State', in C. Crouch (ed.), *State and Economy in Contemporary Capitalism* (London, 1979); and

B. Jessop, 'The Transformation of the State in Post-war Britain', in R. Scase (ed.), *The State in Western Europe* (London, 1980).

75 S. Blank, 'Britain: The Politics of Foreign Economic Policy, the Domestic Economy and the Problem of Pluralist Stagnation', in P. Katzenstein (ed.), *Between Power and Plenty* (Madison, Wisc., 1978); Gilpin, *Multinational Corporations*, ch. 3; and P. M. Kennedy, *The Rise and Fall of British Naval Mastery* (London, 1976).

76 See the essay by Contini in this volume.

2

Dilution, trade unionism and the state in Britain during the First World War*

ALASTAIR REID

The whole history of the shop stewards is the history of a strike wave developing in the engineering centres. It was a revolt against the new conditions imposed by the dilution of Labour which were breaking down the strongholds of the skilled workers. This strike movement was harnessed by the revolutionary socialists of the SLP, the BSP and the syndicalists.[1]

Terse though they are, these remarks by J. T. Murphy in *Preparing for Power* (1934) can still stand as a summary of the conventional view of industrial relations in Britain during the First World War. Naturally those whose political opinions have been closest to Murphy's revolutionary socialism have developed this line of interpretation at the greatest length, but it has also produced a remarkably strong echo in the writing of historians with quite different political perspectives, and almost all of the existing research on labour during the war has focussed on the same events and the same organisations.

The leading exponent of the 'revolutionary' school has been James Hinton, whose detailed study of *The First Shop Stewards' Movement* (1973) made a decisive contribution to the tradition established by early Communist militants like Murphy. Indeed it is largely as a result of this book that the conventional picture has become so firmly established for it was the first, and is still the only major attempt by a non-participant to provide extensive documentation of developments in British industry during the First World War. As in most of the accounts which had preceded it and were to follow it, the focus of attention was squarely on the engineering industry and the centre stage was occupied by the figure of the skilled craftsman. Whereas before 1914 skilled engineers and their unions were seen as having been more or less successful in capturing the new processes introduced in response to foreign competition, Hinton argued that the acceleration of changes in industrial organisation during the war could no longer be contained by the normal methods of craft regulation. In order to deal with vast increases in the use of machinery, the drafting of engineers into the army and particularly an influx of unskilled and female labour, the skilled men had to construct new forms of shop floor organisation. And though these were eventually to be successful in pushing back the tide, Hinton further argued that the shock of the initial challenge jolted many engineers out of their traditional 'craft conservatism' and created new aspirations for revolutionary forms of 'workers' control' in British industry. Moreover, a large part of this process was seen as being the result of a wartime revelation of the true nature of the British state. Again the years 1914–18 were presented as an acceleration of already existing tendencies, this time towards a closer alliance of big business and the civil service in an attempt to gain tighter control over labour, through such schemes as unemployment insurance and labour exchanges. Thus, Hinton argued that behind a public front of concern for the welfare of workers the state was increasing its powers of surveillance and coercion and, by appearing to concede to the demands of organised labour, was able to embroil trade union leaders ever more deeply in the apparatus of an authoritarian, business-dominated, 'Servile State'. In this view, then, skilled workers found themselves confronted during the war by an acceleration of changes in working conditions combined with a rapid growth of state compulsion at the same time as being abandoned by their elected leaders. Thus the new forms of 'rank and file' organisation which began mainly as pragmatic responses to the problems of craft regulation were seen as moving rapidly towards a principled opposition to the compromises of official trade unionism and, especially when they reached the level of regional Workers' Committees, towards a radical challenge to the industrial and political status quo. The only possible response of those in power, then, was to be ruthless in smashing such subversive threats, and the inevitable result was a revolutionary escalation of the opposition between the state and shop floor organisation.

Most of the other views of wartime industrial relations are in fact variations on this central theme; they all focus on the engineering industry, they all see dilution as the root cause of unrest, and they all emphasise the widening gulf between shop floor organisation and official trade unionism. Where they differ is in their political starting points and consequently in their assessment of the nature of state activity and the wider implications of the shop stewards' movement. Thus, what might be labelled the 'corporatist' position, implicit in the work of Arthur Marwick and made controversially explicit in Keith Middlemas's *Politics in Industrial Society* (1979), takes a view of industrial events virtually identical to that of the 'revolutionary' school but portrays the state in more neutral colours. It is no longer seen as a tool of industrial employers but rather as an impartial arbiter striving to defuse conflict by the incorporation of the representatives of both capital and labour in the lengthy and pacifying procedures of joint committees. The seriousness of the threat of 'rank and file' organisation is therefore accepted but it is seen as only one among several influences leading to the creation of a centrist state, and if any sinister elements are identified in this process they do not amount to a conspiracy of one class against another but rather of bureaucracy against the whole society.

Other writers, while still focussing on shop floor organisation in the engineering industry, have been more sceptical about the degree to which it posed an insurrectionist threat and have therefore been able to release government actions from a narrow obligation to defuse revolutionary situations. For example, in his recent study of *The Legend of Red Clydeside* (1983), Ian McLean has emphasised the conservative and divisive aspects of craft regulation and has seen the state's response as being characterised far more by 'muddling through' than by the pursuit of a coherent strategy of any kind. Similarly, most 'administrative' historians have played down the dramatic elements in industrial relations and have emphasised the complexity of the government reaction. At the same time, they have also tended to fill the role of frustrated hero with one or other leading civil servant, for example, José Harris's *William Beveridge* (1977), and have therefore argued that in the midst of the muddle there were still some enlightened individuals attempting to pursue consistent, rational and benevolent strategies. Both of these approaches have the advantage over the 'revolutionary' and 'corporatist' views that they emphasise the complexity of the internal structure of government and a wider range of forces shaping policy, but unfortunately their treatment of industrial issues is far weaker and indeed is generally shaped by the conventional view. Thus rather than advancing a radically different analysis of wartime collective bargaining their divergence has only been over the seriousness of the threat posed by the shop stewards' movement and the degree of consistency and energy shown by the government in repressing it.

Despite the variety of interpretations, then, this spectrum is actually based on a consensus over the central thread in the development of wartime industrial relations; proponents of the 'revolutionary', 'corporatist', 'muddling through' and 'administrative' schools are all united in seeing an opposition between the state and shop floor bargaining.

The rest of the present contribution will offer a thoroughgoing revision of this conventional view, in the first place simply by switching the focus of attention onto another important war industry, shipbuilding, and by examining the extent to which this sector was subject to structural reorganisation and dilution with female labour. Then the argument will broaden out in the course of an analysis of the union response in shipbuilding, for this will involve a reconsideration of some of the most important incidents in wartime industrial relations, the 'Clyde unrest' of 1915–16. The more general questions raised will be pursued in a reinterpretation of government intervention, focussing on the shipbuilding industry but necessarily including a broader consideration of the influences on the formation of state labour policy. Finally, on the basis of this new industrial case study and a reconsideration of the general attitude of the government, it should be possible to make a critical assessment of the conventional view and to advance some alternative conclusions.[2]

I

At first glance there is indeed a great deal of evidence which seems to point to the centrality of dilution not only in the engineering industry but throughout the metal-working sectors, including shipbuilding. From the very earliest sets of wartime negotiations in the autumn of 1914 employers were raising the questions of relaxation of trade privileges, the upgrading of the semi-skilled and possibly even the importation of labour from outside the sector concerned. The increasing pressures of demand for artillery, warships and shells pushed such issues more and more to centre stage and, during the gradual moves towards universal male conscription in early 1916, the question of the substitution of women for men became so prominent that from then on 'dilution' was understood to refer to these new experiments in female employment.

Thus by the summer of 1916 official press releases claimed that dilution schemes were successfully in operation in a wide range of important industries throughout the west of Scotland, particularly in engineering and shipbuilding in which 14,000 women had been introduced into at least half of the workplaces controlled by the government.[3] Going even a little deeper into the archives confirms this impression. It can be discovered for example that at meetings of the Clyde Shipbuilders' Association Lynden Macassey, a leading member of the Clyde Dilution Commission, on several occasions appeared as an almost perfect embodiment of the 'Servile State'. He assured local employers in no uncertain terms that united action behind an agreed dilution programe would be backed up strongly by the government's emergency powers, and that 'all customs opposed to the introduction of unskilled and female labour, and therefore restrictive of output, would be abrogated, their maintenance being contrary to the law'.[4]

However, this impression of the very extensive adoption of dilution conveyed in the official propaganda is a misleading one. Far from being universally implemented throughout the metal-working sectors, dilution was restricted both by the uneven impact of the demand for war materials on different sectors and by the existence of a large number of tasks which were thought to be unsuitable for female labour. Those which *were* deemed to be suitable were normally carried out indoors, in clean surroundings and at moderate temperatures. They were usually already highly subdivided and easy to pick up, as employers were reluctant to waste scarce resources training temporary workers. And they were usually tasks on which women could be employed in self-contained gangs away from the male workforce, not only to prevent sexual incidents but also because women responded best to their own female supervisors.[5]

On one or another of these counts, many tasks in heavy industry were not susceptible to the intensive substitution of women for men, and in shipbuilding most jobs were ruled out on *all* grounds. A large proportion of the indoor work was either near furnaces, and there-fore too hot, or would have required close cooperation with male workers, and little of it was easy enough to pick up to make temporary female workers attractive to the employers. In addition, most of the central tasks of ship construction were done in the open air and also in extremely dangerous conditions for newcomers, due to the chaos of the yards' open bulkheads and high scaffolding.[6]

As a result, the dilution actually achieved in the shipbuilding industry was slight: of the 14,000 women claimed by the government as having been introduced on Clydeside in the first half of 1916 only 1,000 went into shipyards. Indeed 13 yards refused to employ women at all, and, leaving aside Beardmore's and Fairfield's which took larger numbers, the average number of women employed in the remaining 15 cases was only 30.[7] Closer examination of the returns made by firms to the Clyde Shipbuilders' Association (CSA) indicates that the greater part of these women were employed in the marine engineering shops where conditions most closely approached the ideal. For here there had always been a significant amount of repetition production of light and simple components and this could be carried out in self-contained groups in well-lit, temperate shops. Small groups of women were also employed on ancillary tasks like clerical work, time keeping and store keeping, while yet others performed light finishing work like painting and polishing. Only very rarely did they actually assist skilled male workers, though scattered cases can be found of women performing light preparatory tasks for plumbers, joiners and platers.[8]

In other words, all of the publicity about extensive dilution in the shipbuilding industry was little more than morale-boosting propaganda. On Clydeside, for example, though relations between the government Dilution Commissioners and the CSA were at first quite cordial, it soon became apparent that Macassey's strong speeches were only efforts to keep shipyard management quiet and free his hand for the more urgent negotiations in the engineering industry. In fact the Dilution Commission did absolutely nothing as regards shipbuilding for two months after the initial contacts and, though the CSA began to complain loudly about bureaucratic delays, a great deal of the inertia was to be found among its own members who were well aware of the unsuitability of working conditions. Out of 32 member firms only eight showed any enthusiasm at all for dilution and even among those most outspoken in its favour there still remained very strong doubts. As the Greenock firm George Brown and Company remarked:[9]

it must not be lost sight of that the period of training would be a long one, and that the work is not generally suitable for women, being of a hazardous and somewhat dangerous nature and conducted as it is in the open air, subject to the vagaries of our boisterous climate, so that only strong healthy women would be able to stand it. There is also the danger and risk of the class of women that would be employed getting out of control and by so doing making the management and conduct of business worse than it *even* is at *present* with only men employed.

Apart from such explicit objections there was usually also an ulterior motive, particularly strong among the merchant ship-builders: the desire to resist wartime pressures and retain as much skilled labour as possible. Indeed at the end of 1916 a major scandal was unveiled at Harland and Wolff's Merseyside yard which was providing 'accommodation on their premises for workmen in their service and on time-wages but unemployed, in which to smoke, read and play cards during working hours, as an alternative to sending them home with possible risk of military enlistment'.[10]

The Admiralty itself began to adopt a similar attitude as it became clear that the Ministry of Munitions had no real concern for efficiency in the shipyards and only wanted to encourage dilution in order to release skilled men for engineering works and the technical units of the army. Thus Admiralty officials moved from an initial position of cooperation in boosting army shell production to one of insistence on the maintenance of traditional high standards of craftsmanship and 'finish' as a cover-all tactic to protect the skilled labour force in the shipbuilding industry. This attitude became so deeply entrenched that it remained a central part of Admiralty policy even when increasing merchant ship production became a matter of top priority in the last two years of the war. As a result, the Shipyard Labour Department, set up to promote Ministry of Munitions' policies within the Admiralty, was obstructed at every turn by the highly conservative technical departments and was finally made a scapegoat and broken up during the major shipping crisis of February 1918. As one official at the rival Ministry of Munitions then remarked, the shipbuilding industry had remained throughout the war 'notorious for having effected the least possible dilution'.[11]

This was certainly the case taking the Ministry of Munitions' own definition of 'dilution' as the introduction of female labour and the release of as many skilled men as possible for other employment. However, it is probable that for management and government administrators 'dilution' in the case of shipbuilding came to mean the relaxation of demarcation lines and the more flexible deployment of existing skilled male labour. Certainly the so-called 'Dilution of Labour Agreements', reached by the Commissioners with the Clyde committees of the shipwrights' and boilermakers' societies in the summer of 1916, were primarily concerned with the details of demarcation and support for dilution proper was only tagged on at the end as a gesture of principle.[12]

However, even allowing for this distinct interpretation of 'dilution' in the shipbuilding industry, little enough was achieved. As far as the Clyde agreements were concerned, for example, the phrasing that only 'suitable' workers could be transferred across prewar demarcation lines was always interpreted by the unions in their own favour. Thus the shipwrights insisted that the limits of *internal* upgrading be reached before any non-society labour was introduced, while the boilermakers for their part made sure that all transferred men were young enough to fall within the standard system of apprenticeship.[13] While there were some scattered cases of success in the relaxation of demarcation lines among the outfitting trades, no major breakthroughs were made at any stage during the war in the reorganisation of the central tasks of ship construction. This was partly a result of the employers' own resistance to the loss of skilled labour implied in most of the schemes proposed by government departments, but it was, above all, due to the extremely strong position which the unions were able to establish within a very tight labour market. Thus even in the case of the introduction of pneumatic riveting machines in 1917, on which the employers pushed as hard as possible for major reductions from the hand riveting rates and for the employment of unskilled labour on ancillary work, the boilermakers' society was able to enforce its own conception of the fair rate for the job and to insist that only its own members be employed on any task connected with pneumatic work. Wages and conditions were therefore significantly better than had been achieved under the 1905 Caulking Agreement, and the union negotiators were so confident that they self-consciously abandoned their prewar suspicion of machinery: 'in 1905 the argument then adopted by our side was that the moment these machines came there would be no hope for a class of our people. That fallacy has been disabused today. We know that the more the machinery the more work required and the more men'.[14]

II

Far from being faced with a traumatic threat from extensive mechanisation and dilution, then, skilled shipyard workers were able to use the tight wartime labour market to strengthen their collective bargaining position enormously. But, it would be a mistake to conclude that they were therefore 'relatively passive'.[15] Certainly in the first few weeks of the war there were enthusiastic expressions of support for cooperation between workers and employers to increase output on the Clyde. However, the prevalent mood was jokingly referred to by one local union official as 'an armed neutrality', and it very rapidly broke down to be replaced by an intensification of the embittered relations between employers and men which had always been characteristic of the industry in this region.[16]

There was growing suspicion on the part of the unions that management was using the war as an excuse to weaken their controls over the labour market and, as a result, trade union officials became increasingly insistent that all of their members be fully employed before there could be any relaxation of demarcation, let alone dilution. Whatever the Clyde employers' original intentions, when faced with mounting union obstructions they did begin to see the war as a fine opportunity to dispense with a chronic nuisance. There were several incidents as early as December 1914 during which shipyard managements resorted to the police or threatened to call in the Admiralty, and the following month formal proposals were submitted to the Board of Trade by the CSA secretary on behalf of the Shipbuilding Employers' Federation as a whole, calling for legal sanctions against sectional wages strikes, unilateral control over the 'making up' of squads broken by absenteeism, and the outright prohibition of alcohol.[17] However, despite consistent lobbying throughout the first half of 1915, this hard line was frustrated by the more moderate attitudes prevalent in Whitehall, and the small concessions gained corresponded more closely to the attitudes of the civil service than to the demands of the employers. Thus instead of the prohibition of alcohol they were only given restrictions on licensing hours, and instead of general compulsory powers over their workforces they only achieved specific regulations of labour mobility.[18]

The latter were granted under Section 7 of the Munitions of War Act and, while it fell far short of what the shipbuilding employers really wanted, they decided to make the most of their new powers. Section 7 made it illegal for any employer to take on workers who had left government-controlled firms unless they possessed leaving certificates issued by their previous employers guaranteeing that their services were no longer required. Although intended by the government as a means of reducing the movement of workers motivated by the desire for higher wages, this section was increasingly used by the Clyde employers as an instrument of general labour discipline. By threatening to dismiss men without leaving certificates and thereby subjecting them to a minimum of six weeks unemployment, shipyard managers and foremen were able to compel workers to take on dirty, unpopular and less well-paid jobs and also to retain as much skilled labour as they wanted regardless of the availability of work elsewhere.[19]

Naturally this led to an escalation of disputes as the shipbuilding unions and their members began to resist this attempt to undercut the advantages they had won in the tight wartime labour market. One particularly serious strike took place in the last week of September at the Beardmore yard in Dalmuir when a foreman broke up a meeting of caulkers which had been called to discuss a complicated wages question. Although it had apparently been customary to allow such lunchtime meetings to continue for some minutes after the whistle so that all of the business could be cleared up, the foreman on this occasion insisted that the men either return to work immediately or lose their whole afternoon's pay. This provoked a walk-out by 70 of the men concerned and feelings only escalated even higher when 50 of the strikers were fined £2 at a General Munitions Tribunal.[20]

The response at Dalmuir was probably only so explosive because there was already a district-wide campaign of protest against the Munitions of War Act. This had been provoked by an incident at the Fairfield yard in Govan where, on 26 August, two shipwrights had been dismissed for loitering. However, since the reason for their dismissal had been jotted on the note sent to the time office and this raised an old contentious issue of exactly what information about a man's conduct could be communicated between employers, their shop stewards advised them to refuse to go. As a result of a mishandling of the matter by the Fairfield management the dispute rapidly escalated into a strike of 426 shipwrights, and, once again, matters only became worse after 17 of their shop stewards were each fined £10 by a General Munitions Tribunal. In order to fan up more opposition to the way in which Section 7 of the Munitions of War Act was being used on the Clyde, these shop stewards chose to go to jail rather than pay the fines and this case above all the others became the central symbolic issue in a major wave of unrest in the local shipbuilding industry.[21]

The situation became especially inflammable because of its chronological coincidence with the climax of a long campaign of resistance to rising house rents focussed in Partick and especially in Govan, in which shipyard workers and their wives were prominent. The result was that throughout the last quarter of 1915 the Clydeside shipbuilding industry was constantly on the verge of a local general strike in protest against the prosecutions either of shipyard workers under the Munitions of War Act or of tenants refusing to pay rent increases. Indeed on 17 November, just after the problems caused by Section 7 had to some extent been ironed out, there was a one-day strike in six upper Clyde shipyards in protest against the summonsing to trial of 18 rent strikers.[22]

Both because of its direct impact on warship production and because of the fear that this example might affect other sectors and other regions, the Clyde unrest was taken extremely seriously by the government. Investigators were sent in, high-level inquiries were established and sooner or later all of the popular demands were conceded. The prosecutions of tenants planned for 22 November were dropped and a Rent Restriction Act was passed three days later. Then, in January 1916, after a long process of consultation with the unions, the Munitions of War Act was amended to concede the major union demands over Section 7: the form of the leaving certificate was changed, the procedure of Munitions Tribunals was altered and the severity of penalties for offenders was substantially reduced.[23] Without having the space to demonstrate the point at length here, it can be suggested that dilution in the Clydeside engineering industry became such a sensitive issue largely because of the legacy of suspicion combined with organisational confidence left in the minds of local workers by this unrest in the shipyards in the immediately preceding months. This was certainly felt by many of the government officials involved, for example, the Ministry of Munitions' Chief Labour Officer reported on 18 December 1915:[24]

From the experience of the last year (and particularly of the last few months), it is regarded as certain that the Trade Unions concerned would most actively oppose the introduction of semi-skilled or unskilled labour . . . the atmosphere which is essential to permit of such a movement yielding any result does not exist, and the chances of any movement might well be likened to an effort to advance, and sustain an advance, against a solid wall of poisonous gas.

From this rather bald narrative of a complex and frequently discussed set of events a number of points ought to be emphasised. In the first place, the industrial unrest of late 1915 was focussed squarely in the shipbuilding districts and it revolved not around dilution but around the management and control of existing methods of production, particularly the employers' attempts to turn Section 7 of the Munitions Act to their own advantage. While elements of organisation and coordination were clearly present, the unrest was so deep-rooted and widespread that it was impossible to dismiss it as the work of a minority. As Lynden Macassey reported after a month as a government conciliator in the region: 'You find resistance to the Act, and a determination to cripple and crab it exalted into a principle of belief and tenaciously held and publicly preached by workmen, who judged by conventional standards are honest, industrious operatives, are elders in the kirk and have their boys fighting at the Front'.[25] Furthermore there was a very marked overlap of the two strands of protest against rent increases and against industrial discipline. There were frequent indications that workers in Govan and Partick shipyards were prepared to strike over the housing issue, and when the Govan branch of the shipwrights' society sent motions of protest to the Secretary of State for Scotland over Section 7, it not only added a motion about rent control but put it *first*.[26] Finally, this wave of unrest was not characterised by the emergence of a major gulf between trade union officials and their members, nor did shop stewards emerge as organisers of a 'rank and file' revolt against union policy. On the contrary, they were, more often than not, to be found acting just like other trade union officials, caught between the pressures of representing the short term interests of their immediate constituents and the long-term interests of their organisation as a whole. Thus after the dispute at Beardmore's Dalmuir yard one of those directly involved recalled that 'the shop stewards had not time to keep them at their work and as far as I could see, if there had been a little more of it it would have been very hard to keep back a general strike under the circumstances'.[27] Moreover, in shipbuilding, in some contrast to engineering, the relative uniformity of working conditions and rates of pay by the late nineteenth century had made it possible to develop effective centralised trade union policies covering the whole industry and had reduced the autonomy of shop stewards. This was particularly marked in the case of the boilermakers' society within which *district* delegates had always been more important than shop delegates in local disputes and the hands of the national officials had only been tied by employer-imposed procedural rules for a very brief period between 1907 and 1912. Thus the boilermakers entered the war with a more integrated national structure than the engineers and the employers' main grievance was not over 'unofficial' resistance in the shops and yards but rather over the strength and intransigence of institutionalised trade unionism.

Reviewing the shipyard unrest again with this point in mind yields a picture of complex interaction between national and local officials in coordinating resistance to employers' pressures. On 3 November 1914 the national officials of the shipbuilding unions had agreed in principle to increased flexibility in the application of work rules but had simultaneously insisted that all practical details be negotiated thoroughly at the local level: in the ensuing talks the district officials were intransigent. Negotiations were therefore resumed at the national level on 9 December 1914 when the officials of both the shipwrights' and the boilermakers' societies refused to allow any relaxation of union regulations. Throughout these talks both local and national officials were equally firm in refusing to discuss changes in the organisation of work until all of their members were fully employed and, when hard pressed on controversial matters, they always insisted that such issues had to be decided by a wider constituency. In the words of one Clyde official: 'questions of such importance must come before the workmen themselves. We are only representatives and such a thing must come before the men'.[28]

Even after the government began to intervene to loosen up this deadlock, the officials of the shipbuilding unions continued to be successful in their inflexible resistance and were consequently able to win substantial concessions at the Treasury Conference, later embodied in the Munitions of War Act. These included firm guarantees regarding both the temporary nature of wartime changes in the organisation of work and the maintenance of current levels of earnings, as well as promises to set up more effective channels for the arbitration of disputes and the consultation of the unions over matters of labour policy.[29] In the end, this Act may also have contained clauses which could be turned against the unions, but officials in the shipbuilding industry were not reluctant to organise resistance. During the unrest on the Clyde in the Autumn of 1915 the initiative passed largely to the local level where there was no clear-cut distinction between the attitudes of district officials and those of shop stewards.[30] In the case of the first illegal strike on the Clyde (a Fairfield coppersmiths' demarcation dispute on 27 July 1915) the officials concerned paid the fines immediately and remarked that they 'regarded the action of their members as quite legal'.[31] Then, during the far more serious dispute over the shipwrights which later erupted at the same yard, the local officials were solidly behind the shop stewards from the start and were soon able to win over their national leaders. Thus as the conflict unfolded, the crucial strike threat of 23 October was issued by the local officials and, while the national officials formally repudiated it at the subsequent Whitehall talks, they simultaneously insisted that all of the Clyde demands be met.[32]

Officials of all kinds, from shop stewards to general secretaries, had a strong interest in containing disputes within existing bargaining procedures and this made them more cautious in the use of strikes. At the same time they generally backed the majority demands of their members while distinguishing between their own willingness to compromise and the intransigence of 'the men in the yards' in order to leave the maximum room for the subsequent resumption of negotiations. One government official accurately pinpointed this characteristic interaction when he reported from Glasgow at the height of the shipyard unrest: 'Beginning with the Govan Trades Council, the movement had been taken up by the official delegates of the Unions. He had seen several of the latter, who repudiated the actions of the Govan Trades Council, but urged that unless something was done immediately a stoppage was inevitable'.[33]

III

Even if their officials had by no means been incorporated within its apparatus, workers *were* more and more subject to the intervention of the state, an extremely important element in industrial relations during the war which has so far only been mentioned in passing. From some points of view it might indeed appear to have been a 'Servile State', for there was certainly growing pressure from government departments for the reorganisation of production, and this was backed up by emergency powers. At the same time, in its brief appearance in this present paper, the wartime state has already presented a more ambiguous image. It has been evident, for example, that shipbuilding employers were not successful in pressing their hardline demands in the summer of 1915 and also that there could be serious conflicts between government departments responsible for regulating labour. These indications should already suggest that the British state during the First World War was not a simple tool in the hands of industrialists, but this will require some further elaboration given the widespread acceptance of just such a point of view.

In the first place it is important to remember that there were strict limits set on the degree of compulsion which government departments could use in pursuit of their aims. These were partly legal, as became obvious to officials at the Admiralty in the autumn of 1915 when they began to investigate the means available for preventing strikes in the Clydeside shipbuilding industry. They soon discovered that there were no suitable clauses even under the Defence of the Realm Act and when they then pursued the possibility of incorporating new sections into the Munitions of War Act, to allow the prosecution of union officials and the prohibition of financial support to people breaking wartime regulations, the Scottish Law Office replied that it would probably not be worth the trouble:[34]

even when a strike is illegal within the meaning of the Munitions Act, we do not think that the Lord Advocate would succeed in the Civil Courts in obtaining an interdict prohibiting the Trustees of a Trade Union from making strike payments, and, in view of the necessarily protracted character of litigation in the Civil Courts, we doubt if this remedy would be of much practical utility.

As a result nothing further seems to have been done and the only compulsory powers possessed by the wartime state in Britain were those under the Defence of the Realm Act permitting it to deport disruptive individuals from problem areas or, at the other end of the scale, to prosecute individuals for sedition or treason.[35] At no time did any government department have the legal means to force through unpopular industrial policies against generalised resistance.[36]

Alongside this lack of legal power over the civilian population there were also limits on government intervention set by British public opinion. Whenever the question of any form of compulsion was raised, there were outcries from the general public, members of parliament and important pressure groups, especially the unions: it was as a result of just such opposition that the Munitions of War Act did not in the end embody any major compulsory powers. Furthermore, the actions in Glasgow early in 1916, which have come to be seen as major examples of serious repression, appear rather trivial when measured on an international scale. The closure of a newspaper for a month, the deportation of five industrial militants and the jailing of three others for terms of three months to one year would hardly have become so symbolic but for the sensitivity of public opinion. This was given even greater force by the tone of official propaganda for, after all, the war was supposed to be one against dictatorship. It was therefore doubly difficult for the British state to adopt authoritarian measures, and even those who called for them most loudly in moments of crisis revealed something of the more general attitude once the storm had passed. According to the *Glasgow Herald* leader writer, who had earlier demanded general industrial compulsion:[37]

We are incapable of existing under a cast-iron system of rules and regulations such as that which prevails in Germany, and which is so apt to break down when it is over-strained . . . . It is true that we too frequently 'muddle through', but is there any other nation capable of doing this so successfully as we can and coming out on top in the end?

As well as being constrained by the relative absence of compulsory powers, governments were frequently hampered by internal differences between their departments. Thus the Ministry of Munitions and the Admiralty, the two major branches of the state responsible for war production, frequently clashed with each other over the allocation of skilled labour and even scarcer supplies of steel. The Ministry of Munitions wanted to extend its policy of dilution as far as possible throughout metal working in order to release skilled men for its own use in the production of guns and shells. The Admiralty, for its part, became increasingly uncooperative, even going as far as to establish a special 'Priority Department', in January 1916, to identify and resist Ministry of Munitions' encroachment on its resource base. This became a real nuisance as it not only directly reduced the amount of skilled labour freed for munitions' production, but also indirectly began to undermine the dilution campaign as a whole by setting bad precedents.[38]

Eventually a truce was reached on 18 October 1916 under which the Admiralty was given full control over labour in shipbuilding in return for an acceptance of the Ministry of Munitions' list of firms with labour priority.[39] But unfortunately this agreement collapsed almost as soon as it had been signed. For the German submarine campaign began to make huge inroads into the merchant marine and from early in 1917 production priorities were shifted away from land artillery and towards the building of cargo vessels. In order to minimise friction over labour policy in merchant shipbuilding the powers of the Ministry of Munitions were then transferred to a 'Shipyard Labour Department' which was set up within the Admiralty. However, while this certainly reduced inter-departmental conflicts it also kept the Admiralty traditionalists only too happy: they were able to block the development of an effective dilution and reorganisation policy and finally, in April 1918, to dissolve the new department amid severe criticism from most of the rest of the Cabinet.[40]

Within this narrative of the incompetent administration of shipyard labour the Ministry of Munitions seems to be a paradigm of progressive views and centralised administration, but within its own areas of responsibility it was frequently far less efficient than it would have liked to appear. In the first place there were serious frictions between its creator, Lloyd George, and his leading officials springing from the classic conflict between politicians and civil servants. For Lloyd George was continually faced with the pressures of public opinion and trade union lobbying and frequently had to make major concessions; meanwhile, in the background, protected from such immediate political pressures, the Ministry's leading officials generally disapproved and wished to stick to the letter of existing legislation. Moreover, there were significant differences of opinion even within this group of powerful administrators, with Hubert Llewellyn Smith and William Beveridge pursuing a tough line on left-wing militants, while Christopher Addison was rather more hesitant and prepared to look for compromises. Naturally such differences emerged most sharply under the stress of crises, so that far from functioning as a monolithic manipulator of labour, the Ministry of Munitions was more often indecisive and contradictory in its behaviour.[41]

Whatever the interpretation of its policies, then, it would be important to bear in mind the limits to state activity set by the law, public opinion and its own internal divisions. However, an even more crucial weakness in the standard account of the wartime state is the assumption that its policies conformed to the interests of industrial employers. It is certainly the case that some industrialists wanted a more coercive approach to labour matters and that they sometimes won the attention of important politicians, especially during the period of the initial establishment of the Ministry of Munitions in the summer of 1915. However, they were not on the whole very influential. Thus the influx of businessmen into the new ministry was primarily for the purposes of giving technical advice to the production departments, working out the mundane details of design, for example, and dealing with the placing and costing of contracts. The same pattern was repeated in 1918 when two leading private shipbuilders, James Lithgow and Lord Pirrie, were given control of merchant shipbuilding. Instead of marking the beginning of a major offensive against the unions, this coincided with the abandonment of a coherent Munitions' style labour policy and the focussing of attention on design details and the priority of building contracts.[42] While employers were sometimes acknowledged as having expertise on the handling of labour, this was emphatically not one of the skills which was required of them by the government.

Similarly, while the war saw the formation of many employers' pressure groups, including the Federation of British Industry, this was largely an indication of weakness rather than of strength. Initially established as a result of concern over the increase in government intervention in industry and the question of postwar economic policy, the tone of all these organisations was one of annoyance at not being consulted. This was especially true over labour matters on which it was almost universally felt that far too much was being conceded to the unions, particularly during the amendment of the Munitions Act and during the wage arbitrations of the last two years of the war.[43]

Labour policy, then, remained squarely in the hands of the professional civil service and primarily in the hands of men who had already served at the prewar Board of Trade Labour Department. In terms of their background they were either metropolitan progressive liberals or else ex-trade-union officials and, however it is interpreted, their policy before 1914 had been biased against hard-line employers and in favour of moderate trade unionism.[44] Wartime conditions, far from reversing this general orientation, markedly reinforced it. Not only were the unions strengthened by full employment and rapidly rising membership, the main government priority was clearly national security not private profit. While government bureaucracy could be substituted for the laws of the market and the hierarchies of private management there was no substitute for labour: its consent had to be won. There did remain quite serious frictions between trade unions and the government, especially over the slowness of wage arbitration which often meant that settlements were already rendered obsolete by rapid price inflation. However, that the state was generally responsive to pressure from the unions may be made clear by a brief review of the development of its labour policy in the first two years of the war.

From the very start the officials concerned refused to be used by the employers as a new weapon against the unions. On the contrary, they were experienced arbitrators quite conscious of the complexity of industrial relations and sensitive to the views of trade unionists. Llewellyn Smith, later to become the general secretary of the Ministry of Munitions, outlined his attitude as follows:[45]

the men are full of suspicion as to the real motives of the employers and the ultimate result of any concessions that they may make. I have considerable hope that by the exercise of patience and tact a successful result may yet be achieved. I am strongly of the opinion that nothing but disaster would attend any attempt to rush the position by a frontal attack on union policy, or by any Government action which would give the unions the impression that the Government in this matter were acting as the mouthpiece of the employers.

The first major initiative, by Sir George Askwith, highlighted the official willingness to overcome union worries by offering important assurances. The central strand of his approach was an attempt to negotiate the exchange of a relaxation of union restrictions on output for a government guarantee of a return to pre-1914 conditions once the war was over.[46] In other words, it was a clear renunciation of the employers' desire to use the war to make a permanent breach in trade union power. Furthermore, during the first upsurge of wage strikes in the spring of 1915, and largely in response to labour protest over 'profiteering', Askwith added to the government side of the bargain the control of wartime profits, a major concession to union demands that 'there should be an equal sacrifice on the part of employers and workmen'.[47]

This policy, developed in the course of almost continuous talks with union officials from January 1915, was the backbone of the 'Treasury Agreement' of 19 March 1915 and, as a result, provoked something of a backlash from many employers who demanded the prohibition of alcohol and stiff measures of industrial compulsion.[48] There was some support for prohibition at the Home Office but little at the Admiralty, and the line taken by Lloyd George's own industrial advisers was that this was very much a secondary problem which would respond best to careful treatment, namely the restriction of licensing hours and more wholehearted attempts to provide works' canteens.[49] Under heavy pressure from William Weir, among others, Lloyd George temporarily swung heavily towards the side of industrial compulsion and gave a controversial speech on this theme in Manchester on 3 June 1915. However, the ensuing storm of protest from trade unionists and members of parliament, combined with tactful pressure from leading members of his own staff at the Ministry of Munitions, led to a hasty retraction. Instead, the new ministry focussed its energy in the first months of its existence on mobilising all the untapped resources of the country's metal industries and on the careful implementation of the 'Shells and Fuses Agreement' (5 March 1915) in close consultation with the Amalgamated Society of Engineers (ASE).[50]

The Munitions of War Act in the end, then, gave statutory force to the 'Treasury Agreement' which was an agreement between only two parties: the government and the unions. Although there were clauses in the Act which could be used by hard-line employers as the nearest approximation to industrial compulsion, the government response to this was clearly favourable to the union side from the start. Sent to the Clyde in October 1915 both Lord Balfour and Lynden Macassey made clear their very strong criticisms of the Fairfields management, their equally strong sympathy for the union case, and their private opinion that the imprisoned shipwrights should be released immediately.[51] Indeed during the subsequent full-length hearings of their inquiry, in November 1915, the employers were effectively on trial for they were put in the position of answering union charges and were prevented from making a positive statement of their own case. Not surprisingly, then, the resulting Amendment Act removed all the causes of grievance which Clyde workers and union officials had raised over Section 7 and it was strongly opposed by industrial employers.[52]

Apart from its reaction to such tense dramas, the government in its day to day operations pursued a policy of detailed negotiation with shop stewards and local officials. Thus during the introduction of dilution on the Clyde in early 1916 the local commissioners were quite explicitly opposed to the principle of general compulsion, according to Lynden Macassey:[53]

Day by day our work is appreciably lightening and we do not feel we are

confronting the same dead weight of suspicious hostility. It has the characteristic that it is working quietly and by degrees, and not comprehensively
with possibly a general conflagration. It makes the most exacting and
exhausting demands upon the endurance and judgement of the Commissioners for transcending that involved in the deliverance of a more or less
general ultimatum.

This hallmark of Ministry of Munitions' procedure was also
evident in the approach adopted by the Shipyard Labour Department in 1917 and once again it evoked strong hostility from
industrial employers who both opposed the initial formation of the
department and then complained that it functioned mainly as a
channel for trade union grievances.[54] Lynden Macassey, who reap-
peared as its director, did not dispute such charges and indeed
summarised his strategy as 'the exercise of considerable tact, very
great patience, numerous meetings with the District Committees,
and a very full knowledge of shipyard conditions, Trade Union
practices, and the workman's point of view'.[55]

IV

Thus it seems that behind some of the most familiar episodes of
industrial conflict during the First World War there lay an unfamiliar
industrial dynamic. The sector concerned in many of the disputes
was shipbuilding rather than engineering, the conflicts did not
revolve around dilution nor did they produce a 'rank and file' revolt,
and there is no evidence that the state adopted a repressive attitude
towards organised labour. It would be surprising if events in other
sectors were identical to those in shipbuilding and it would certainly
be valuable to have a more systematic analysis of developments in
coalmining, for example, or steel making. However, some general
conclusions can already be drawn about the conventional picture.

In the first place, the importance of dilution and independent shop
floor organisation has been exaggerated, even in the case of engineering. With a few exceptions, British employers stubbornly maintained
conservative attitudes and had little faith in proposals to rationalise
labour-intensive methods of production. Indeed it was frequently
managements which put up the strongest opposition to dilution,
because each firm wanted to retain as much skilled labour as
possible. This attitude was clearly favourable to the existing trade
unions which, assisted by the high wartime demand for labour, were

able to expand their membership from four to six-and-a-half million. Thus, though there was often friction over short-term tactics between officials and their members in particular shops or districts, only a very small minority accepted the radical critique of officialdom as such.

Industrial conflict during the war continued to revolve around wages and working conditions within established systems of production and, on the whole, the representatives of workers' grievances still came from within official trade unionism. The emergence of new forms of shop steward organisation in the engineering centres should, therefore, be traced mainly to the strains imposed on the wage structure by the wartime demand for labour and the effects of government intervention. There were major shifts in the regional and sectoral distribution of labour requirements and this led to quite sudden changes in the relative strengths of different groups within the workforce. Meanwhile the government was attempting to control wage drift and inflation by imposing periodic national wage rises, but this was only partially successful because they had to be supplemented by *ad hoc* 'war bonuses' appropriate to local conditions. Wage bargaining in the engineering industry became rather a mess, then, and the complex readjustments required to maintain something like the old differentials between skilled and unskilled, time and piece workers could only be carried out really effectively at the level of the individual workplace. Shop stewards, who had existed as dues collectors before the war, therefore, found that their collective bargaining functions were greatly increased and, on the whole, this was welcomed by both national union leaderships and the main government arbitrators. Indeed, if there was any element of incorporation in the state's labour strategy it was aimed at this layer within the unions: the need for someone to bargain with in the new situation produced government schemes for establishing shop floor organisation where it did not exist and for strengthening it where it was weak.[56]

Only on the Clyde is there any evidence that dilution was a contentious issue or that it produced a strong impulse towards independent shop floor organisation, and even here both of these tendencies need to be seriously qualified. In the first place it is not at all clear that the problems over the introduction of dilutees were the result of a greater intensity of reorganisation in this region. Indeed, one local shop steward, Herbert Highton, thought that the overall impact of dilution had been marginal. There were 1,500 women working in general engineering by the middle of 1916, but 500 of them were doing unskilled work and most of the rest were doing jobs which had been classified as 'semi-skilled' before 1914. As well as being only minimally threatened by the changes, many of the local skilled men seem to have expected that the clarity of the sexual distinction involved in wartime dilution schemes would actually help them in their postwar struggle against the encroachment of the semi-skilled.[57] The explanation of the severity of the conflicts on the Clyde in the early months of 1916 therefore probably lies partly in the after-effects of the previous six months of successful protest in the local shipbuilding industry and partly in the chronic disarray of the local organisation of the ASE. Moreover, it is not at all self-evident that the revolutionary impulse towards independent 'rank and file' organisation was the most significant aspect of these struggles, for that would be to overlook the more protracted and ultimately more successful dispute at Lang's of Johnstone which was, after all, supported by both local and national officials.[58]

Whatever our precise analysis of the contentious events on the Clyde, the second main conclusion about the conventional picture should be clear by this stage: there was no serious revolutionary crisis and no sustained government strategy to contain it. This removes the foundation of two of the main interpretations of the role of the state during the war, for both the 'revolutionary' and the 'corporatist' views begin with the premise that it was faced with a major insurrectionary threat. The 'revolutionary' view is further vulnerable because of its assumption that government policy was determined by industrial employers when in fact there is a growing body of evidence that they had only a marginal influence before and especially during the war. Industrialists were therefore a profoundly discontented group and, in combination with the persistence of serious economic conflicts between capital and labour, this also further undermines the 'corporatist' notion of an emerging consensus between employers, unions and the state. The creation of certain formal institutions did not determine the nature of the proceedings within them.

Of the four approaches outlined at the beginning of this paper, that which emphasises 'muddling through' has much more to recommend it, for it highlights both the *ad hoc* nature of government responses and the openendedness of long-run outcomes. This was after all the *First* World War. The economy had never been mobilised on such a scale before and few civil servants had enough experience of the country's industrial regions to be able to calculate in advance the effects of their interventions. At the same time, they were almost always pursuing some goal, even if pragmatically. So here there is also a great deal of value in the approach of the 'administrative' school with its emphasis on the intentions of leading civil servants, and that especially because the war years saw a massive expansion of state intervention in domestic affairs.

Thus it is important that those government officials most centrally involved in the development of labour policy were not only concerned with achieving the highest possible levels of output but also with creating a framework of industrial relations which would be fair to both employers and workers. Some of the most interesting and important differences between them were, therefore, over which side had to be held in check to guarantee a just outcome, and it is significant that those who were the most hostile to the unions gradually lost ground. How much this was due to shifts in personal influence and in the political consensus within Whitehall and how much to external pressures is not yet clear. But it is certain that both were important; and the main shortcoming of the 'administrative' approach is, therefore, in its lack of attention to the social context of government activity. Whatever the internal developments within the civil service, it was under increasing pressure to adopt a loosely pro-labour strategy during the First World War because of the tight labour market, the growing strength of the unions, the representation of the Labour Party within the coalition government, the indispensability of winning consent from manual workers and the cumulative effect of its own policies.

In conclusion, it is therefore important to highlight a feature of the war years which has been rather obscured by much of the recent literature: that the changing relationship between the state and the economy was largely favourable to organised labour and that this had a major impact on popular political attitudes. There were two important developments during the war. First, many trade unionists made collective bargains over wages and working conditions with the state for the first time, and this began to undermine their habitual separation of economic and political issues. Secondly, many groups of working people had the experience of putting pressure on the government over a wide range of issues and winning. Taken together, this meant that it seemed increasingly valuable to have workers' representatives in parliament, both to guarantee higher wages for those involved in bargains with the state and to expand the growing sense of influence over government policy. A further development tilted the balance in favour of a specifically socialist attitude towards politics. For the demands of war production had forced the government to adopt comprehensive controls over markets and even to intervene in the ownership and management of key industries. Thus it was demonstrated that private enterprise was not the only viable form of economic organisation and that some form of collectivism might really be possible on a permanent basis.

As well as a different industrial dynamic there was, at the centre of the war experience, a different political dynamic from that frequently assumed. Here the emphasis should be on the achievements of official labour organisation rather than the missed chances of a 'rank and file' revolt, on the growth in strength and ambition of the Labour Party rather than on the search for an intangible 'revolutionary situation', and on what was actually achieved through existing institutions rather than on the explosion that might have been.[59] As a counterpoint to the opening quotation from J. T. Murphy it is therefore appropriate to close with one from another contemporary, the Glasgow writer, J. M. Reid:[60]

Governments had taken over or controlled transport, the supply of goods to the shops, house rents, the allocation of labour. For almost a century before 1914 Socialism had been written and talked about, but comparatively few had taken it seriously. It had been widely felt that State control of the means of production, distribution and exchange 'wouldn't work'. So long as most active-minded men hoped to be their own masters the idea that all ought to be servants of the State was fiercely resisted. But generations of industrial wage-earning had gradually destroyed among most working-class people the ambition to win economic independence by getting property of their own, and the war had produced something very like practical socialism.

NOTES

* I would like to thank Joseph Melling, Steven Tolliday and Jonathan Zeitlin for valuable comments on the original draft of this paper.
1 J. T. Murphy, *Preparing for Power* (1972 reprint), p. 145.
2 A more complete treatment of all of the issues can be found in A. Reid, 'The Division of Labour in the British Shipbuilding Industry 1880–1920', unpublished Ph.D. thesis, University of Cambridge, 1980.
3 *Glasgow Herald*, 17 June 1916; *The Times*, 23 August 1916.

4 Papers of the Clyde Shipbuilders' Association in Strathclyde Regional Archives TD 241/12/32. CSA Special General Meeting with Dilution Commission 21 March 1916, verbatim minutes.

5 *Report of the War Cabinet Committee on Women in Industry*, Cmd 135 and Cmd 167, PP 1919, xxxi, especially pp. 258, 272, 333–6, 353, 606. See also G. Braybon, *Women Workers in the First World War* (1981), and D. Thom, 'The Ideology of Women's Work 1914–1924', unpublished Ph.D. thesis, CNAA, 1982.

6 Papers of Sir James Lithgow in Glasgow University Archives 49.35.12.71, 'Merchant shipbuilding position', 3 September 1918.

7 TD 241/12/32, returns of CSA members.

8 *Ibid.*; papers of the Ministry of Munitions in Public Record Office, MUN. 5.72, A. McDermott Service, 'Lists of operations performed by women in various industries', 21 January 1917, p. 8; MUN. 5.73, L. Macassey, 'Dilution of Labour in Clyde district', 29 February 1916; MUN. 5.73, J. B. Adams, 'Progress of the dilution campaign from January 8th to March 1st 1916', 1 March 1916.

9 TD 241/12/32, CSA circular 9th March 1916, p. 2.

10 MUN. 5.57, L. Macassey, 'Report on the present serious unorganised condition of shipyard labour', 14 December 1916, pp. 7–8.

11 Papers of the Admiralty in Public Record Office, ADM 116.1602, L. Macassey, 'The reorganisation of Admiralty labour organisation', March 1918; ADM 116.1609, Director of the Labour Department of the Ministry of Munitions, 'Shipyard labour', 17 April 1918, from which the quotation is taken.

12 TD 241/12/32, 'Agreement between the Clyde Dilution Commission and the Clyde District Committee of the Shipconstructors' and Shipwrights' Association', 15 June 1916; 'Agreement between the Clyde Dilution Commission and the Clyde and West of Scotland District Committees of the United Society of Boilermakers and Iron and Steel Shipbuilders in reference to the Dilution of Labour', 10 June 1916.

13 TD 241/12/32, A. J. Inglis to CSA 16 November 1916, 22 and 25 May 1917, 4 and 7 June 1917; Dunlop Bremner to CSA 26 June 1916.

14 TD 241/12/41, 'Memorandum of Agreement between the Shipbuilding Employers' Federation and the United Society of Boilermakers and Iron and Steel Shipbuilders re Working on Pneumatic Rivetting Hammers (Merchant Work – New and Repair)', 11 January 1918, and Proceedings in Central Conference between SEF and USBISS, 12 September 1918, Verbatim Minutes, pp. 48–9 for quotation.

15 J. Hinton, *The First Shop Stewards' Movement* (1973), p. 155.

16 Verbatim minutes of these early talks will be found in TD 241/12/13, see minutes of the conference of 16 November 1914, p. 15, for the quotation; also, on the general character of relations in Clydeside shipbuilding, see ADM 116.1608, L. Macassey, 'Report on proposals for labour reorganisation by the SEF and the Shipyard Trades' Standing Committee and the Boilermakers' Society', 11 March 1918, p. 6.

17 TD 241/12/13, CSA Executive Committee Minutes, 4 December 1914; T. Biggart memorandum for G. R. Askwith, January 1915.

18 Reid, 'The Division of Labour', pp. 300–28.
19 MUN. 5.79, memorandum on Section 7 of the Munitions of War Act, August 1915; details of the cases which arose will be found in MUN. 5.80, 'Clyde Munition Workers' Inquiry held by Lord Balfour of Burleigh and Lynden Macassey on the 4th, 5th, 11th, 12th and 22nd of November 1915', verbatim minutes.
20 Ibid., pp. 96–150.
21 History of the Ministry of Munitions 4, 2, pp. 50–6.
22 Reid, 'The Division of Labour', pp. 346–69; J. Melling, Rent Strikes (Edinburgh, 1983), especially pp. 74–103 for the events of October and November 1915.
23 Reid, 'The Division of Labour', pp. 361–9; Melling, Rent Strikes, pp. 99–103.
24 MUN. 5.73, J. Patterson memorandum, 'Dilution of labour', 18 December 1915, pp. 12 and 15.
25 MUN. 5.73, L. Macassey memorandum, 'Causes of unrest among munition workers on Clyde and Tyne-side which are peculiar to those districts', 18 December 1915, p. 3; see also the remarks in the annual review of shipbuilding by Noel Peck (CSA chairman) in Glasgow Herald, Shipbuilding, Engineering and Commerce in 1915, October 1915, p. 33.
26 Papers of the Scottish Office in Scottish Record Office HH 31/22, Shipconstructors' and Shipwrights' Association to Secretary of State for Scotland, 9 October 1915; also Melling, Rent Strikes, pp. 70–1, 86, 91.
27 MUN. 5.80, 'Clyde Munition Workers' Inquiry', p. 102.
28 Reid, 'The Division of Labour', pp. 274–92, which draws on letters and minutes in TD 241/12/13; quotation from Adjourned Special Conference, 16 November 1914, verbatim minutes, p. 28.
29 Reid, 'The Division of Labour', pp. 306–25.
30 See MUN. 5.80, 'Clyde Munition Workers' Inquiry', pp. 509–12, for details on the cooperation between officials and shop stewards on the Clyde Shipyards Joint Trades Vigilance Committee.
31 History of the Ministry of Munitions 4, 2, pp. 49–50.
32 Ibid., pp. 50–6; Shipconstructors' and Shipwrights' Association, Quarterly Report, July–September 1915, p. 6; MUN. 5.73, L. Macassey memorandum 'Causes of unrest', 18 December 1915.
33 Isaac Mitchell quoted in History of the Ministry of Munitions 4, 2, p. 55.
34 ADM 1.8436, Parliamentary and Financial Secretary to First Lord, 21 October 1915; H. Llewellyn Smith to Secretary to the Admiralty, 15 November 1915 from which the quotation is taken.
35 History of the Ministry of Munitions 4, 2, pp. 81–2.
36 Ibid., 4, 2, p. 35, and 4, 4, pp. 100–1; also revealing comments to this effect by Beveridge in MUN. 5.70, W. H. Beveridge, 'Suppression of the "Forward"', 6 January 1916.
37 Glasgow Herald, 17 June 1916.
38 ADM 116.1608, L. Macassey, 'History of the various arrangements determining the relations between the government and labour', 11 March 1918; MUN. 5.23, 'Points of difference between the Admiralty and the Ministry of Munitions', 5 October 1916.

39 MUN. 5.57, L. Macassey, 'Report on . . . shipyard labour', 14 December 1916, pp. 18–20 and Appendix C.

40 *Ibid.*, pp. 23–6; ADM 116.1602, L. Macassey, '. . . Admiralty labour organisation', March 1918; ADM 116.1609, Navy Controller, 'Sir Lynden Macassey and the Admiralty Labour Administration', 1 May 1918; ADM 116.1609, Director of the Labour Department of the Ministry of Munitions, 'Shipyard labour', 7 April 1918.

41 J. Harris, *Beveridge* (Oxford 1977), pp. 212–15; I. McLean, *The Legend of Red Clydeside* (Edinburgh 1983), p. 30.

42 Lithgow Papers 49.35.12.71, circular letter to shipyard owners 5 March 1918, and Controller General of Merchant Shipbuilding memorandum, 'Merchant shipbuilding position', 3 September 1918.

43 J. A. Turner, 'The politics of "organized business" during The First World War', in J. A. Turner (ed.), *Businessmen and Politics* (London 1984).

44 R. Davidson, 'The Board of Trade and industrial relations 1896–1914', *Historical Journal* 21 (1978), pp. 571–91, and 'The myth of the "Servile State"', *Bulletin of the Society for the Study of Labour History*, 29 (1974), pp. 62–7.

45 MUN. 5.9, H. Llewellyn Smith, 'Supply of armament labour', 23 January 1915, quotation from p. 4.

46 MUN. 5.9, G. R. Askwith, 'Shortage of labour – shipbuilding and engineering', 28 January 1915, and 'Shortage of labour – shipbuilding and engineering', 5 February 1915.

47 *History of the Ministry of Munitions* 1, 2, pp. 57–80; quotation from A. Wilkie in *Parliamentary Debates, House of Commons* 172, 28 June 1915, vols. 1585–91.

48 MUN. 5.10, Treasury Conference, 17–19 March 1915, verbatim minutes; one of the more outspoken employers being, of course, William Weir in the *Glasgow Herald*, 21 May 1915 and later in MUN. 5.73, W. Weir memorandum to Lloyd George on dilution of labour, December 1915.

49 *Report and Statistics of Bad Time Kept in Shipbuilding, Munitions, and Transport Areas* (220), May 1915, PP 1914–16, 4; MUN. 5.100, T. J. MacNamara to Lloyd George, 7 June 1915; MUN. 5.91, W. L. Hichens, 'The influence of drink on the production of war materials', June 1915.

50 *Parliamentary Debates, House of Commons* 172, 8 June 1915; MUN. 5.48, Conference between representatives of Trades Unions and Lloyd George, 16 June 1915, verbatim minutes; C. Addison, *Four and a Half Years* (1934), pp. 85, 91; *History of the Ministry of Munitions* 4, 1, pp. 22–88.

51 MUN. 5.79, 'Threatened Clyde Strike', 16 October 1915; Balfour Papers TD 82/12/134, Balfour and Macassey to Ministry of Munitions, 28 October 1915.

52 MUN. 5.80, 'Clyde Munition Workers' Inquiry', pp. 299–302; *History of the Ministry of Munitions* 4, 2, pp. 64–83.

53 MUN. 5.73, L. Macassey, 'Procedure and progress of the Commission', 5 February 1916, pp. 11–12; see also *History of the Ministry of Munitions* 4, 4, pp. 119–23.

54 ADM 1.8480, 'Organisation and control in the shipyards and marine engineering shops', 15 February 1917, pp. 1–2; TD 241/12/32, Inglis to CSA, 4 June 1917, 16 November 1917.
55 MUN. 5.57, L. Macassey, 'Report on . . . shipyard labour', 14 December 1916, p. 31.
56 Hinton, *Shop Stewards' Movement*, pp. 86–91; G. D. H. Cole, *Workshop Organisation* (Oxford, 1923).
57 H. E. R. Highton, 'Report on engineering industry, Clyde District', July 1916, printed as Appendix 1, pp. 113–33 in B. Drake, *Women in the Engineering Trades* (1918).
58 For an important revision of the 'revolutionary' view of events on the Clyde see McLean, *Red Clydeside*, pp. 6–110.
59 For work which points in this direction see R. Harrison, 'The War Emergency Workers' National Committee, 1914–1920' in A. Briggs and J. Saville (eds.), *Essays in Labour History 1886–1923* (1971), pp. 211–59; J. Winter, *Socialism and the Challenge of War* (1974).
60 J. M. Reid, *James Lithgow* (1964), p. 72.

3

Public policy and port labour reform: the dock decasualisation issue, 1910–50*

NOEL WHITESIDE

Few sectors of the modern British labour market have been so influenced by state policy as the docks. Persistent public concern with the problems of casual and irregular employment – whose symbol became the waterfront – led policy makers and administrators to focus their attention on the organisation of port labour. Their favoured remedy, decasualisation – as its name suggests – required more effective coordination of labour supply and demand, but was certain to alter traditional working practices. Although statutory regulation was to prove politically unfeasible, these reforming initiatives appealed to certain labour leaders on the docks, who saw that cooperation with official agencies might enable them to consolidate union organisation and thereby increase their members' security of employment and regularity of earnings. In the event, however, the pursuit of such strategies strained the relationship between the union executive and its rank and file. These tensions erupted into open conflict after the Second World War, when it became clear that officially sponsored decasualisation schemes demanded extensive changes in industrial relations on the waterfront. These changes were opposed not only by a number of port employers, but also by large numbers of the dockers themselves, who were drawn thereby into confrontation with their union and the state. Viewed from one angle, decasualisation offered major concessions to workers in the industry: it promised to safeguard earnings, rationalise the distribution of work, promote unionisation and secure an equal voice for workers' representatives in the management of port labour. But despite the popularity of job protection and income guarantees, dockers came to resent the transfer of authority to a remote bureaucracy insistent on dismantling established patterns of local bargaining.

Although central government's concern with the docks remained consistent, both the objectives and the instruments of public policy underwent considerable revision. Decasualisation had originally developed as a response to the more general problem of unemployment at the turn of the century; then official policies had to cater for the chronically underemployed as well as for the totally redundant. But during the two world wars, manpower shortages and the national emergency transformed both the motives and methods of decasualisation, as the government negotiated direct controls on dock labour in order to remove and conscript surplus workers. Between the wars, by contrast, the advantages of a rigorous rationalisation of port work appeared less evident, and the ability of the state to enforce such changes more questionable. On the one hand, decasualisation threatened to exacerbate rather than alleviate mass unemployment; on the other the moral and social arguments for the reform of port labour had not lost their force. But such issues were no longer deemed the proper province for public intervention; by the 1920s it had become generally accepted in official circles that the reform of employment practices should be left to the discretion of private management and, within reason, should not be subject to administrative interference. It was only after the Second World War, with the more general reappraisal of the role of the state, that the emergency of continuing labour shortages in a key export-linked sector made the introduction of permanent controls on both workers and employers politically acceptable and economically desirable.

Support for dock decasualisation – or at least the greater regulation of the labour market – was more prevalent among trade unionists than among employers in the industry. The latter generally suspected that decasualisation was simply a strategy for increasing union bargaining power by restricting their labour supply. Indeed, the port employers proved unwilling to negotiate any collective solution to the casual labour question until the eve of the Second World War. Employer hostility, together with the problems of organising a fluctuating and overstocked labour market, encouraged union leaders to look outside the industry for the means to secure recognition and organisational stability. During the First World War, dock union representatives made little secret of their ambition to use official controls to impose a closed shop. Throughout the interwar period, Ernest Bevin – the chief union advocate of decasualisation – argued consistently that regular employment and guaranteed earnings would not only eliminate poverty on the waterfront, but would also increase commercial efficiency by improving the quality of dock labour and enhancing workers' loyalty to the industry they served. A similar blend of arguments was in turn used to promote the union version of the state's prewar decasualisation scheme, adopted by Bevin as Minister of Labour to regulate dock employment during the Second World War.

The marriage of state and union policies proved uneasy in practice. The administration of decasualisation on a centralised basis presumed a complete restructuring of port employment and a transformation of established practices on the part of both employers and dockers, if it were to work effectively. There had always been signs that such cooperation might not be forthcoming and this became fully apparent during the 1940s. Although happy to accept the protection offered by the new system, the rank and file were reluctant to abandon the local job controls developed to safeguard their position in a chronically overstocked labour market. Official policy assumed that the industry could be run on the basis of a 'normal' working week and that all port work – and therefore port workers – were effectively interchangeable: assumptions that proved ill-founded. The largest union, the Transport and General Workers (TGWU) had been prepared to defend local working agreements and bargaining procedures before the war. But during postwar negotiations, union officials agreed to cooperate with the employers in revising working practices in return for concessions on a minimum weekly wage. In the context of full employment, income guarantees lost their appeal and dockers generally concluded that the benefits of decasualisation did not justify the sacrifices demanded in exchange. In short, union leaders and their members differed over the appropriate strategy for coping with the threat of future unemployment; the dockers continued to place their faith in the preservation of workplace controls rather than in bargaining with the state. In the postwar period, a more aggressive form of industrial unionism appeared on the waterfront, which sought to take advantage of the new system's benefits while repudiating the compromises struck by Bevin's successors.

In the account which follows, my purpose is less to rehearse the history of port unionism than to draw out the ways in which state policies reshaped the administration of labour and helped to redefine the pattern of industrial relations on the docks. But as we shall see, the constraints on state intervention in industry proved as striking as its extent: schemes for the reform of port employment rarely produced the effect that policy makers had intended, since dockers and employers alike turned out to be adept at modifying official initiatives to suit their own ends.

I

The structure of the port transport industry in the early twentieth century was both heterogeneous and complex; in most respects it was less a single enterprise than a conglomeration of independent concerns, bound together more by geographical proximity than by the common nature of their business. Large areas around the major estuaries – the Mersey, the Clyde and the Thames – were covered with docks and wharves; divisions between port employers were further aggravated by competition for business – among the wharfingers, between the wharfingers and the dock companies, between the dock companies and the shipowners and so on. Ownership of port facilities was similarly splintered; few ports were managed by a single enterprise. Bristol (owned by the City Corporation), Manchester (owned by the Ship Canal Company) and a number of small railway ports like Barry and Garston were the exception rather than the rule. Throughout this period, the diverse size and profitability of port employers made for partial and sporadic investment in port facilities and new technology; the introduction of mechanical handling was slow. Well into the interwar period, old methods of loading and unloading persisted alongside the new, perpetuating the demand for skills and experience which were, in principle, redundant.

A fractured industrial structure supported a fractured labour market. The demand for labour fluctuated widely – according to the season for particular cargoes, the nature of the weather and the general state of trade. Numbers needed for work on the docks varied, in an unpredictable fashion, by the day and by the week, as well as by the time of year. In effect, throughout this period, the waterfront supported a multiplicity of separate local labour markets, each characterised by idiosyncratic methods of work and systems of payment and each 'followed' by a number of dockers whose aptitudes and experience suited the nature of the business concerned. It is a mistake to assume that all port workers possessed similar abilities and skills, or that they all lived constantly in the shadow of poverty, although the renowned association between casual labour and destitution was well founded. At the upper end of hierarchy, however, gangs of dockers with particular strength, skill or experience with certain processes or on various cargoes – such as stevedores, coal trimmers, deal and corn porters – could command higher wages than the ordinary quayman and would rarely deign, when trade was slack, to compete with the crowds at the dock gate for a common casual's rate. Such men could get high earnings for strenuous work in a given season, or for a number of days a week, and then take time off, or turn instead to other forms of industrial or agricultural employment, quite commonly away from the waterfront altogether. Such dockers, together with those who aspired to a similar status, valued their 'freedom' – highly illusory at times of bad trade and rising unemployment – to work as their needs dictated rather than submit to the soul destroying routine of the factory hand or other manual trade. For them, the offer of a regular job held little appeal. It was these 'specialists' who formed the hard core of the dock labour force and early union membership, with sons following fathers into the trade.

Such a system offered obvious advantages to the port employers; it gave their foremen access to experienced men who knew the work (or who were willing to pay for the chance of a job). For smaller firms, such arrangements were essential for their business. Where the need for labour was sporadic, speed essential and profit margins low, there was little opportunity or inclination to train up new men for each consignment or to invest in the unnecessary expense of a permanent workforce. This mutual interdependence fostered sectional agreements, idiosyncratic piece-rate and payments systems and highly localised arrangements for determining manning levels and the rate for each job. Early forms of industrial bargaining were dependent on a particular type of solidarity found on the docks – a recognition among more regular men that it was counterproductive, even immoral, to encroach on another man's territory. When times were hard, more regular dockers made every effort to share available work among as many men as possible.

The solidarity and mutual support found on the waterfront provided the foundations from which trade union organisation developed. However, the position of any docker was insecure. Preference depended largely on physical attributes as well as experience and this was easily undermined by illness, accident or old age. Any spell of absence could lose a man his place. And, at the other end of the spectrum, the huge crowds of casual labourers – many incapable of regular work – made up the bulk of an overstocked labour market. Chronic poverty on the docks shocked middle-class opinion and provided the basic justification for social reform. During periods of recession, the numbers competing for work rose as the general unemployed resorted to the waterfront on the off-chance of getting a job.

Union organisation had to accommodate all sectors of the labour market in order to be effective, and to counter the other major threat to the dockers' livelihood, namely the anti-union attitudes of the more intransigent port employers. The Shipping Federation, using blackleg labour recruited in agricultural regions, perfected strike breaking techniques to a fine art before the First World War.[1] Port unionism became indistinguishable from other types of general labour organisation due to the drift of men on and off the docks. To paraphrase Eric Hobsbawm, every type of union could be found on the waterfront by 1914.[2] Following the 1912 dock strike, 29 unions could be found in the port of London alone and still most of the dockers there were unorganised.[3] In the prewar period, unions were plagued by a high incidence of lapsed membership, partial and erratic recognition and interminable inter-union rivalries and disputes.

The creation of the National Transport Workers Federation (NTWF) in 1911 can therefore be seen as an attempt by labour leaders to set their house in order, as well as being a broad manifestation of the solidarity found among dockers, mentioned above. Even so, there were continuing disagreements about whether port workers were best protected by the establishment of a national union of dockers or through the development of local organisations for all general labourers.[4] Adopting the former strategy made it necessary to draw distinctions between dock labourers and other casual workers; members had to be confined to port-work if out-siders were to be banned from the waterfront. To win recognition and secure stability, outside assistance was needed; to establish a closed shop, the union would have to guarantee an adequate supply of labour to meet fluctuations in demand and this would require greater mobility of labour between employers and more regular attendance at the call. How to provide such changes in working practices without disrupting membership loyalty was to prove a persistent problem. Union leaders, however, were not alone in their efforts to contain the effects of casualism. At the turn of the century, public attention was directed to casualism in general – and the waterfront in particular – because of its association with poverty and general social distress. The conclusions drawn by the philanthropic investigations of Charles Booth, Eleanor Rathbone and the Charity Organisation Society (COS) were reinforced by the experience of the distress committees set up by the 1905 Unemployed Workmen's Act and the evidence presented to the Royal Commission on the Poor Laws.[5] Casual labourers were a major component in the problem of pauperism: a burden on the communities in which they lived because of their reliance on the rates. If this source of individual demoralisation and urban degeneration was not to spread, major casual markets like the docks had to be subject to more rational management.

Demonstrating a correlation between casualism and pauperism was not, in itself, an argument for state intervention. Indeed Booth himself publicised a system, already used by some of the major shipping companies, which encouraged port employers to concentrate work in the hands of a limited labour force by maintaining formal lists of 'preferred' men – or principles very similar to those recommended by Lord Devlin's committee in 1965. Decasualisation became a subject of public policy for two principal reasons. First, casualism was not seen as the problem of a particular industry, but as part of a more general evil threatening the fabric of the whole nation and the foundations of Empire. Casual labour markets gave no reward to good character or industry. They potentially demoralised all who worked for them; they were a haven for the dissolute and the petty criminal. It was the duty of government, furthermore, to eliminate sources of underemployment and rationalise the distribution of jobs. In this way the idle and incapable would be excluded from the labour market, work would be concentrated in the hands of the efficient and industrial performance would improve. Indeed, the national system of labour exchanges, introduced in 1909, was designed chiefly to do just that. It vested control over job placement in the hands of impartial officials, thereby guaranteeing that employers would be sent suitable labour to fill notified vacancies. It was this system which was adopted for special application on the docks.[6] Secondly, proponents of decasualisation focussed their attention on the waterfront not only because of the quantities of casual labour to be found there, but also because inefficient port labour management might undermine Britain's position in world trade and commerce.[7]

The rationale behind official decasualisation was unchallengeable but the opposition that any compulsory scheme was likely to arouse was unlimited. The 'exchanges and insurance' package was the first tentative step towards the rationalisation of the labour market; the prewar Liberal government did not want to alienate either side of industry, especially after the TUC had given such a hostile reception to the proposal for state labour exchanges.[8] Hence decasualisation was limited to voluntary arrangements, allowing employers to reduce their individual contributions under national insurance if they hired casual men through the local exchange, which would thus be in a position to concentrate work in the hands of *bona fide* applicants.[9] By the end of 1912, a handful of schemes had been set up involving cloth porters at Manchester, corporation workers in Birmingham, ship repairers in South Wales and – by far the most ambitious enterprise – a port labour scheme in Liverpool, created by a joint agreement between employers and unions at the end of the 1911 dock strike.[10]

This was not, from the Board of Trade's point of view, an overwhelming success. The introduction of clearing houses (sub-labour-exchanges) on the waterfront brought all dockers in Liverpool and Birkenhead out on strike and the objectives of the scheme caused Tillett to remark in his union's journal that its authors were of the opinion that labour surplus to the port's requirements ought to be poisoned or shot.[11] Once it became clear to both workers and employers (and 20 of the latter refused to have anything to do with the experiment) that as the scheme was voluntary no sanctions could be brought to bear on those who ignored its rules – industrial peace was restored. The port continued to work exactly as it had always done. The 33,000 brass tallies – allocated to registered dockers – were freely sold, loaned and hired; a large number vanished without trace.[12] The sole consequences of the scheme were to harden the heart of the Treasury against approving any further decasualisation proposals under the 1911 National Insurance Act and to consolidate the position of the local union – the National

Union of Dock Labourers (NUDL) – at the northern end of the port.[13] The Liverpool experiment was isolated largely because no other group of port employers was willing to vest the union with joint control over a registered labour force. In London and Manchester, by contrast, the Port of London Authority (PLA) and the Ship Canal Company responded to the call to decasualise by drawing up extensive preference lists, following the scheme advocated by Charles Booth. These effectively increased the control of the employer over the men who worked for him and aimed to exclude union labour completely. On the other hand, the association of Board of Trade schemes with labour exchanges aroused suspicion in ports where union labour had managed to secure control over the allocation of work. When the scheme was discussed in Glasgow, at a mass meeting of the Scottish Union of Dock Labourers (SUDL) in 1912, it was thrown out – the first of many rejections. Even before 1914, registration of port labour had proved far from popular.

II

In the context of the war, the whole purpose of decasualisation changed. Various state departments developed a direct interest in the efficient operation of the ports. Central government became more involved in port labour management – less to eliminate the inefficient than to release the younger, fitter men for service overseas. The idea of a port labour register was adapted to suit wartime purposes; local labour shortages were supplemented by the use of Transport Workers Battalions (TWBs), composed of enlisted dockers, which were capable of being directed from port to port. Not surprisingly, hostility to the conscription of dock labour for civilian purposes provoked labour opposition. At local level, the TWBs provided an easy way of breaking sectional stoppages. At national level, the NTWF saw that organisational advances and their own central influence would be undermined if the use of conscripted labour spread. Hence in 1917 negotiations opened between government departments and labour representatives to seek an alternative solution.

As elsewhere, the war fundamentally strengthened labour organisation on the waterfront and allowed the advocates of national dock unionism to further their cause.[14] The influence of this NTWF executive was increased through its involvement with the implementation of wartime controls. The Federation gained representation on local port and transit committees, created to prevent congestion, and on the port labour committees which managed the registers of exempted dockers.[15] In response to the crisis over the use of the TWBs[16] and the general manpower squeeze of 1917–18, the union leadership – principally inspired by Ernest Bevin – produced a peacetime formula designed to consolidate new won gains and prevent the recurrence of earlier organisational difficulties. This scheme married registration to union membership and – in place of unemployment insurance benefits – demanded the introduction of a minimum weekly wage, conditional on regular attendance and mobility of workers between employers. This was to be funded by a levy on goods going through the ports.[17] It was a plan which, with some modifications, Bevin was to support for the next quarter century and to introduce as Minister of Labour during the Second World War.

The NTWF proposals were viewed in the interim with considerable ambivalence. The chief difficulty concerned the maintenance wage. Should this be seen as part of normal labour costs and be added to the industry's wage bill or was it actually a special form of unemployment relief for casual workers and therefore the proper responsibility of the state?[18] The Federation preferred the former interpretation, but the National Association of Port Labour Employers (NAPLE) did not. Few NAPLE members wished to perpetuate wartime controls over port employment, fewer still to add to their industry's labour costs in this fashion. Neither the Ministry of Labour, nor the Treasury, on the other hand, wanted special privileges under the national insurance scheme – whose extension was under discussion in 1919 – to be granted to particular sectors of the industrial unemployed.[19] Generally, state policy in the immediate postwar period aimed to dissolve wartime controls and – through the promotion of 'home rule for industry' – to encourage collective bargaining as the means to promote industrial peace. Such a strategy repudiated the more interventionist type of policy developed by the Board of Trade before the war. Throughout the interwar period, the Ministry continued to support voluntary registration as an essential first phase in decasualising the docks, but to argue that this was a matter for industrial negotiation alone. Rising unemployment and enforced wage cuts in the early 1920s altered the situation completely; negotiations on the maintenance wage went into abeyance.

Without the compensation of guaranteed earnings, voluntary registration lost its support among the rank and file. Indeed, in the interwar period, such schemes degenerated into little more than partial closed shop agreements, allowing preference for union men at the call.[20] While state support – largely confined to moral encouragement and free stationery – allowed both registration and TGWU branches to be introduced in the small ports of Cumberland and in the south-west, the hostility of local port employers on the Tees and the Thames prevented the union from using the scheme to enforce a closed shop and delayed the introduction of any register at all in a number of ports – notably on the Tyne.[21] As registration remained voluntary its sanctions were non-existent and individual employers all round the coast periodically evaded local regulations, using outside labour as and when it suited them. Indeed, after the General Strike, the scheme in some ports was turned on its head, as employers, following the example set by the PLA in 1912, gave preferential employment to non-union, unregistered dockers.[22] Only in the late 1930s, when the TGWU was once again strong enough to force the issue on wages, did the NAPLE take any serious interest in registration and maintenance. Even then, the employers were looking for a solution which would raise the income of lower paid dockers without involving the industry in the greater expense consequent on a general wage rise.[23]

As a means for consolidating organisation, voluntary registration proved to be a mixed blessing. In theory, dockers could be expelled from the register for a variety of misdemeanours; however, failure to pay union subscriptions was not among them and the TGWU continued to be plagued by the problem of lapsed membership.[24] Furthermore, because registration schemes created joint administrative controls, they were attractive to labour organisers where unionism was weak but, in ports where union control was secure, the scheme could work to the advantage of the employers. In Glasgow, all regular dockers were union members; a closed shop had been conceded before the First World War. Here, mass meetings repeatedly rejected registration because it gave port employers greater control over the composition of the labour force. In an attempt to bring the branch into line with union policy, Bevin replaced local officials with his own nominees in 1929. The ensuing fracas was eventually resolved in 1931, when the Scottish Transport and General Workers Union (STGWU) broke away from TGWU.[25] Similar tensions developed elsewhere in Scotland; the schemes at Aberdeen, Greenock, Grangemouth, Ardrossan and Kirkaldy were all abandoned during the 1930s, but the TGWU chose not to make an issue of these developments and the ports stayed within the union.[26] The unpopularity of registration among dockers continued to be a problem.

While trying to wring any possible advantage from official interest in dock decasualisation at national level, the TGWU also used more traditional methods to consolidate organisation and share available work. Such defences were imperative in the circumstances of the interwar period, when technological advance, the slump in the export industries and the general decline of the British share in world trade – all guaranteed a steady decline in the numbers needed to work the docks. In London alone, which suffered least from the consequences of the recession, the numbers finding work each week fell from around 34,000 in January 1921 to 26,000 in the first half of 1930.[27] In Liverpool, where the slump was particularly severe, the value of goods handled in 1931 dropped to just under 42% of the sum total for 1924.[28] Under these conditions dockers were caught in a crossfire; local industry shed labour and the numbers competing for jobs multiplied in inverse proportion to the amount of work available.

Hence local union officials worked to defend manning levels rendered obsolete by mechanisation, to increase both the opportunity and rewards for overtime and generally to ensure that union members got the best deal possible from both the employers and the official unemployment insurance fund. Far from rationalising port labour management, registration was used to protect casualism. In the absence of any concessions from the employers over a minimum wage, such strategies seemed justifiable. As one union official put it, 'the individual has as much right to regulate his life as the employer has to regulate his business'.[29] Hence the tradition of specialisation and the rigidity of the port labour market were reinforced. Of the 14,750 men engaged on average each week in Liverpool in 1923, 11,310 worked for only one employer and very few indeed for more than two.[30] Working agreements remained local, unique to the port, or the dock, in which they operated; their popularity guaranteed their observance, even though the system exacerbated variations in wages and conditions. Hence local bargaining – rather than national negotiation – re-emerged in this period as the chief means of protecting dockers' interests.

By combining worksharing agreements with registration, the TGWU succeeded – within limits – in concentrating employment in the hands of union men. This was, in itself, a step towards mitigating the worst effects of casualism, although the labour market was hardly 'decasualised' as such. Even after the General Strike, an official observer could see how union membership was affecting the distribution of work in London:

a man stands a poor chance of obtaining work unless he is a member of the Union; the Union is unwilling to admit and secure registration for a man who is not likely to get a livelihood in dockwork and a man who does not so obtain his livelihood will fall into arrears with his Union membership and cease to be a member.[31]

By 1936, official returns showed that port employment was concentrated among a limited number of dockers, probably union men – even in Glasgow where registration as such did not exist.[32] In spite of the slump in demand and the high rate of unemployment on the waterfront – which rose to 40% in 1931 – the distress and deprivation which had been so prominent among dock workers in the Edwardian era had largely vanished, among registered men at least. Credit for this achievement can only be partly attributed to the success of union tactics; for a further explanation we must turn to the impact of state unemployment benefits on dockers' income.

In the context of mass unemployment, the problem of casual labour dwindled into insignificance when set against the major structural problems of the economy and the collapse of industry in the depressed areas. Officials in the Ministry of Labour were always far less inclined than their predecessors at the Board of Trade to use welfare benefits for the purposes of reforming industrial employment. For them, the worker's economic well-being was generally less entangled with his moral and social behaviour. Indeed, the problem following the unemployment crisis of 1921 was less to rationalise the supply of and demand for labour than to give the unemployed any work at all. In what was assumed to be a temporary measure to deal with exceptional circumstances, the Cabinet was persuaded in 1921 to condone the payment of benefit in advance of statutory contributions, to introduce dependents' allowances and – in recognition of the desirability of spreading available work – to allow the limited payment of benefit to those forced to work short-time because of the recession.[33]

Concessions to short-time workers operated to the advantage of casual dockers. Certainly the political and economic climate was not conducive to decasualisation. For the state, there was little to be gained by swelling the numbers of totally redundant men (who would make no contribution to the insurance fund) while provoking resentment from within the port transport industry by intervening in management affairs. Attempts, in 1923, to persuade the NAPLE to accept some responsibility for maintaining unemployed dockers came to nothing.[34] The port employers resolutely refused to extend voluntarily their existing financial burdens. In view of the uncompetitive state of the industry – dues in British ports in 1924 were 300% higher than those charged by their Continental rivals[35] – no government was going to force them to do so.

As a result, public policy for the unemployed had entirely different consequences from those envisaged by the prewar Board of Trade. All governments still acknowledged that decasualisation was desirable and that voluntary registration should be encouraged. In 1925, Bevin managed to persuade Ministry officials that, in order to prevent the drift of labour on and off the docks, registered men should not be required to search for work away from the waterfront; this effectively exempted dockers from the exigencies of the 'Genuinely Seeking Work' regulation under the unemployment scheme.[36] As total long-term unemployment was comparatively rare, most dockers managed to maintain their contributions and therefore their right to statutory benefits. Hence the habit spread of using benefit to 'top up' weekly earnings (under the insurance scheme's three day continuity regulation) for up to 26 weeks in the year. 'Three days in the book, three days on the hook' became a common pattern on the waterfront. In an overstocked labour market, it was relatively easy, and sometimes financially advantageous to avoid the call. In the course of the 1920s, the Unemployment Fund received £6 million in contributions from the industry and paid out £22 million in benefits, a balance which moved the Royal Commission on Unemployment Insurance to recommend that the Minister of Labour give the situation on the docks his urgent attention.[37] Instead of encouraging decasualisation, the unemployment scheme, by subsidising irregular earnings, was reinforcing casual working habits.

Of course, port transport was not the only industry where unemployment benefit was used to support an overstocked labour market. In areas where short-time working was the traditional response to recession – in cotton and textile finishing, in leather goods, in some collieries and shipyards and in some branches of light metal manufacture – industrial agreements developed which allowed workers to claim benefit to supplement reduced earnings. Such arrangements might prevent demoralisation and degeneration consequent on unemployment but they discouraged the movement of labour away from declining sectors and forced industry to support a workforce in excess of possible future requirements.[38] A change of policy developed during the early 1930s, due to arguments in favour of rationalisation, the impact of the slump and the influence of industrial employers, who argued consistently that relief for the long-term unemployed should be a charge on the Exchequer and not on industry, which basically financed the Unemployment Fund. The 1931 Anomalies Regulations redefined the terms on which benefit might be claimed by short-time workers. At the same time, the Exchequer took over the relief of all unemployed who had exhausted their right to statutory unemployment benefit and introduced a household means test. And the Ministry of Labour gave support to the creation of a permanent jointly representative Standing Committee to coordinate local registration schemes and promote decasualisation on the docks.

None of these developments, however, changed working practices in the ports. Registration schemes were introduced in the north-east but no progress was made in Scotland where opposition remained strong. Employment on the docks remained concentrated among unionised, registered workers; however, these comprised only half of the 164,770 men identifying themselves as dockers at the labour exchanges in 1932.[39] Chronic unemployment remained concentrated among outsiders. Only 12 of the 564 dockers applying for poor relief in Wallasey in 1929, for example, actually possessed tallies.[40] Even at the height of the slump, official statistics showed that only 10,000 of the 164,770 dockers had amassed too few contributions to qualify for statutory unemployment benefit.[41] Hence, only a minority of dockers (except on Merseyside) came under the aegis of the Unemployment Assistance Board and the means test – and these would have been mostly unregistered non-union men. The relative ease with which dockers could supplement their earnings with state benefit – together with union support for worksharing practices – protected registered men during the recession. Like other sectors of the industrial unemployed who were temporarily laid off, dockers saw official benefits as designed to tide them over the inevitable gaps that appeared between jobs. There was no sense in moving away from the work they knew to take another job which might disrupt their understanding with their regular employer and make access to work more precarious. In short, the interwar experience did nothing to prepare dockers for decasualisation. For the more peripheral workers, Bevin's scheme had even less appeal, for, if applied efficiently, they would be removed from port-work altogether.

The failure of the state to remedy this 'abuse' of the unemployment scheme is not as surprising as it might appear. Both sides of the industry rejected the recommendations of the Holman–Gregory Report.[42] The TGWU would not agree to any measures which would limit their members' access to benefit unless concessions were forthcoming on a minimum weekly wage. Employers were not going to make such concessions and lose the subsidies provided by the state scheme towards their wages bill. The Ministry had no desire to impose compulsory controls on a recalcitrant industry; such a step would be administratively expensive as well as politically unpopular. Further, the main policy problem for the state insurance scheme concerned those who, having exhausted their right to statutory benefit, were still claimants on public funds. Dock workers were not a prominent category in this group, but might become so should decasualisation be effective. By the mid-1930s the Unemployment Fund was out of debt; generally, policy aimed to keep as many of the unemployed as possible on statutory benefits, which were funded principally by industrial contributions, and off unemployment assistance, which remained the liability of the Exchequer. In short, the cost of underemployment on the docks was being met by other industries and there was no incentive for any of the parties more directly involved to change this state of affairs.

III

The Second World War produced an even greater strain on the ports than the conflict of 1914–18; the use of convoys and the rise in transatlantic shipping put increased pressure on western harbours and made greater mobility of labour both within and between the ports imperative. To promote the effective deployment of manpower while minimising the risk of resistance from the dockers themselves, Bevin adapted his union's scheme of registration and maintenance to the wartime emergency. This was first introduced on the Clyde and the Mersey in 1941 and extended to all other ports – under the management of a new agency, the National Dock Labour Corporation (NDLC) – in the following year. Both the Ministry of War Transport and the NDLC aimed to secure regular attendance and maximum mobility from the registered men. As registration retained its traditional links with union membership, the TGWU hoped that the new system would finally remove all outsiders from the docks.

The union therefore wanted to see the wartime experiment converted into a permanent peacetime scheme. During 1945, negotiations opened between both sides of the industry, with a view to determining the precise form this should take; the following year the Attlee government committed itself to giving the expected agreement statutory force. However, discussions broke down. The TGWU proposals were only acceptable to the NAPE if management powers were vested in port authorities dominated by the port employers themselves and if the dockers contributed to the cost of the guaranteed wage. The NAPE's position was, however, weak. The 1937 negotiations on registration and maintenance had shown that the Association's members generally did not support change; in 1938 the Employers' Association of the Port of Liverpool had explicitly denounced the proposals made by the NAPLE executive. During the war, these tensions became even more evident; in the course of postwar negotiations the NAPE could not develop any viable alternative proposals for real reform. Hence the Labour government, fearful lest manpower shortages impede the operation of the ports, followed the TGWU proposals closely when the National Dock Labour Board (NDLB) was created by statutory order in 1947. This solution was endorsed by three independent inquiries. Port labour management was subject to joint control at local and national level; a guaranteed weekly wage was introduced for all dockers.[43]

The TGWU hailed this as the triumphant culmination of a 30 year struggle to win security of employment and income for their members. Through the constitution of the NDLB, the closed shop could be guaranteed. The problem of partial organisation had constantly undermined the bargaining position of the national executive in the interwar period; this would be finally overcome. Bevin had always argued that the interests of the state and of his union in matters of port labour management were quite reconcilable; the creation of the NDLB seemed to prove him right.

The dockers themselves proved less enthusiastic. A wave of militant strike action hit British ports in the 1940s and early 1950s; this re-established the men's reputation for industrial militancy and attracted copious quantities of official and academic analysis. The number of man-days lost annually through strikes rose from an average of 49,000 in 1930–8 to 344,400 in the period 1947–55, peaking at 400,000 in 1949.[44] As strikes were illegal until 1951, most of these stoppages were unofficial. Indeed, it was the inability of either union or government to control the high incidence of dock strikes that brought compulsory arbitration to an end in that year. In the interim, the TGWU's role was not to support the men but to urge a return to work, pending an official settlement. This advice was commonly ignored.

Resistance is best understood if both wartime and postwar schemes are interpreted in the context of government manpower policies and are not seen simply as concessions won by the TGWU on behalf of the dockers themselves. Wartime regulations aimed specifically to replace traditional practices which had been designed to share work, protect jobs and preserve local autonomy in determining pay and conditions. Normal methods of working were thrown abruptly into reverse. The definition of dock work was extended, both geographically and professionally, in order to raise both the number of registered dockers available for port work and the number of employers liable to the levy which financed the minimum wage.[45] This brought onto the docks men who had little or no direct experience of the shipping trade. Apart from the new schemes themselves, official 'Speed and Output' committees were created in major ports to prevent overmanning and encourage the efficient use of labour.[46] Port labour officers secured priority for essential supplies, thereby imposing another layer of official controls in the allocation of men to jobs. All these attempts to raise productivity were far less successful, however, than the traditional financial incentives – in the form of war bonus and piece-rate systems – introduced by employers on the Mersey, the Clyde, in Bristol and Southampton. Dockers were paid more to speed up the turn-round of ships and to make the best use of daylight hours when work was not impeded by bombs and blackout.[47] Extra payments also helped make transfer between ports more acceptable. This extensive use of financial inducements transformed dockers' earnings, making them among the best paid workers in the war economy.

Stricter controls, introduced in the context of the wartime emergency, were not, however, to be abandoned when peace returned. The government was sharply aware of the importance of the ports in achieving economic recovery and reviving exports. Port employers were determined to modernise port facilities and restore commercial competitiveness. In return for concessions on the issue of a minimum wage, the NAPE sought to abolish restrictive practices, reduce manpower costs and raise productivity within the industry.[48] Hence the transition from war to peace did not see any relaxation of pressure on either the ports or the registered labour force. Like its antecedents, the NDLB tried to prune registers and reform working agreements in accordance with these aims. For the dockers, this contravened Bevin's promise, made in 1942, that prewar practices would be restored when peace returned.

In the context of continuing full employment and high earnings, the income guarantees provided by the new schemes proved insufficient inducement for dockers to modify traditional working practices – either during the war or after it. The TGWU tended to argue that this was because the sums of money involved were too low: 'In point of fact we find,' Arthur Deakin told a committee of inquiry in 1945, '. . . the value of the dock labour scheme has produced no more money than unemployment insurance. So the much warranted advantage we have had from the national scheme . . . is not quite as real as it is supposed to be.'[49] Insurance benefits had, of course, acted as a supplement to casual earnings and had helped perpetuate casual employment; now earnings were higher, it was unlikely that similar sums would provide an incentive for regular work. Maintenance offered nothing to well-paid men; even in the mid-1950s only a tiny minority of dockers had their wages 'made up' to the guaranteed minimum wage.[50] Most were prepared to forego these financial benefits and continued to break continuity, evade the call and refuse allocated work when it suited them. In absence of an effective carrot, the scheme came to rely increasingly on the stick. Jointly representative local disciplinary committees – not the individual employer – were vested with powers to punish dissidents. The incidence of insubordination remained high; in the early 1950s some 15,000 individuals – 18% of the labour force – were appearing annually before these committees, accused of infractions against the scheme and other similar offences.[51] The scheme thus disrupted traditional forms of mutual obligation between the foreman and the men who 'followed' him. The very quantity of disciplinary cases also reflects the inability of either national or local boards effectively to break traditional work practices.

Resentment of change was not founded on blinkered conservatism; the new regulations bred injustice. The specialist sectors found the scheme put their superior status in jeopardy, for their work could be allocated to fringe casuals while they were tied, by continuity,[52] to poorly paid work or to inconveniently sited ships.

> The stevedores have always hated the scheme ... because it destroys the privileged position they formerly held. It breaks up their gangs and makes them share the cream of the work in the port with others. It makes it difficult for them to absent themselves when they desire to do other things. As the scheme is largely dependent upon the acceptance of [clause] 84b, its rejection would mean the destruction of the scheme and a return to casual conditions in the docks, but this would not trouble those who find the clause restricts their freedom of action.[53]

Declining recruitment rates within the industry also made it more difficult for men in this class to hand on their jobs to their sons.[54] At the same time, pressure on the ports necessitated extensive overtime, which became virtually compulsory, even for men working a six-day week. Both the allocation of work and the discretionary granting of 'excuse stamps' (to 'deserving' absentees or dockers incapable of extensive overtime) were vested in board officials; in exercising these powers, they were frequently accused of victimisation or unwarranted favouritism by those who found they were getting a hard deal.[55]

More fundamentally, the new methods of labour management disrupted industrial relations on the waterfront by increasing central authority over industrial bargaining. Determining the rate for the job was supposedly subject, at the final count, to official arbitration. Increased mobility exposed the discrepancies in rates and methods of pay not only between ports but also between employers in each port. During the war, the National Joint Council for Dock Labour (NJCDL) adjudicated over a number of queries concerning payment appropriate to particular cargoes; refusal to accept the NJCDL's decision led to a rash of stoppages in Newcastle in the opening years of the war.[56] Central intervention destroyed the right of employers and men to decide local conditions. Before the war, industrial agreements were negotiated locally – within the broad framework set out by the National Joint Council. Such practices allowed particular disputes over badly stowed or dirty cargoes to be decided on the spot; the ship remained untouched until agreement was reached. Strike action had always been most effective if it was a prompt response. The introduction of lengthy arbitration procedures weakened the dockers' position since, once the cargo was stored and the ship sailed, the employers were less inclined to make concessions. The national scheme assumed an uniformity in the nature and methods of dockwork which did not exist and, by imposing standard rates on varied conditions, reinforced the determination of the shop floor to restore local control over questions of pay.

Resistance to the new system was manifest, as we have noted, in an escalating number of strikes. Small stoppages were often converted into port-wide disputes; this showed the collective determination of the rank and file to reject the sacrifices required of them by the scheme. Support for those penalised by the new regulations led to mass industrial action. Hence compulsory overtime caused strikes in Liverpool in 1943, in Manchester and London in 1951 and led to an overtime ban by the London stevedores in 1954.[57] Suspension of recruitment and attempts to reduce the number of registered casuals produced stoppages in London in 1946 and in 1947, in sympathy with a strike in Glasgow over the same issue.[58] An attempt to serve compulsory redundancy notices on 30 elderly London dockers led to a port-wide 'ineffectives' strike in 1949.[59] The Thames region was peculiarly sensitive to any modification in working practices; militant resistance was the prompt response to any new obligations or controls.

In order to analyse this collective resistance, we need to distinguish dockers' attitudes to the TGWU scheme itself from their response to other aspects of the postwar settlement, specifically the extension of central control over industrial arbitration and port labour management. There is no sign that the dockers wanted to abolish the postwar dock labour scheme; on the contrary, even the most militant elements valued the protection it offered and used the safeguards it provided to protect traditional practices – as will be shown below. What was resented was the way in which the NDLB threatened industrial democracy by repudiating local involvement in determining working procedures. An example will help illustrate the point. In June 1948, a gang of London dockers refused to unload a cargo of zinc oxide at the official rate and were threatened with disciplinary action. Replacement gangs sent by the local dock labour board refused to touch the work, the whole port stopped work and Liverpool dockers came out in sympathy shortly afterwards.[60] The strike did not result from a common conviction that the cargo was dirty and the official rate unjust. Rather, dockers argued that the local board had no right to punish men who had been following traditional procedures by refusing to touch a ship until the rate for the job had been determined to the satisfaction of both sides. The issue of procedure and penalties converted a particular incident into a common cause. The main reason for unrest was collective resistance to a new source of authority and managerial discipline.

In the short term, this resistance was successful; the scheme was never implemented as originally intended. Registers remained unpruned, attendance stayed sporadic, disciplinary powers were under-used as employers learnt that formal procedures generated more trouble than they were worth. The influence of officials in allocating work remained marginal. In short, the NDLB – whose powers over the activities of local boards were negligible – never decasualised the docks. The state was aware that the system had failed from an early stage but, by the end of this period, was far more concerned to prevent dock strikes than to promote port labour reform. This strategy persisted into the 1950s; the Conservative administration was to prove much less enthusiastic than its Labour predecessor had been about using official controls to regulate port employment. The scheme became, as one Ministry of Labour official noted privately in 1951 'a pretence at organisation which is really no organisation at all'.[61]

The port employers had never been strongly in favour of the scheme; it failed to make the industry more efficient and competitive. It also reduced their authority in the management of port labour. Faced with rising disruption, the NAPE argued consistently for the abolition of joint controls, while most employers reverted to traditional methods of reinforcing their authority – by increasing the number of permanent or semi-permanent men and demanding compensatory cuts in the casual quota. Such tactics provoked opposition at the local level and revived old tensions between casual and permanent men.

Hence restrictions on registration persisted and, in face of the constant reductions in the numbers of casuals, the ageing docker was faced with an uncomfortable dilemma. He was susceptible to pressures to turn permanent on the grounds that, if he did not, the next man would and this lead to his expulsion from portwork.[62] Fears of compulsory redundancy, reflected in the 'ineffectives' strike in London in 1949, haunted the casual workforce. In the end, of course, it was this strategy which was adapted to decasualise the docks under the Devlin Agreement – over 60 years after the idea had first been broached.

Labour shortages had always raised the bargaining power as well as the earnings of casual dockers; in the late 1940s unofficial port workers' committees developed to coordinate collective action in defence of local involvement in industrial bargaining. Joint representation on local dock labour boards was used to protect casual quotas and traditional working practices, not to promote the more rational deployment of labour.[63] In London, the National Amalgamated Stevedores and Dockworkers (NASD), which had never recruited permanent men, was expelled from the NDLB in 1949 for refusing to implement cuts in the port labour register.[64] The general move to assert local democracy, in face of the twin threats posed by the bureaucracies of Arthur Deakin and Lord Ammon, became centred on the 'blue' union (as the NASD was called) in the early 1950s. Branches appeared in the north-west and in Hull at this time. A form of industrial unionism – strongly reliant on collective loyalties to protect local rights – re-emerged on the waterfront; in form and nature this was reminiscent of earlier forms of dock labour organisation. While happy to defend the advantages offered by the dock labour scheme, unofficial leaders specifically repudiated the corporatist tactics used by the TGWU to promote the interests on the rank and file.

The consequences for the TGWU are relatively well known; far from consolidating union organisation on the waterfront, the new system undermined its very foundations. The union was found to support the regulations and procedures that provoked hostility;

during disputes it was the TGWU official who pleaded for a return to work and on disciplinary committees, it was the TGWU representative who – while ostensibly representing the men – helped determine punishment for breaches in regulations which the dockers resented and whose legitimacy they questioned. The union had long been viewed as over-bureaucratic and undemocratic; in the context of the postwar struggles, it was incapable of responding to rank and file opinion. The low point was reached in the early 1950s; the NASD had made successful inroads on TGWU organisation in Manchester, Merseyside and Hull and had secured representation on local negotiating machinery. Unwilling to become embroiled in a complex interunion dispute, the Ministry of Labour decreed in 1955 that men could not be excluded from the register for the lack of a TGWU card. As in the interwar period, registration proved an unreliable way to secure a closed shop.[65]

During the 1950s, the TGWU used all means in its power to discredit its rival at national level but at the same time was re-evaluating local organisational tactics. The lack of central control over local dock labour boards did not help decasualisation but it did afford greater autonomy to regional officers and local organisers. Similarly, the abolition of compulsory arbitration reduced central regulation of bargaining procedure. Official shop stewards appeared on the docks; under the recommendations of the Devlin Committee in the mid-1960s, these became vested with greater authority in local bargaining and the establishment of collective agreements. The damage was not, however, easily repaired; in the major ports old rivalries continued and non-unionism remained a problem. The strategy of 'unionisation from above' had proved singularly unsuccessful.

IV

Postwar dock strikes show that rank and file dockers resented the loss of local autonomy in industrial bargaining and rejected not only the introduction of stricter managerial discipline but also the objectives that management sought to achieve. The powers nominally vested in the NDLB and its local counterparts were disliked by both sides of the industry; we cannot interpret these stoppages as a straightforward expression of class conflict. Peter Weiler's well-researched essay on the 1949 Canadian Seamen's strike[66] draws attention to the close links that developed between government and union at this time and points out, quite correctly, that communist infiltration played only a marginal part in stimulating unrest, although the cold war gave this explanation much credibility in official circles. However, Dr Weiler asserts that the interests of the port employers were well served by the dock scheme, a viewpoint evidently not shared by the employers themselves who argued persistently for the restoration of their former managerial authority throughout the 1940s – as Richard Morgan's research has shown.[67] At local level, there is evidence to suggest that employers made every effort to reduce the impact of official regulations and to undermine the influence of dock labour board officials in the allocation of work – in much the same way as they had done under the voluntary system before the war. Postwar legislation proved little more effective in re-shaping employment on the docks than had earlier initiatives. Locally, collectivist solutions gained little support from either side.

In retrospect, we can see that the postwar decasualisation scheme held little attraction for dockers. It threatened older and weaker workers with removal from the labour force; it subjected more autonomous elements to more rigorous industrial discipline. In other words, it removed the advantages of a casual's life style for those who showed little desire for permanent employment while taking off the waterfront those who might welcome greater protection. It also operated on the assumption that dockers could and should be capable of working on any number of different tasks; the assumption that port-workers were interchangeable undermined, at least in theory, the hierarchies of port-work which had provided the foundation for traditional forms of industrial bargaining.

How far structural features of the port transport industry justified these divisions by the mid-twentieth century is a complicated question. On the one hand, technological innovation and mechanical devices, already in common use among major port employers before the war, had reduced the strategic importance of the old specialist gangs. The war itself and the postwar drive to modernise the industry encouraged this development, which was to culminate with the introduction of containers during the 1960s. On the other hand, new technology, manpower shortages, the form of industrial ownership and investment and the nature of port-work itself, all combined to reinforce divisions within the labour force and to make the postwar dock labour scheme an inappropriate measure for raising productivity. The strategic importance of 'specialist' groups did not disappear. Mechanical handling generated a demand for particular skills in driving cranes and manipulating winches. Continuing manpower shortages during the 1940s justified the extension of registration to incorporate riggers, checkweighmen, coal trimmers and similar groups for the first time, but the new system constantly exposed the need for experienced men on particular processes which could not be efficiently carried out by any docker who happened to be available. At the same time, industrial investment remained uneven because industrial ownership remained basically unchanged. Even in the 1960s, large numbers of small employers were still in business; these were less able to afford new technology and were traditionally more reliant on the availability of gangs who knew their work. Finally, the very nature of the industry did not encourage greater mobility of labour or allow dockers to work a 'regular' week. Once in dock, the ship had to be dispatched with all possible speed. This was best achieved by gangs who knew the job and worked round the clock; intensive work for short periods made problematic the effective integration of inexperienced, or reluctant labour. Thus, a degree of interdependence between an employer and his men persisted throughout this period and this provided the foundations for traditional forms of industrial bargaining.

Hence we see that postwar port-workers' committees were similar in their objectives and their methods to local TGWU branches in the interwar period and, thanks to full employment, probably operated with considerably more success. Both forms of local organisation used registration to strengthen their bargaining power by keeping outsiders off the docks. While the guaranteed weekly wage exercised little influence on working practices in the 1940s, access to state benefits in the earlier period helped reinforce established working methods. In practice, the unemployment insurance scheme acknowledged that the port transport industry was, effectively, a multiplicity of discreet concerns, each with its own labour force. Although an important financial reinforcement for casualism, the state scheme was not a fundamental factor shaping dockers' attitudes. In Liverpool, for example, the impact of the slump forced large numbers of port-workers onto means-tested assistance; in the postwar period Merseyside retained its reputation as one of the most stalwart defenders of casualism. In this instance, reduced access to benefit 'as of right' did not restructure dockers' attitudes to port labour reform.

If anything, memories of the interwar period reinforced collective determination to protect traditional forms of workplace control. These at least vested the dockers themselves with the responsibility for safeguarding access to work and rates of pay. The alternative was to allow authority in such matters to pass to a remote bureaucracy under professional management whose chief concern was apparently to raise productivity at all costs.

This is not to suggest that dockers were indifferent to the protection of their work opportunities; in periods of rising unemployment this was manifestly not the case. However, the TGWU was never able to whip up rank and file support for its decasualisation policies. When the union was strong enough to win concessions, dockers were least threatened by outside labour; when unemployment rose, the prospects of welfare intervention became more attractive, but the union bargaining position weakened. It was in such periods that local bargaining strategies proved fundamental to safeguarding the union's survival. Except in wartime, dock unionism was largely national in name alone. In the interwar period, as at the turn of the century, organisation was patchy, the closed shop only partially and sporadically enforced and bargaining was vested in local – virtually autonomous – branches committed to the defence of established practices.

Like Tillett and Sexton before him, Bevin was aware of the advantages cooperation with the state could bring, in terms of consolidating organisation on the waterfront itself and raising the influence of the executive in national bargaining. However, from the viewpoint of the rank and file, the introduction of Bevin's dock labour scheme represented a transformation in the nature of union politics and the location of union power. The consequences of 'unionisation from above' was resistance at local level; this was first manifest in the 1911 disruption on Merseyside and subsequently in the determined defence of local autonomy, shown chiefly in Newcastle, Aberdeen and Glasgow between the wars, and in Liverpool, Manchester and Hull in the later 1940s. The TGWU used two, possibly contradictory, strategies to promote unionisation. One looked back to traditional workplace bargaining and the other emphasised the benefits that could be gained by collectivist solutions. The political debate over the boundaries between the industrial and political spheres of the British labour movement, visible in a variety of other areas, here spilt over into open confrontation.

Except in periods of war, the extension of official controls over the operation of the industrial labour market has been subject to continuous political debate. By and large, the acceptability of state intervention has reflected prevailing opinion about the ability of government to stimulate industrial growth and economic prosperity. Certainly, the Board of Trade Labour Department – before the First World War – was convinced that the correct application of scientific solutions to the problems of urban degeneration, industrial inefficiency and under-utilised labour would benefit the whole of society. This interventionist stance contrasts strongly with the position held by the Ministry of Labour during the 1930s; by then, the generation of industrial efficiency was not considered a concern of central government and the ministry was eager to shed even the remnants of its responsibilities for the decasualisation of dock labour. Even when pressed by both sides of the industry, ministry officials would not intervene. It was only the Second World War itself, and the crucial role played by the ports both in the military emergency and in postwar reconstruction, that produced a change of policy.

As far as official attitudes towards organised labour were concerned, the pattern of state policy is reasonably clear. In periods when the efficient operation of the ports was vital to the survival of the country, the state tended to make common cause with the dockers' leaders, evidently preferring to negotiate with a single national executive than with a plethora of small and partially organised unions. In the interwar period, by contrast, official interest in decasualisation waned and, with it, official interest in safeguarding any particular kind of unionism on the docks – or any union organisation at all. In periods of relatively full employment, when industrial unrest was likely, central government took more positive steps to safeguard the establishment of collective bargaining than at other times. Such a strategy was, however, emphatically not anti-union; one of the main characteristics of official decasualisation policy during the first half of this century lies in the reliance the state placed on the unions – not the port employers – in furthering its objectives.

In general, economic assumptions and political factors both played a part in shaping the role of the state in this area. While governments all conceded that decasualisation was desirable, the involvement of official agencies and statutory powers remained a more open question. In this respect, the history of decasualisation is similar to that of other areas of employment and training policy, of which it originally formed an integral part. Except in periods of war, these have tended to rely on voluntary incentives. Civil servants and politicians alike have been wary of introducing compulsory controls over industrial employment; such intervention would fail to achieve any constructive purpose if it disrupted established bargaining practices, thereby provoking confusion or unrest. Nonetheless, state policy – through its various systems of income maintenance – has affected working conditions and practices, although not always in the way that policymakers intended. Like industrial training and transference, the advisory employment services and temporary measures of job creation, official efforts to decasualise the docks had only a marginal influence on the structure of the job market and the allocation of work. But interwar unemployment insurance and the postwar port labour schemes actually helped protect casual employment practices and concomitant forms of workplace control that they were designed to remove from the docks. In the event, earlier fears that official regulation might stimulate unrest proved justified. In major ports, dockers fought to protect traditional forms of local bargaining. The results of this confrontation did not vindicate the state's authority but exposed its limitations. Generally, port-workers proved adept at using official concessions and incentives for their own purposes.

NOTES

Abbreviations used

NAPE	National Association of Port Employers
NAPLE	National Association of Port Labour Employers
NUDL	Nation Union of Dock Labourers
SUDL	Scottish Union of Dock Labourers
DWRGWU	Dock, Wharf, River and General Workers' Union
NTWF	National Transport Workers' Federation
NASD	National Amalgamated Stevedores and Dockworkers
STGWU	Scottish Transport and General Workers Union
SACPTI	Standing Advisory Committee of the Port Transport Industry
NJCDL	National Joint Council for Dock Labour
PRO	Public Record Office
BLPES	British Library of Political and Economic Science (LSE)

* This paper is drawn from G. A. Phillips and N. Whiteside *Casual*

*Labour: The Unemployment Question in the Port Transport Industry,
1880–1970* (Oxford, 1985). I wish to record my debt to my co-author
for material produced here. My thanks are also due to Richard Morgan
for his useful comments on an earlier draft of this paper. Unless otherwise stated, place of publication for works cited below is London.

1 L. H. Powell, *The Shipping Federation* (1950). Union recognition was
confined to small port employers: see R. Bean 'Employers Associations
in the Port of Liverpool', *International Review of Social History* 21
(1976).
2 E. Hobsbawm, *Labouring Men* (1964), p. 205.
3 R. Williams, 'Map of British Isles, showing present methods of organisation among dockers, waterside workers etc.' (1912) NTWF pamphlet in
BLPES.
4 NTWF, *Federation or Amalgamation?* (1912), Webb Coll E/B, vol. CV
BLPES.
5 COS, *Report on Unskilled Labour* (1908); E. Rathbone, *Enquiry into
the conditions of Labour at the Liverpool Docks* (1904); *Royal Commission on the Poor Laws and Relief of Distress: Appendices: Minutes
of Evidence* vols. VIII and IX, Cd 5066 and Cd 5068/1910.
6 N. Whiteside, 'Welfare Insurance and Casual Labour', *Economic
History Review*, 2nd series, 32 (1979), pp. 508–10.
7 J. Broodbank, *History of the Port of London*, vol. 2 (1921), gives a
detailed description of the debate and of the work of the Royal
Commission, set up at the turn of the century, to reform port facilities in
the capital.
8 TUC, *Annual Report*, 1909, especially p. 103 and pp. 156–8.
9 National Insurance Act, 1911, section 99.
10 See R. Williams, *The First Year's Working of the Liverpool Docks
Scheme* (Liverpool, 1914) and 'Memorandum on Schemes set up during
1912', PIN 3/8/22, PRO.
11 DWRGWU, *Annual Report*, 1912, p. 12. Tillett was the leader of the
rival London Dockers' Union.
12 R. Williams, *Liverpool Docks Scheme*, and memorandum, by
Beveridge, 16 June 1913, LAB 2/1484/ LE 23987/27, PRO.
13 For evidence of Treasury opposition, see LAB 2/1483/ LE 2211/24 and
PIN 7/2, PRO.
14 In London at least, membership had shown signs of declining after the
upsurge of 1910–12; J. Lovell, *Stevedores and Dockers* (1969), p. 202.
15 See 'Final Report of the Port and Transit Committee, 1921' on file MT
25/62, PRO. For union representation on port labour committees, see
minutes and papers in MT 10/1891; MT 10/1930; MT 10/1949; MT 10/
1956; LAB 2/169/ LE 50041. For files on individual ports, see LAB 2 boxes
1042–5, PRO. These show how, for example, in Glasgow, Liverpool
and Bristol, the military authorities conceded exemption to all union
card holders – as *bona fide* dockers.
16 Description of the formation and work of the TWBs in MT 10/1906.
Evidence of the resistance they engendered can be found in the NTWF,
Weekly Record during this period; see, for example, 20 Jan 1917; also
MT 10/1930 and MT 10/1949, PRO.

17 On file LAB 2/1045/DPL 244, PRO.
18 In 1916, Beveridge renewed his efforts to effect decasualisation by extending a special scheme of unemployment insurance to dockers, see Beveridge Papers III/42, BLPES; LAB 8/52, PRO and R. J. Scally *Origins of the Lloyd George Coalition* (Princeton, NJ, 1975) pp. 307–13. Attempts to negotiate a compromise agreement between Bevin and Beveridge in the summer of 1919, following both men presenting their ideas to a committee of inquiry into casual labour in the port of London (Roche), came to nothing. Generally, the Ministry of Labour favoured a modification of the insurance principle while Bevin opposed any idea of contributions and wanted the scheme to be run by the industry, not the state. See PIN 7/36 and LAB 2/1042/DPL 131/20/1919, PRO.
19 N. Whiteside 'Welfare Legislation and the Unions during the First World War', *Historical Journal* 23 (Dec. 1980) especially s. IV and 'Welfare Legislation and the Unions After the First World War: A Reply', *Historical Journal* 25 (May 1982).
20 Memorandum by L. G. Dennys, 2 April 1924, LAB 8/52, PRO.
21 Agreements for minor ports documented in TGWU files at Transport House. A member's registration card did double duty as a TGWU membership card and a registration certificate. Difficulties with employers were also experienced in Hull and Southampton: individual files in LAB 2/boxes 1041–7, PRO.
22 TGWU, *Minutes and Record of the General Executive Committee* vol. 6, Nov. 1927; Min. 1018.
23 LAB 8/190–1, PRO.
24 TGWU, *Minutes and Record*, vol. 5, Aug. 1927; Min. 745 and Min. 971.
25 Summary of Clydeside resistance to registration, see LAB 8/51, PRO. An account is also given in A. Bullock, *The Life and Times of Ernest Bevin*, vol. 1 (1960), pp. 465–8.
26 Standing Advisory Council for the Port Transport Industry: Annual Report for 1937, LAB 8/191, PRO.
27 H. Llewellyn Smith, *New Survey of London Life and Labour* vol. 2 (1931) pp. 399–401.
28 D. Caradog Jones, *Social Survey of Merseyside*, vol. 2 (Oxford, 1934), p. 63.
29 J. Hilton, et al., *Are Trade Unions Obstructive?* (1935), p. 120.
30 E. C. P. Lascelles and S. S. Bullock, *Dock Labour and Decasualisation* (1924) p. 186. Figures taken from the Liverpool Dock Scheme.
31 Minute by Reid, 29 March 1927; on file LAB 2/1042/ED 2100/28, PRO.
32 SACPTI, *Annual Report*, 1936 and LAB 2/2177/STATS 297/1935.
33 These were, of course, seen as temporary concessions, embodied in the Unemployment Insurance (Amendment) Act of 1921. For the policy to allow benefit to those on short time, see Ministry of Labour memorandum to the Cabinet Committee on Unemployment, 15 Feb. 1921, CAB 27/135, PRO. The arrangement was still upheld in 1925; see correspondence T 161/250/526 827, PRO.
34 See minutes of conference, NJCDL and Minister of Labour, Feb. 1923; LAB 2/1039/IR 553/1923, PRO.

106   NOEL WHITESIDE

35 *Port Facilities of Great Britain* (1924) pp. 280–1. Comparisons were made with Antwerp, Rotterdam, Le Havre and Dunkirk.
36 LAB 2/1954/ED 37606/1925, PRO.
37 Ministry of Labour's Statement to the Maclean Committee (1930) on file LAB 2/2036/ED 2668, PRO. Also *Royal Commission on Unemployment Insurance Final Report* Cmd 4185/1931–2, ch. 2, para. 129. For the industry's reactions to this recommendation, see SACPTI memorandum, in LAB 8/39, PRO.
38 Evidence of Price to the Royal Commission on Unemployment Insurance, 31 Dec 1930. Evidence, vol. 1 (1931–2), pp. 107–11.
39 Report, Feb. 1933, p. 4, in PIN 6/71, PRO.
40 F. G. Hanham, *Report of an Enquiry into Casual Labour in the Merseyside Area* (Liverpool, 1930), p. 11. For similar ratios in West Derby, see p. 86.
41 See note 39 above. Only 10,000 had collected fewer than 20 stamps in one year.
42 NJCDL 'The Final Report of the Royal Commission on Unemployment Insurance', appendix 2; on file LAB 2/1051/ET 6339/1932, PRO.
43 More detailed accounts of postwar negotiations and the establishment of the NDLB can be found in V. H. Jensen, *The Hiring of Dock Workers* (Cambridge, Mass., 1964), pp. 134–41 and M. P. Jackson, *Labour Relations at the Docks* (Farnborough, Hants, 1973), pp. 31–39. The NAPLE changed its name to the National Association of Port Employers during the war.
44 *Final Report of the Committee of Enquiry into Certain Matters concerning the Port Transport Industry* (Devlin), Cmd 2734/1965. Table of man-days lost through strikes 1947–55.
45 Discrepancies between ports were widespread, even after the war. See LAB 8/1382, PRO.
46 These had the full official support of the TGWU when introduced in the spring of 1942 and were endorsed by an independent enquiry into unrest on Merseyside. See Forster, Report, p. 23, in MT 63/217, also papers on file LAB 8/1379, PRO.
47 Evidence of Donovan (TGWU) to Committee of Inquiry on a National Minimum Wage (Evershed), minutes, 4 Dec 1945, p. 25: BK 1/85, PRO.
48 Hence their general opposition to any expansion in the port labour registers; see C. M. Cunningham, 'The Dock Industry on Merseyside', in R. Lawton and C. M. Cunningham (eds.), *Merseyside Social and Economic Studies* (London, 1970), pp. 235–56.
49 Evidence of Deakin to Committee of Inquiry (Evershed), p. 14.
50 *Commission Appointed to Enquire into the Operation of the Dock Workers (Regulation of Employment) Scheme 1947: Report* (Devlin) Cmd 9813/1956, p. 17.
51 *Ibid.*, p. 21.
52 In the interwar period, continuity agreements protected the casual docker's right to finish the job for which he had been hired, thus preventing his replacement by a permanent hand. During the war, the regulation was extended to all ports and prevented men leaving one job

unfinished in order to get another, which was more attractive or better paid.

53 Whitlock report on the Canadian Seamen's strike in London: 16 July 1949, on file LAB 10/904, PRO.

54 'My grandfather and father were stevedores and I am a stevedore' protested a member of a NASD delegation to the Ministry of Labour in May 1946. 'My son was demobilised yesterday and he cannot get a stevedore's book to carry on his grandfather's job.' Minutes, p. 16, on file LAB 8/1359, PRO.

55 In June 1943, a conference recorded fines levied on dockers in Bristol, Immingham, Grimsby and Liverpool for non-attendance at the call, following spells of overtime: BK 1/21, PRO.

56 See LAB 10/184, PRO.

57 For Liverpool strike, see LAB 10/259, PRO; the Manchester strikes are recorded in T. Simey, *The Dock Worker* (Liverpool, 1954), appendix 1 and in M. P. Jackson, *Labour Relations at the Docks*, pp. 51 *et seq.* For the stevedores' overtime ban, see *Enquiry into Dispute in the London Docks: Interim and Final Reports* (Evershed), Cmnd 9310/1954.

58 See LAB 10/735, PRO.

59 See LAB 10/831, PRO.

60 Official papers on the Zinc Oxide Strike of June 1948 are on file LAB 10/783, PRO.

61 Minute on file LAB 8/1707, which also includes evidence on port employers' reluctance to impose the scheme's regulations in full, for fear of stimulating a dispute. Departmental discussions on the Doughty Report (*Review of British Dock Strikes*, Cmd 7851/1949) reveal that departmental officials were fully aware that the scheme itself was the chief cause of unrest, but were extremely reluctant to criticise openly the new system which, ostensibly, was still promoted as a desirable and progressive measure of port labour reform. See LAB 8/1709, PRO.

62 D. Wilson, *Dockers: the Impact of Industrial Change* (1972), p. 114.

63 In the north-west at least, dockers had long fought against any extension in the use of permanent men or preference systems. Hence local control of the register became a new means to realise traditional objectives.

64 The NASD, unable under the dock labour scheme to recruit new members, had long felt itself threatened by 'senile decay'. Minutes of delegation, 29 May 1946, p. 6, on file LAB 8/1359, PRO.

65 More detailed accounts of this renowned interunion dispute can be found in M. P. Jackson, D. Wilson and elsewhere. See also J. Dash, *Good Morning, Brothers* (London, 1970).

66 P. Weiler, 'British Labour and the Cold War: the London Dock Strike of 1949' in J. E. Cronin and J. Schneer (eds.), *Social Conflict and the Political Order in Modern Britain* (London, 1982).

67 Cooperation between state and port employers remained circumscribed by the diffuse nature of the latter's interests in port labour management; this was reflected in the NAPE's resistance to collectivist solutions (paper to King's College Research Centre seminar, March 1983).

4

Government, employers and shop floor organisation in the British motor industry, 1939–69

STEVEN TOLLIDAY

In the last few years, a picture of the history of the development of shop floor organisation in the motor industry has consistently appeared in a variety of works by historians, economists and sociologists. Broadly speaking, the view is that trade union organisation established itself in the motor industry by the end of the Second World War, taking advantage of the tightening labour markets of the prewar rearmament boom and the favourable conditions of wartime production. In the postwar period the car firms found themselves facing a soft sellers' market, particularly in Europe, and a tight labour supply at home. In order to achieve continuous and expanding output, they conceded high wages and a considerable measure of job control to powerful shop steward organisations. By the time that international competition began to intensify in the mid-1950s, they had largely lost control of the shop floor and were unable to dislodge the deeply entrenched shop steward organisations that faced them.[1]

This picture is a highly misleading one. It is largely based on generalisation from the cases of Standard Motors and some of the smaller motor firms in and around Coventry, and in certain respects it may be an accurate picture of this sector of the industry.[2] But these firms produced less than a fifth of British car output in this period, and if we look to the volume car producers the picture is very different. The level of unionisation shows the contrast. In 1956 Morris Motors was only 25% unionised; Vauxhall was well below 50%; Ford was in the same range and was notorious for its limitations on shop stewards. Austin fluctuated between 60% and 90% during most of the 1950s, but the shop floor organisation had made only very limited inroads on managerial authority in this period.[3] In most of these firms, which accounted for some 75% of

British car output at this time, the key period for the consolidation of shop floor organisation was in fact the late 1950s and early 1960s – and at Vauxhall it is arguable whether there has ever been a powerful shop steward organisation.

Such a revision of the conventional periodisation of development leads one to be wary of looking at shop floor organisation as some sort of reflex of the labour market and to query the extent to which shop steward organisation has primarily been built from the bottom up by autonomous action in the workplace. Clearly much *does* depend on particular workplace issues, local labour traditions and strategic groups of workers. But the growth of workplace organisation also depends crucially on the strategies and organisational structures of unions and management. Moreover, government actions have played an important role in both of these areas. There was little *direct* government intervention in the industry in this period, yet the government was highly influential in shaping the bargaining environment, often in pursuit of policy aims in other areas, in ways that offered a varying pattern of opportunities and constraints for both management and unions. Government action was always important, and during the war, the late 1940s, and the late 1950s, fairly decisive in the emergence, shaping and consolidation of workplace organisation. The turn towards direct legal intervention by government in the late 1960s should not be seen as the emergence of a new actor into a framework of previously bilateral collective bargaining, but as one further shift of gear in a long-running ambiguous relationship between government, employers and unions.

I

For most of the 1930s the motor industry was a trade union desert. Despite the prosperity and expansion of the late 1930s which offered certain possibilities for union recruitment, by and large the major firms were able to keep their workers out of unions before the war. The only significant exception was at Pressed Steel in Oxford where a significant shop floor organisation had been built up following the big strike of 1934. Apart from this, the rapid expansion of unionisation that had occurred in other sectors of engineering and in aircraft production was absent.[4] It is against this background that wartime developments have to be seen.

Many wartime conditions appeared to favour union development in motor companies and other firms. The drive for production, tight labour markets and growing union confidence symbolised by the presence of Bevin in the government were accompanied by government policies that tended to mitigate employer hostility, such as cost-plus contracts and the priority accorded to conciliation. But though the war undoubtedly constituted a watershed in the unionisation of the motor industry, the advances that took place were restricted and partial. Most of the big motor firms came through the war with their unions still in a fairly weak position. Union density at Ford and Vauxhall at the end of the war was probably below 25%, at Morris 30% and at Austin around 50%. Only in the smaller Coventry firms was the advance more dramatic.[5] Trade union gains seem to have depended heavily on wartime conditions and often receded along with them.

In the first place, the most spectacular inroads of the unions were made not in the core motor factories themselves but in the 'shadow' aircraft factories managed by the motor companies. At Austin the new Aero works became the focus of a powerful shop steward organisation;[6] at Vauxhall the tank shop was the nucleus of unionisation;[7] at Standard organisation spread outwards from the new Bristol aircraft shop;[8] at Morris the newly established Metal Produce Recovery Department was the leading shop, while the nearby Radiators' factory which was entirely engaged on the mass production of jerry-cans, oil coolers and radiators for the desert war, saw the most dramatic developments of unionisation.[9] New jobs and new timings, the urgency of production and the new framework of government cost-plus contracting, made rapid union advances possible. Moreover, management often found it advantageous to make substantial concessions to the shop floor to stimulate production and to enlist shop steward cooperation in the smooth running of the factory. At Morris Radiators, for instance, a management that had previously been bitterly hostile to the unions sought to resolve the problem of widespread absenteeism and indiscipline among its numerous women workers by giving the shop stewards and Communist Party activists free rein to recruit the women into the unions and thus provide greater discipline and control on the shop floor. The unions made significant gains from this trade-off, but their enhanced role in the factory did not outlast the war. A slack period of work and the great freeze-up of 1947 following the war gave management the opportunity to conduct a major purge of activists and by 1950 the Amalgamated Engineering Union (AEU) organisation at Radiators had been virtually dismantled.[10] At Longbridge, Cowley and Vauxhall, closure of the special wartime departments also meant the dispersal of the new organisations.[11]

In those parts of the old motor factories where prewar work organisation remained more intact, prewar traditions of subordination to management were often slow to break down: jobs changed less, prices were stickier and wages often much lower than on the new jobs. As a result, union strength was more apparent than real in motor firms in wartime. Management frequently found it tactically advisable to ally with the growing pushfulness of the shop floor and turn it towards productivism rather than meet it head on. But the exceptionality of war work often meant that concessions to unions could be relatively easily recouped at the end of the war.

A partial exception to this pattern is to be found in the Coventry motor firms where, in the tightest concentration of light engineering works in the country, the unions, and particularly the TGWU, were able to entrench themselves more thoroughly by exploiting to the full the opportunities presented by wartime legislation and administrative structures. Before the war, union organisation was thin on the ground in the Coventry motor firms, and this changed only slowly in the first two years of the war. But as the groundswell of workplace dissatisfaction grew as the war effort intensified, the unions were able to bolster face-to-face bargaining in the shops with the judicious use of the new framework of legal regulations from the time of the Essential Works Order. The unions were able to push for the implementation of Essential Works Order welfare provisions if management were slow to provide them: if they succeeded, the unions were able to take the credit for canteen or nursery provisions. Similarly, the new institutions of manpower policy could be used to advantage.[12]

The Labour Supply Inspectorate (LSI) had been set up to prevent excess labour and to assess the requirements of management for new labour. A large number of the LSIs were ex-trades unionists and several of them were directly nominated by The Confederation of Shipbuilding and Engineering Unions (The Confed.).[13] If shortages of materials were leading to under-utilisation of manpower, unions could call in the LSI and thus exert pressure over issues such as the loss of earnings through short time. Once in the factory, the LSI would talk to shop stewards or union members to get information about labour practices that management might wish to conceal from them.[14] Both here and in other collective bargaining areas, the threat of third-party scrutiny made managers more willing to negotiate directly with unions. Conciliation officers urged management consistently to negotiate and the threat was always present that if a settlement was not reached internally, the matter would eventually go to arbitration and the decision-making power would be taken out of the hands of management.[15] Management were therefore under pressure to negotiate and the prevalence of cost-plus contracts made it relatively easy for them to pass on wage costs. Hence, a small trade union presence in a factory could quickly find ways of getting results and, therefore, demonstrate the benefits of union organisation to others in the factory.

The lack of pre-existing organisation, however, meant that effective unionisation often depended on establishing a small nucleus of activists in the first place. The Essential Works Order crucially undermined hire-and-fire policies: if their case was weak, management would find themselves forced to reinstate by an Appeals Board, and though victimisation continued almost throughout the war, it was an increasingly risky operation for management.[16] Against this background the TGWU were also able to utilise their contacts with sympathetic labour exchange clerks to slip key activists into strategic plants. This was especially useful in making maximum use of the influx of experienced unionists from hosiery, docks and steelworks. For example, a batch of Tinplate workers from South Wales who became the nucleus of organisation at Morris Engines Foundry in Coventry were got in in this way,[17] and it was also particularly effective in the initial establishment of a core of unionists at Standard Motors.[18] Until the latter years of the war, there does not seem to have been a groundswell of militancy throwing up activists in the shops, and union members in the factories were as likely to need to be encouraged by their branch or officials to push their claims in the factory as to need to be restrained. The emergence of a core of shop stewards often *preceded* the establishment of significant membership. Stewards would often be elected by a few members and then push outwards to organise the rest of the plant and demand recognition.[19]

Hence, union opportunism and effective recruitment policies could utilise the potential leverage of the wartime framework of regulation. But it seems that the most extensive developments were achieved where, in addition, managements saw the cooperation of labour as essential for maximising output. In this situation the union officials in Coventry were often able to develop a relationship with management to 'win the war', and to negotiate the establishment of Joint Production Committees and other cooperative relationships involving unions in the maximisation of output and control in the works.[20] It seems that in Coventry the unions were able to push further along these lines than in most other parts of the country, but even here recalcitrant firms such as Carbodies and Singer were able to keep unions out of their works all through the war.[21] Moreover, the end of the war saw a city-wide offensive on the wage front which was only partially resisted.[22] In general, however, union organisation came out of the war in good shape and largely survived intact during the transition to peacetime production, though it was only at Standard Motors where the Managing Director, Sir John Black, pursued a unique strategy that the wartime practices of conceding substantial shop floor control to the unions survived into peacetime.[23]

If the Coventry case is one end of a spectrum, the example of Ford is near the other end. Ford systematically resisted unionisation for almost the entire duration of the war, and their case illuminates how little pressure the government was prepared to exert in a context where the unions did not prove able to help themselves. Friedman and Meredeen have argued that pressure from Bevin on Ford was directly responsible for the 1944 recognition agreement,[24] and Nina Fishman has described recognition as 'a foregone conclusion once Bevin became Minister of Labour'.[25] In fact, however, the government seems to have been anxious *not* to get directly involved in the Ford issue and their involvement was quite ambiguous. Government did play a significant role in the breakthrough of union organisation at Ford's Manchester works and at the works of Briggs Bodies, their close associates and suppliers on a neighbouring site at Dagenham. At Briggs, the Doughty Inquiry, set up by Bevin after threats of disruption of production in 1941, was directly instrumental in securing shop steward recognition,[26] while Manchester is an interesting case of a combination of shop floor pressure intensifying as a result of government labour market regulation and combining with pressures for production in a wartime bottleneck to produce a strong union presence. In the early part of the war the Manchester factory was reopened to fill a vital gap caused by Rolls-Royce's inability to mass produce sufficient Merlin engines for Spitfire aeroplanes. In order to secure sufficient skilled labour for the new works, the Ministry of Labour's LSIs had scoured Manchester for labour and the local firms had used this opportunity to pass the hot potato of their militant workers on to Ford. The result was a Toolroom full of ex-shop stewards and victimised militants.[27] Ford tried to resist their efforts to organise, sacked a number of leading stewards and provoked a major strike in the Toolroom. Ford were found by a tribunal to be in breach of the Essential Works Order in their sacking and Sir Percival Perry, the Managing Director, was called in to see the Ministry of Aircraft Production (MAP) where Craven, one of the most senior officials, 'did a good deal behind the scenes to try and secure recognition'.[28] In the event, squeezed between the unions and MAP pressure for production, Ford had to back down and concede recognition.

But at Dagenham, despite the fact that the TUC saw Ford as a pivotal issue – or perhaps because of its symbolic centrality – the Ministry of Labour kept out of it. The matter received attention at the highest levels of the Ministry of Labour, and Ford workers consistently lobbied for government action to assist the unionisation of Dagenham. But Bevin and the Ministry were reluctant to follow the precedent of Briggs lest they appeared to be legislating unions into firms and instead preferred to leave it to the TUC to attempt to negotiate a recognition agreement, even though it was quite apparent that Ford were procrastinating and unwilling to make concessions.[29]

The recognition agreements at Briggs and Manchester had come before the entry of the Soviet Union into the war, and in both cases Communist Party activists had been prominent in the shop floor struggles leading up to it. After Hitler's invasion of Russia, however, the communist and left-wing stewards and activists at Dagenham were reluctant to disrupt the war effort by going all out for recognition.[30] They were prepared to hold back shop floor discontent and place a great deal of reliance on the TUC, who were unable, and the government, who were unwilling, to deliver the goods. At firms where unions were already established the self-denying ordinance on strikes was often no great sacrifice, but at Ford it meant the loss of a major weapon. The Party discouraged the use of explosive everyday grievances as a basis to build up an organisation. In the end they were by-passed by a ragged coalition of angry workers, Catholics and CP dissidents who forced the issue by direct action in occupying the management's offices and forcing Ford to negotiate with the TUC.[31] The resulting settlement, much to the satisfaction of Vic Feather of the TUC, largely excluded shop stewards from any role in collective bargaining and placed industrial relations firmly in the hands of management and full-time union officials. The Ministry of Labour privately found the agreement quite unsatisfactory and liable to store up trouble for the future, but as it solved the immediate problem, they were not prepared to do anything about it.[32]

　　This pattern of wide variations according to local initiatives and managerial responses, dependence on specific wartime conditions and the appearance of government legislation as a resource and framework for activity rather than a set of policies and instrumental actions, reflected the nature of Bevin's wartime labour policy. This was certainly in no clear sense a pro-labour strategy in the sense of state sponsorship of union development: the Essential Works Order, for instance, completely lacked the sort of positive provisions for union recruitment and negotiating rights of the American Wagner Act. Instead, Bevin's programme was a complex combination of labour budgeting, social peace, welfarism and Bevin's own conception of collective bargaining – and it shifted gear as the war progressed through different mixtures of reform and repression.[33]

　　Bevin's policy, as Bullock has shown, was first and foremost a manpower policy centred on a strategy of labour budgeting to maximise production. His aim was to minimise coercion and manage working-class opinion so as to make limited compulsion acceptable. Formal industrial discipline was generally not allowed to move ahead of what was strictly necessary for industrial mobilisation. It was also a policy for wage restraint. Bevin believed that legal control of wages would promote discontent and industrial disruption and in the end prove counter-productive. Government control of wages would politicise *all* wage claims and push wages to the centre of the political stage, unions would inevitably be pushed into demanding the socialisation of industry as a *quid pro quo* for wage control and this would unacceptably heighten social conflicts and place the coalition under great strain. Bevin therefore looked to voluntary restraint promoted by the unions in the context of popular support for the war.[34]

But it was not to be restraint *imposed* through the unions either. Bevin saw clearly that union leadership could only hold the line if they were able to preserve their own credibility and authority over their members – and to do so they needed the ability to bargain independently. The use of legal controls could undermine the position of union officials. Even warnings by officials to their members of the legal consequences of their actions could be seen as the officials threatening their members with imprisonment. Bevin relied primarily on the unions, using their enhanced bargaining power to establish themselves and then accepting his leadership in a form of 'guided' voluntarism. He could ensure that management and labour were brought together on more equal terms than ever before and faced with the necessity of working out an agreed solution which, in the last instance, he could back up by statutory regulation.

Bevin's conduct in office displayed many continuities from his prewar policies as leader of the TGWU. His strategic aim for the labour movement was the recognition of the unions by the government as a powerful interest to be consulted at the highest level, and this was embodied in his claim to be seen as the representative of the working-class in government. At the level of the workplace, his aspiration had never been for workers' control but rather for the fullest consultation and the fullest recognition of the unions as the legitimate representatives of the workers. Partly because of this pragmatic outlook and partly because of the constraints of his wider political role, his accession to power had no clearly articulated relationship to the development of the organisation, structure and policy of unions either nationally or in the workplace. Bevin was in government as an economic and political manager and the precondition for the continuation of this role was success in manpower policy and wage restraint: the promotion of collective bargaining was necessarily subordinate to these ends and had to take a form compatible with them. His successes were most notable at the level of national consultation and in industrial relations in munitions and aircraft where employers were working more or less as government sub-contractors in purpose-built facilities and where 'responsible' unions could largely grow up with the enterprise. Beyond this, however, the results of Bevin's wartime policies were patchy. His measures had different implications depending on the past history of industrial relations, the demands of production, and the varying responses of management. In catering, the conditions of war did not promote union growth and Bevin was not able to find a form of legal regulation that would be both politically acceptable *and* promote collective bargaining in this area.[35] In coal, where prewar organisational traditions were strong, Bevin's rejection of nationalisation in order not to disrupt the coalition forced him into using his powers of direction to restrict the miners when wartime conditions gave them a powerful hand against their old antagonistic employers for the first time in 20 years.[36] In motors, the underlying strong hand of the employers remained intact after its wartime vicissitudes.

While Croucher has stressed the repressive aspects of Bevinism, Middlemas has interpreted it as the admission of the unions to power as a 'governing institution'.[37] While the first view pays disproportionate attention to one aspect of Bevin's policies, the second exaggerates the extent to which Bevin was in a position to apply positive policies to promote union organisation and growth. Bevin was able to deny employers any significant advantages from wartime conditions, but was politically restrained from throwing his weight into the scales on the other side. Organised labour's admission to the corridors of power was contingent and limited, and these weaknesses became increasingly apparent as employers regained their freedom of action after the war.

II

The growing political influence of the unions under the Labour Government of 1945–51 was not mirrored by progress at shop floor level in engineering in general or motors in particular. The new political influence of the unions was not a direct reflection of their shop floor strength and indeed was in a certain degree of tension with their local bargaining power. One of the things that the unions offered to a political partnership with Labour was the ability of the leaders to control their members and deliver restraint in the work place, and government policy determinedly set itself to support their authority.[38]

The leaderships of both the TGWU and AEU believed that they could get an adequate *quid pro quo* for their support in the form of social reforms and wider class progress, and in the era of postwar nationalisations and the establishment of the National Health Service this was not wholly unrealistic. But such wider political considerations and loyalties meant that they tied themselves to the

government in a way that made it difficult for them to satisfy many of
the aspirations of the shop floor. In the docks, for instance, the
TGWU were prepared to take on a quasi-managerial role in return
for the fulfilment of certain of their long-term goals in the industry –
namely decasualisation and greater stability. But this brought them
into conflict with other aspirations of dockers for job control and the
maximisation of earnings based on their strengthened bargaining
position. The result of the TGWU's policies of restraint was a crisis
of authority for the union. The schism with its workplace membership in a well-organised sector like the docks resulted in the
emergence of a strong unofficial movement.[39] In motors, shop floor
discontents had different outlets. The motor industry was only one
relatively small section of the diverse industrial constituencies of the
TGWU and AEU, and in the absence of positive policies geared to
motors, developments on the shop floor in the industry in the late
1940s largely by-passed the two big unions and resulted in a period
of stagnation for their organisations.

In the major motor firms the late 1940s were a difficult period for
the unions. Despite the postwar boom, supply problems made
production discontinuous and periodic layoffs facilitated the victimisation of activists and disrupted organisation. At Austin there
were attempts to victimise leading stewards in 1946, 1948 and 1951,
though in the first two cases the men were eventually reinstated after
appeals to tribunals.[40] Morris pursued a policy of weeding out
leading stewards, and buying them out if they could not kick them
out: in 1948–9 a senior manager told the AEU Convener that he had
arranged a higher paying job for him at an estate agents in Oxford. If
he did not take that, the manager warned him, he was likely to soon
be made redundant. The convener took the job.[41] At Ford the late
1940s were dominated by problems arising from the TUC backed
National Joint Negotiating Committee's (NJNC) unwillingness to
support the establishment of normal shop steward negotiating rights
along the lines of Engineering Employers' Federation (EEF) Procedure. Resistance from management and only half-hearted support
from the union leaders on the NJNC, meant that Ford organisation
remained weak and politically divided throughout this period.[42]
Vauxhall remained a weak spot for union organisation.[43] These
problems show up in the membership figures. In a period when
engineering employment expanded, TGWU Engineering membership at first stagnated and then declined between 1948 and 1950.[44]

The AEU lost 30,000 members in these two years, and in Birmingham AEU membership stagnated just below 31,000 between 1945 and 1948 and then fell to 28,747 in 1949.[45] The motor firms outside Coventry continued a modified form of their prewar policy of combining high wages with anti-unionism. Their main concern was to get adequate supplies of labour and speedy output and in pursuit of this they were often ready to make *ad hoc* concessions to workers on the shop floor even *without* the pressure of union-organised shop floor activity. In 1948–50, while the TGWU and AEU leaders were throwing themselves behind the government's pay-freeze, shop floor bargaining in motor firms was largely escaping these constraints and going its own way, producing increases of around 5% annually between 1948 and 1951. This may well have had as much to do with loose shop floor management as with union pressure, and in this situation, the shop floor impetus to join a union may well have been fairly limited where unions were neither prepared to pursue aggressive bargaining nor to launch active organising campaigns.[46]

Something of the deleterious effects of TGWU's and AEU's commitment to the Labour Government on their workplace growth can be seen from the contrast between their stagnation and the vigorous growth of the third major motor industry union, the National Union of Vehicle Builders (NUVB) in this period. While the big unions stood still, the NUVB, though still much smaller, expanded rapidly, recruiting numerous semi-skilled production workers for the first time. In January 1947 their membership stood at 39,119: within two-and-a-half years, by July 1949, it had grown to 57,606.[47] A small union like the NUVB did not have any of the national political responsibilities being shouldered by its giant colleagues. Instead, it was able to use the opportunity of its rivals' commitment to the Labour Government to carve out a sphere of influence for itself in the workplaces. Vehicle-building skills were in decline, but for the time being they remained very much in demand in the postwar years and the NUVB were able to take advantage of this to pursue a strategy of moving from defending their craft skills to that of claiming a particular area of work as their own, in this case 'all above the chassis', the body, paint and trim shops.[48] They made their claims effective through a two-pronged strategy. First, they used aggressive sectional bargaining to claim demarcation rights in particular areas and enforce them by establishing a closed shop.

Secondly, they sought to establish a distinctive NUVB wage structure for the area. By restricting their demands to these particular shops they made it possible for small, well-organised groups to exert great strategic pressure on the motor firms through small strikes involving very little cost to the union supporting the strike. The Executive were frequently willing to give official support to 'wildcat' type strikes over demands for a closed shop, notably at Fisher and Ludlow, Rover, and Jaguar, and their willingness to support such actions gave them a reputation for being a 'Communist' union in these cold-war years.[49] But what gave an additional cutting edge to their closed shop strategy was that once they established a closed shop, they could also claim a higher rate for the workers in that shop, and in doing this they were able to take a significant tactical advantage out of the continuing existence of the wartime framework of legal regulation, especially the National Arbitration Tribunal (NAT).

The basis for this strategy went back to the Engineering Woodworkers' Agreement made between the NUVB and the UK Joint Wages Board for the Vehicle Building Industry of 1920, as amended in 1922. This was an agreement made under very different technical and market conditions which by the late 1940s had unforeseen implications. The Agreement laid down 'vehicle-builders' rates' for specified occupations in the industry in two grades: one for first-class private body-work and commercial vehicles and a second lower one for batch production. In effect, though not in conception when drawn up, this defined a skilled and semi-skilled 'vehicle-builders' rate' for workers in particular occupations. The skilled vehicle-builders' rate was 1d above the AEU skilled fitters' rate and the semi-skilled vehicle-builders' rate was 1d below, which nevertheless put it 1d above the AEU semi-skilled fitters' rate and, thus, also above TGWU semi-skilled workers who followed the AEU target rate. In other words, if the NUVB could force recognition that their agreement was applicable to particular jobs, they could claim the vehicle-builders' rate for it. Thus, being in an NUVB shop carried with it a defined higher rate. Before the war the enforcement of this agreement was confined to NUVB strongholds in high-quality work, but in the late 1940s they sought to use NAT rulings to extend it throughout the areas of work that they laid claim to.[50]

They had some success with this approach, most notably at the Austin where it was central to their relatively rapid growth in the late 1940s which far outpaced the other unions at Longbridge. They gained a major success immediately after the end of the war when Lord Teddington ruled in NAT Award No. 899 in November 1946 that the rates provided for by the Engineering Woodworkers' Agreement for the semi-skilled should be paid to all trimmers and finishers employed on bodywork at Austin.[51] Following this, NUVB were able to recruit vigorously: as George Evans, the Birmingham District Organiser put it, 'we used the NAT as our recruiting base'.[52] The Agreement gave both a higher rate and a sanction to NUVB claims for recruiting rights on these jobs. As a result, the Body Shop became 100% NUVB at a time when the overall level of unionisation at Austin was below 50%.[53] As Evans described it, 'We had no opposition from anyone then [i.e. other unions] because we'd been to the NAT, we'd got a NAT ruling that the workers were vehicle builders so other unions couldn't come in.'[54] The other unions did not accept this, and the TGWU and the Confed. strongly resented the NUVB position. But armed with the 'vehicle-builders' rate' the men in the shops were effectively able to 'put the squeeze' on TGWU members in body or trim shops to get them into the NUVB, and to assist in closing the shops and establishing a sphere of influence.

At other firms, the NUVB had more mixed results with this approach, and no other case approached the way in which shop floor organisation and NAT judgements were able to ratchet off each other for maximum effect at the Austin. In the late 1940s, moreover, the NAT and the Ministry of Labour became increasingly wary of creating similar precedents that could turn out to be hostages to fortune.[55] They feared that continuing recourse to the NAT on closed shop or demarcation issues could lead to a creeping legalisation of industrial relations that they were anxious to avoid, and by the late 1940s the Ministry were strongly advising employers to settle issues outside of the framework of arbitration to avoid precedents that might make inroads on managerial functions or place the onus of settling disputes on the government.[56] Nevertheless, the interaction of the internal politics of the big unions and their relationship with the Labour Government had already affected their bargaining strategies in such a way as to provide the opportunity for a third union to use the legal framework and its own distinctive organisational strategy to revive its waning position in the industry and to establish the pattern of multi-unionism that was to characterise the motor industry until the early 1970s.

III

There was no sharp shift in government policy towards the unions following the victory of the Conservatives at the 1951 General Election. Churchill was anxious to 'keep industrial relations out of politics' and to maintain as far as possible the harmonious relation with trade union leaders that his Labour predecessors had enjoyed.[57] The appointment of Walter Monckton as Minister of Labour was significant. As Monckton described his role: 'Winston's riding orders to me were that the Labour Party had foretold grave labour industrial troubles if the Conservatives were elected, and he looked to me to do my best to preserve industrial peace.'[58] Between 1951 and 1955, Monckton pursued this course assiduously. He had no party political background before his appointment, and he sought to distance the Ministry from the government and to build a reputation for impartiality between employers and unions. At times this went to absurd lengths, such as refusing to speak at a Tory Party Conference lest he impair his image. Industrial peace was a high priority for the government.[59] Their other aims, such as the growth of output, the balance of payments and electoral advantage, seemed to require above all an absence of industrial disruption. As Harold Macmillan put it, 'It may well be argued that with the critical state of financial affairs, and in view of the slender majority by which we governed, any extensive or prolonged industrial dispute might have proved disastrous'.[60] The relative prosperity of the early 1950s made crisis avoidance appear a sensible option, especially since rising wages and inflation did not appear to be the principal threats to the economy.

Conservative labour policy was, therefore, designed to contain and limit conflict as its first priority, and compromise was therefore an inbuilt feature. Under full employment this meant a climate relatively favourable to unions, either because arbitrators tended to split the difference, or because the Ministry of Labour was often prepared to lean on employers to increase their last offer so as to give the union leaders sufficient for them to assuage their members. Arguably, the unions could have gained more by aggressive bargaining but in the early 1950s both the TGWU and the AEU feared the internal political consequences of such a strategy, and their right-wing leaders were committed to vigorously curbing their left-wing members. At the same time, there was a certain degree of uncertainty about the support they might get for militant action. In 1950 when the AEU and the Confed. called for national strike action by their membership in support of a national pay claim, they were voted down 3:1 by a ballot of their membership in favour of arbitration.[61] The Engineering Employers' Federation were one of the toughest groups of wage bargainers from the late 1940s onwards and regularly resisted union claims throughout procedure: the threat of a national confrontation, however, regularly brought ministerial action in the form of arbitration or a Court of Inquiry to settle the matter. Half of the engineering wage claims between 1946 and 1957 went to one of these bodies for settlement and nine out of 15 cases were only finally resolved after the intervention of the Minister of Labour. The EEF developed a strong sense that they were being betrayed on wage restraint by government policies of appeasement.[62] There seemed to be a danger of the emergence of a going rate for settlements fixed by arbitration decisions. The EEF saw wage decisions gradually being taken out of the hands of the employers themselves and settled under pressure from Whitehall in the form of 'politically determined' compromises. While exhorting employers to resist excessive wage claims, the government were not willing to see the employers indulge in the sort of all-out confrontation necessary to hold the line.

This position was tolerable as long as the economic climate was easy, but the period 1955–6 saw a sharp 'stop' in the government's stop–go policy superimposed on a picture of generally tightening international competition. A large body of employers, spearheaded by the Midlands' motor firms, began to reject the government's view that industrial conflict was more dangerous than wage increases. Hitherto, this had not been the case among the motor firms. They and the Coventry employers were notorious for paying high wages and for a willingness to make concessions to shop floor organisation at plant level to keep production going. Until 1955, their prosperity and rising productivity had enabled them to do this, but the sharp economic squeeze of 1955–6 brought fears of an end to the soft postwar sellers' market. As Peter Dunnett has shown, the postwar trading strategy of the motor firms was severely constrained by government demand management policies: balance of payments criteria resulted in tight controls over their balance between export and domestic sales, and allocations policy in regard to restricted supplies of steel and power, along with governments armaments contracting procedures, tended to freeze the pre-existing fragmented industrial structure. At the same time, demand management policies induced a sharp boom–slump cycle for the industry. Whenever it was necessary to improve the balance of payments, the government would reduce internal demand usually through purchase tax or hire-purchase controls, and consumer durable demand, especially for cars, was particularly sensitive to such changes.[63] Dow's view that government budgetary and monetary policy in the 1950s had a 'positively destabilising' effect, and that the major fluctuations in the rate of growth in demand in this period were chiefly due to government policy, has been widely accepted.[64] In the light of this, it is not surprising that following the 1955 credit squeeze, the motor manufacturers both blamed the government for much of their plight and looked for government support to do something about it.

They were encouraged in such hopes by developments inside the Conservative Government in the mid-1950s. In 1955 the 'arch appeasers', Churchill and Monckton, had been replaced by Eden and MacLeod, and in his White Paper of May 1956, 'The economic effects of full employment', Macmillan, the Chancellor of the Exchequer, made a major appeal for wage restraint on the part of both employers and unions.[65] Meanwhile, the anti-conciliation faction in the Cabinet around Peter Thorneycroft and Enoch Powell had become increasingly influential.[66] In taking up a strong position in favour of resisting wage increases, the motor employers and the EEF had good reason to believe they were swimming with the tide. In the summer of 1956 the Birmingham and West of England Districts of the EEF successfully lobbied the organisation to reject *in advance* any wage claim from the Confed. They believed they had received personal assurances from the Cabinet that the government would not intervene if the EEF fought it out with the unions.[67]

But over the next nine months the apparent close alliance of government and employers broke down. When the Confed. responded with a national strike, the President of the EEF was called to personal meetings with the Minister of Power and the Prime Minister and told that the country could not afford what might grow into something close to a general strike, which could precipitate devaluation and perhaps the collapse of the government. Under unremitting ministerial pressure, the EEF were forced to accept arbitration and a subsequent compromise settlement.[68]

What accounts for this collapse of the government–EEF front? In the first place, the Suez crisis in the summer of 1956 had changed the economic terrain considerably. The crisis in itself had resulted in a loss of confidence in sterling and this was exacerbated by the threat to price stability posed by the rise in oil and petrol prices. Macmillan, the new Prime Minister, felt that devaluation was on the cards if there was a major shock to the domestic economy.[69] And simultaneous developments in the unions made such a shock more likely. From 1951 to 1955 the big unions had been fairly monolithically right-wing, malleable and willing to curb their militants. In 1955, however, Frank Cousins had stepped into the recently vacated shoes of Arthur Deakin at the TGWU with a policy of revitalising the union by fighting for higher wages. In sharp contrast to his predecessors, Cousins rejected cooperation in wage restraint and showed the TGWU willing to give official support to strikes in support of wage claims in various sectors. For the first time in the life of the government, strikes in 1956 rose significantly above the level of striker-days lost during the previous Labour Government. Cousins' leadership reflected the importance of currents of aggressive and successful bargaining at shop floor level percolating through to the top of the ossified structure of the TGWU.[70] With rail and dock strikes also on the agenda, the government felt its position too weak and the stakes too high and reversed their earlier policy. As Macmillan put it, 'In the long run and for the common good, the umpire is better than the duel'.[71]

The EEF decided that they could not pursue their chosen course without government support, or at least benevolent neutrality. The Coventry Association felt 'they had been completely let down' and there was considerable bitterness towards MacLeod for twisting the EEF's arm in private and then denying that he had done so in public.[72] The unreliability of the government forced the engineering employers to take a hard look at their capability of acting without government support. As Ivan Yates, the Deputy President of the Birmingham District Engineering Employers' Association put it during the extensive post-mortems on the stoppage conducted with the EEF:

If the Government bring great pressure to bear on us, *can* we resist that pressure? I suspect that the Office Bearers of the Federation think we can *not*. But many of our members think we can and should. Whatever the right answer to this question may be, one thing is clear. We must agree among ourselves *now* whether or not Government intervention is inevitable, and, if so, whether we must yield to it. Our *tactics* must be adjusted accordingly.

We must not encourage our members to support a certain line of action when we know perfectly well that it can't and won't succeed.[73]

Clearly, the internal coherence and unity of employers was decisive in answering this question. But did the engineering employers have this sort of internal solidarity? The evidence is that they did not, and that in fact government support was the only thing that could hold together some sort of alliance between the diverse engineering employers in pursuit of a common goal.

In the first place, despite large votes in favour of confrontation tactics in EEF ballots in 1955–7, it was clear to both the government and the EEF leaders that not all the engineering employers were as determined as the motor manufacturers. Iain MacLeod had privately expressed such doubts to the President of the EEF in the autumn of 1956 and B. Macarty, Secretary of the EEF, feared 'a slight outbreak of weakness at the knees in certain quarters' in the run-up to the strike. Arbitration tribunals were awarding a going rate of 3%, roughly equivalent to the rise in the cost of living, and there were some indications that certain firms would prefer a settlement of 3% to an all-out struggle.[74] Over and above this, was the long-run persistent conflict of interest between the Federated motor employers plus the motor-related Coventry and Birmingham firms and most of the other districts.

From the late 1940s onwards, the motor manufacturers had led the resistance to wage concessions by the EEF in national bargaining. But there was a paradox to their opposition. While leading the call for wage restraint, they ignored the fact that, through local payment-by-results systems, they themselves had a much worse record in allowing earnings to rise than their fellow engineering employers. As table 1 shows, the Coventry firms and the motor companies paid well above the national average of Federated firms throughout the period. More importantly, only 32% of the increase in the Toolroom rate – the day-rate for skilled toolmakers calculated on the basis of the average earnings of skilled pieceworkers in the Coventry district – was attributable to national settlements: the rest was the result of shop floor bargaining.[75] Thus, the motor firms' hard line at national level contrasted with the much softer bargaining environment in their workplaces. The significance of their opposition lay only partly in their support for wage restraint per se. They also wanted to see restraint combined with changes in engineering wage structures to their particular advantage. From 1949 they had argued that national

Table 1 *Average hourly earnings of semi-skilled adult male motor workers in selected firms, 1948 and 1955*

	Jan. 1948	Sept. 1955
National average in Federated engineering firms	3/4½d	5/3½d
Average of Coventry Federated firms	4/3¼d	7/3½d
Morris Motors (Cowley)	3/10d*	5/11d
Ford	3/10d*	6/3d
Jaguar	4/3d	6/9d
Austin (Longbridge)	4/3d	6/9d
Rootes	4/4d	6/10d
Standard Motors	4/5d	7/10d
Coventry Toolroom Rate: day-rate for skilled toolmakers	3/8½d	7/4¾d

* Estimated figures
Sources: EEF records and Turner, Clack and Roberts, p. 139.

increases should be confined to *minimum* rates rather than percentage increases on national rates. This would leave them wide scope for local bargaining and would avoid the sort of immediate ratchet effect on the wages of their highly paid pieceworkers that general rate increases produced. Only in 1950 did they succeed in getting this policy adopted. But in the aftermath of this agreement the other engineering employers, particularly those in the heavy engineering sectors of the north-east and north-west, found that they were able to make much less satisfactory bargains in face of continuous local claims than the Midland employers were able to achieve: local bargaining proved excessively costly to them in terms both of money and industrial disruption. Thereafter, the other Associations – apart from the west of England who often voted with the Midlands – continuously outvoted the motor firms and their allies on this issue. They felt the motor firms were trying to offload the problems arising from their lax payment-by-results systems on to the shoulders of the lower-paying engineering employers by trying to achieve settlements with the unions based primarily on increases for lower-paid engineering workers.[76] In 1956–7 both groups had a common interest in giving no increase at all, but once compromises became an issue, divisions lurked in the background.

Hence, not surprisingly, the issue of a motor breakaway from the

EEF which had simmered in the background since 1953, came sharply to the fore after the 1957 climb-down. Led by George Harriman of the British Motor Corporation (BMC) and William Lyons of Jaguar, they voiced strong dissatisfaction with the conduct of the EEF and hinted at leaving.[77] In the end, however, nothing came of it. The voice of the motor firms remained that of a dissident group, unhappy with many aspects of EEF policy but neither willing nor able to strike out on their own. Why were they in this position? In the first place, it should be remembered that the motor firms were weakly represented in the EEF in comparison to their size and significance in engineering. Ford had always preferred to maintain a free hand on labour matters and had never joined the EEF: Vauxhall had left it to go its own way in 1921. Morris came in only belatedly in 1943, and Standard, who had been a member before the war, left it in 1945 and did not rejoin until 1956. In that year only just over half of British car output was produced by Federated employers.[78] BMC and Rootes were the really important Federated motor firms, but before the late 1950s they were little involved in the leadership of the EEF. They could not hope to dominate, and if they withdrew to form an independent motor association, there was little hope that they could draw in Ford and Vauxhall to make it broadly based and comprehensive. In that situation there would be grave dangers of the unions playing off the rival associations against each other. Even among the British motor firms there was still the danger – epitomised by the recent career of Standard Motors – that if the going got rough one or more of the motor firms might break ranks, for instance, in the case of a prolonged strike.[79] On top of this, the senior management of BMC who were the obvious candidates to lead a new body, felt that they were quite simply 'too busy' to run an association. After 1958, therefore, discussions about motor autonomy in the EEF were mainly centred around possibilities of coordination through some sort of 'action committee', *within* the Federation.[80]

Thus, the existence of positive government support for the EEF in pursuit of wage restraint was important both in papering over the cracks in employer solidarity that might otherwise undermine determined resistance, and at the same time it gave the motor employers within the EEF leverage for a hard-line position that they might not otherwise have been able to exert. The significance of the 'hard line', however, was not the same for all the motor firms with their diverse industrial relations histories. For the smaller motor companies such as Jaguar, Rootes, Standard or Rover, fears of an end to the postwar sellers' market were pushing them to reconsider the problem of controlling established union organisations, often with significant controls over the process of production, that had emerged and consolidated themselves during and after the war.[81] If they were to re-establish control of their rather slack piecework systems, they, along with their fellow West Midlands engineering firms, needed a much more concerted and confrontational approach to wage bargaining. Their problems were much the same as those of other firms in the Coventry and Birmingham engineering districts and were not peculiar to motor employers. With the exception of Standard Motors, the Midlands motor firms do not seem to have been wage leaders in the area in this period, indeed, Knowles and Hill have suggested that Coventry motor firm wages tended to be pulled upwards by the general Coventry wage level rather than vice versa.[82] For example, as table 1 shows, in September 1955 both Rootes and Jaguar were paying below the average hourly earnings of Coventry Federated firms.

BMC, however, had a very different set of shop floor relationships, more in line with other big-volume car producers like the non-Federated Ford and Vauxhall. These firms accounted for some 70% of motor employment and produced some 75% of British car output in the mid-1950s. In these firms the war had produced the first real breakthroughs in shop floor organisation, but this had not really been consolidated and had pushed forward only slowly and discontinuously over the next decade. These firms had maintained strong traditions of hostility to unions, while at the same time paying relatively high wages. Their core works at Longbridge, Cowley, Dagenham and Luton, were located in areas without strong local trade union traditions, and in the absence of this they had proved hard to organise effectively. As table 1 shows, even with relatively weak unions, wages at Ford, Morris and Austin remained well above the engineering average and rose at a comparable speed to those in the Federated motor manufacturers – again with the exception of Standard Motors. Relative prosperity based on rising productivity and easy profitability, combined with managerial non-cooperation had made the task of shop floor militants in organising the plants an arduous one. Only from the time of the 1956 redundancies and the highlighted role of the national union organisations in mounting resistance to them did recruitment begin to climb to significantly higher levels at the core plants of Cowley and Longbridge. In addition, unionisation at BMC and at Ford was rolling in from the edges as the firms began to take over well-organised body-making firms and suppliers who had previously been independent. The industrial-relations history of Ford in the 1950s is dominated by their attempts to push back the more highly developed shop floor organisation of their newly absorbed Briggs Bodies suppliers to a level comparable to that of their weakly organised main plant.[83] Similarly, in the 1956 redundancy strike at BMC, the weakness of organisation at Cowley and Longbridge where strike rates were below 25% despite the most dogged efforts of the minority of shop floor militants, was made up for by the well-organised solidarity of the unions in their suppliers, notably the recently absorbed and well-organised Fisher and Ludlow body plant.[84] Sustained shop floor pressure from below had not yet been able to make big incursions on managerial control at the core of BMC, Ford and Vauxhall. But BMC's anti-union policies were becoming increasingly hard-pressed inside its own factories and increasingly isolated among Federated employers, and during the early and mid-1950s, their hard line put the firm at odds with the EEF on several occasions.

In 1952–3, for instance, Austin took on and decisively defeated the NUVB in a major confrontation following the victimisation of the NUVB Convenor, John McHugh. During the dispute, the EEF, both locally and nationally, felt that Austin's position in terms of the facts and the legalities of the case was very weak and had urged the Company to compromise: the sort of hostility towards unions that still prevailed at Austin and BMC was out of line with the general drift of EEF policy in this period.[85] Leonard Lord, Austin's Managing Director, was again rebuffed by the EEF and the District Association three years later when BMC made 6,000 workers redundant overnight without warning in the summer of 1956. The announcement of the redundancies came on the day following the EEF's public announcement that they intended to reject any Confed. wage claim submitted that year. Lord and Joe Edwards at BMC saw this as an appropriate moment to signal that as far as they were concerned, they were no longer going to put up with the 'velvet glove' methods with which prominent motor firms like Standard Motors were associated. The result of the sackings was a grave shock to BMC. The Minister of Labour delivered a public rebuke to the Company in the House, and the press condemned the high-handedness of the action.[86] BMC had also underestimated the capacity of the unions to respond. The sackings were concentrated at Long-bridge and Cowley where the unions were weak. However, Cousins quickly made the dispute official for the TGWU, and by pulling out strategically placed, well-organised factories in the BMC group, such as Fisher and Ludlow and the Morris Engines plant in Coventry, and backing this up with systematic blacking by TGWU lorry drivers and the dockers, they were able to bring BMC to a halt. Against this background the EEF pushed BMC into making *ex gratia* payments to the dismissed men – in effect, though both Company and EEF denied this, a precedent for redundancy payments.[87]

Such conflicts fuelled BMC's prominence in the breakaway move-ment which we have already noted and made the Company increas-ingly wary of hoping for support for conflictual policies from the EEF. If they were to sustain their resistance to the cumulative grass-roots pressure of shop floor activity at Cowley and Longbridge, they would need more sympathetic and consistent backing from the EEF. Solid government backing for the EEF's 'new course' in 1956–7 might have provided this, but the reversion to a political climate and labour policies more characteristic of the early 1950s both pulled the props out from under the united front of the engineering employers and torpedoed any prospect that BMC might have had of gaining a wider constituency of support for revanchist workplace policies among other employers. The period after the events of 1956–7 marked a turning point in shop floor relations in BMC, since at both the main plants union organisation finally consolidated itself against waning managerial resistance over the next six or seven years. The evidence is that by the early 1960s 100% unionisation had finally come to Longbridge and Cowley and the unions were beginning to contend seriously for control over wider aspects of the production process.[88]

This turning point shows up clearly in the data on strike activity presented by Turner, Clack and Roberts. The motor industry was not a particularly strike-prone industry until the late 1950s. Until then, most disputes had been over union recognition, wage increases and closed shop and dismissal issues: but between 1959 and 1964–5, disputes over the hours and conditions of work, wage *structures*, work loads, relativities and the rights of management to control the mobility of labour and engage or dismiss workers as they thought fit, which had never been above 25–30% of all disputes before 1960, moved sharply upwards to 40–45% of all disputes between 1960 and 1964. As the unions consolidated their position in the motor factories, they began to contest new areas of workplace control: as Turner, Clack and Roberts note, 'the most recent strike movement, ... is treading very closely into the area of "managerial functions" '.[89] The problems of workplace control that had long faced the smaller firms had now spread into the heart of the big corporations.

IV

In the 1960s, the strength of shop floor organisation in motors was at its peak. It was always somewhat partial and more in the nature of a countervailing force than an actual power over the process of production, and it ran across a spectrum of strengths between plants, ranging from Vauxhall where the unions were never very strong, through Dagenham, Cowley and Longbridge where it was sporadically powerful though still reactive, patchy and uncoordinated, to Coventry firms such as Standard–Triumph or Rootes where it was most consistently effective and fringed on more positive or purposeful job control. The long rearguard action by Austin, Morris or Ford to keep the unions at arms length had petered out, and some form of accommodation with workplace organisation that recognised its legitimacy and permanence was now the order of the day throughout the industry.

The transformation of the motor industry in the late 1950s and early 1960s from an industry that was not very prone to strikes to one that was comparable to the notoriously strike-prone sectors of shipbuilding, mining and the docks, rapidly made it a major concern for the government. It was a *new* problem area and it came in a key export sector on which the delicate balance of payments situation was thought to depend heavily. From 1958, unofficial strikes in motors were beginning to loom large in the government's pantheon of causes of relative industrial decline, and the prospects of effective wage restraint became increasingly associated with the problems of curbing the supposed anarchy of shop steward militancy.[90] In 1959, Edward Heath, as Minister of Labour, had intervened behind the scenes to secure a compromise settlement in a major strike at Cowley, following the sacking of the TGWU Convenor, Frank Horseman,[91] and a year later his successor, John Hare, in a novel initiative, brought together leading representatives of the employers and of the principal unions for a series of meetings under the Minister's chairmanship to discuss the situation in the industry. The talks resulted in a certain measure of agreement which was embodied in a joint statement (referred to as the 'charter') in April 1961, the main feature of which was an acceptance by both sides that existing grievance procedures were 'generally adequate if operated in the right spirit' and a commitment by both sides to 'act in accordance with their respective constitutions to secure observance of these procedures by employers and union members'.[92] In many respects this echoed the traditional preoccupation of the Ministry of Labour with procedure that had been most clearly embodied in the Courts of Inquiry of the 1950s with what McCarthy and Clifford have described as their 'uncompromisingly hostile attitude to unconstitutional action of any kind'.[93] In this case, however, the statement was more significant than a reaffirmation of these proceduralist values. Both sides found common ground in the desire to foster 'responsible' unionism in the motor industry. If the unions could not be dislodged, then motor employers would have to work with them and, if possible, get them to control their members as the price of this cooperation.

The authority of the motor unions over their members was, however, somewhat problematic. For both the AEU and the TGWU their motor membership was only one component of a far wider and much older membership constituency, and it was a component that had received little systematic attention at national level. There had been no significant coordination pattern and inter-union rivalry was strong. In an industry where fragmented shop floor bargaining through payment-by-results systems was the order of the day, the important bargaining agents were self-reliant shop steward and workgroup networks. By the late 1950s, however, Bill Carron, the right-wing President of the AEU, was becoming seriously concerned at the AEU's lack of control over these workplace organisations. In May 1959, he confided to the President of the EEF privately that he could not control what he called the 'wild boys'. He argued, however, that in many cases managements were responsible for the troubles that were arising. 'They were apt to give in rather easily and the result was that the men derived benefits from unofficial action. . . . This was a bad thing for the Union leaders whose authority was weakened by such events.' His point was well taken by the engineering employers. Hague, the President of the EEF, was recorded in the minutes of the Birmingham Association as declaring himself in favour of 'strengthening the hand of Carron and similarly well-disposed trade union leaders. . . . It was necessary to make sure that we would have the support of the 'good' leaders before we took official steps. . . . So far as he was concerned, he trusted Carron and his kind.'[94] Thus, in certain respects and for the time being, the strategic goals of the motor employers and of key union leaders were moving in parallel, and the interest of the Ministry also provided the motor employers with a platform from which to rebuild inter-employer solidarity. The talks for the first time brought together both Federated and non-Federated motor employers in talks with unions, and Joe Edwards and others saw the talks as the possible basis for a 'new-look' alliance of motor employers to coordinate their approach to labour problems and ensure that 'when one motor company is attacked all are attacked'.[95]

The ministerial helping hand had provided a stepping off point for both employers and unions to perceive definite mutual advantages in a certain degree of cooperation. Against a background of persistent urging by the Minister of Labour and his officials, the result of this temporary *rapprochement* was the appearance of a new 'firm line' in industrial relations centring on an insistence on rigid adherence to procedure. The 'firm line' lasted through two major disputes in 1961–2 at Pressed Steel's Swindon plant in April 1961 and at Rootes' British Light Steel Pressings subsidiary at Acton in August to October 1961. In both of these disputes a core of militant shop stewards were isolated and defeated with the assistance primarily of the AEU, and the Pressed Steel dispute, which began a week before the 'charter' was signed in April 1961 was clearly seen as a test case, particularly as the boss of Pressed Steel was Joe Edwards, one of the leading exponents of the new employer solidarity.[96]

But the very successes of the firm line undercut the viability of the compromise on which it was based. In these cases relatively isolated groups of militants were picked off and defeated; but that did not necessarily bring Carron any closer to 'control' over his wider membership. Acquiescing in the elimination of pockets of militants was not the same thing as integrating shop stewards into the union through the development of more orderly conduct of industrial relations. Carron had no love for militants and he was prepared to go a long way in the cause of anti-communism; but he was a right wing trade union leader, not a management stooge. It was difficult to argue that the 'firm line' was not benefiting employers far more than unions, and a hard-line anti-militant posture had risky implications for Carron in other respects within the union. The AEU rarely had exclusive jurisdiction in workplaces and rival unions were likely to take advantage of any persistent restrictions on militancy in the AEU imposed from above. However, Carron's 'strong' leadership of the AEU was more apparent than real – effective at the level of national politics, but severely constrained in industrial matters by the union's strong traditions of local autonomy, and by the growing success of the left in electoral competitions within the union in the mid-1960s, developments which culminated in the election of Hugh Scanlon as President after Carron's retirement in 1967. The AEU was not an oligarchy; its leadership had to remain responsive in a certain degree to the membership and had to deliver the goods.[97] In the early 1960s, Carron was willing to compromise with the employers, but he had to have a *quid pro quo*. Without this the 'firm line' quickly became defunct by 1964. Carron felt that he had been let down by the employers, and his bitterness as well as his wider perspectives come out clearly in the evidence he gave to the Donovan Commission in February 1966. As he put it, 'The automobile manufacturers complaining bitterly as they now are, are really complaining about themselves.' The shop floor had decided that the way to succeed was not to go through Procedure but to 'turn on the heat': the motor manufacturers had developed a habit of conceding *only* under pressure. 'They refuse through all the levels of Procedure and then at a certain point, there is a threat of action or something similar and then they concede. This,' he concluded, 'is making nonsense of Procedure.' Employers were conceding under pressure what they would not concede through reason. What Carron wanted was for them to concede through reason most of what they now concede through threat – *not* that they should stop making concessions altogether.[98]

From 1961 to 1964, the Conservative Government was pursuing an incomes policy, partly through attempts to win union cooperation in restraint and the 1961 charter and subsequent 'firm line' fitted into this approach.[99] From 1964, however, strike rates in the motor industry were rising sharply again and the motor employers were shifting their approach.[100] While successive governments continued to stress joint solutions and to seek to involve both sides in bipartite or tripartite organisations – notably the Motor Industry Joint Study

Group in 1964 or the Motor Industry Joint Labour Council under Jack Scamp from 1965 – these were looked upon by both sides as fairly non-controversial adjuncts to existing bargaining procedures, and a sign to the government that they were trying to put their house in order so as to forestall more extensive government action. The flurry of activity during the strike peak of 1965 seems to have been as much to block suggestions of some form of compulsory arbitration emanating from Downing Street as from any conviction in the likely efficacy of Scamp's 'fact finding commission'.[101]

The main developments in the late 1960s, however, took place not through these formal joint bodies, but in the evolution of new employer strategies and the responsible chord that they struck in the wider movements of government policy. Their thinking centres around various forms of statutory support for Procedure. In the conditions of the mid-1960s with extensive and often well-organised workplace trades unionism in an industry characterised by highly interdependent flow systems, small work groups could have highly disruptive effects on production.[102] A loss of output at any stage of the production process could have wide repercussions. The most notable example was perhaps the summer of 1968 which was a period of boom demand following several rather slack years. Yet there were almost incessant interruptions through strikes in the major component suppliers (Pressed Steel, Automotive Products, Girling Brakes and Lucas Electricals) which were then compounded by strikes in the assembly plants resulting from lay-offs due to shortages of components.[103] Hence, the motor employers saw the observance of Procedure and 'industrial discipline' as at a premium. Because of their inability to get their act together in terms of multi-employer bargaining or re-establishing control of their own internal piecework or labour control systems, they turned towards trade union restraint and legal controls.

In the position that they developed in their submissions to the Donovan Commission between 1965 and 1968, they argued for legislation to reinforce procedure which would make strikes more difficult, and thus make wage claims harder to pursue, and at the same time oblige the unions to control their own members. According to their proposals, unions would only continue to enjoy the unfettered right to strike where the negotiating Procedure had been exhausted. The substance of collective agreements would remain voluntary, but procedure would become a matter of law. This would be backed up by sanctions based on either fines or expulsions from unions. In this context they were prepared to concede 100% trade union agreements to the unions to enable them to better police the agreements.[104] The response of the unions was to launch a sustained defence of voluntarism before the Commission. George Woodcock of the TUC argued that the employers were trying to bring in the unions to 'do their job for them'. The employers were taking a 'glib' view of the workings of unions and of their ability to enforce their views on their members.[105] The introduction of legal regulation would have wide implications which the employers had not thought out; without intending it, Kahn-Freund argued, the motor employers were proposing 'a complete transformation of industrial relations'.[106] Three years later the Ford Motor Co., in an unprecedented initiative, sought to force the issue by means of a test case seeking an injunction against the AUEW and TGWU, alleging that their strike action was a breach of Procedure and therefore a breach of contract. Their case was a weak one and was decisively defeated. Instead, the judgement upheld and formalised existing presumptions that collective agreements were not legally binding unless contractual force was *explicitly* intended by both parties.[107]

The motor employers formed a vanguard among other groups of employers in turning towards increased legal regulation of collective bargaining. Before 1964 such views had been held by only a minority in the Tory Party and among employers. But the motor employers' view was supported first by the EEF and later by the National Confederation of Employers' Organisations before Donovan and on the wider stage. In the period between 1964 and 1970, during the period of Tory opposition, this view gradually captured the Party. The main difference between the employers and the Party that remained was that while the employers wanted the state rather than themselves to be responsible for legal action against workers, the Party as a whole was reluctant to see a detailed involvement of the state in industrial conflict.[108]

By the late 1960s, however, the influence of these ideas was extending across party lines and was to strongly influence policy in the last years of the Labour Government. Despite the fact that Donovan finally came down firmly on the side of 'voluntarism',[109] the Labour Government's policy embodied in *In Place of Strife* in 1969, echoed many of the themes that the motor and engineering employers had argued to the Royal Commission, particularly in the form of the proposed statutory 'conciliation pauses' and government powers to order strike ballots.[110] Like the employers, the Wilson Government saw legal reform as an indirect form of wage restraint, a brake on collective action that they mistakenly hoped would be less politically controversial than an incomes policy. But the convergence was not a simple capitulation by the government to the demands of employers. *In Place of Strife* arose out of the interaction of the Wilson Government's economic policy requirements with its wider conceptions of the government's relations with the trade unions and the needs of electoral strategy.

Above all, what Labour as a party of government valued was effective voluntary cooperation by the unions in incomes policy. The prevalence of shop floor bargaining, of which the motor industry was the *locus classicus*, vitiated both the will and the capacity of the unions to respond in this area. Barbara Castle, the formulator of *In Place of Strife*, in particular resented the damage that union sectionalism did to the Labour Party and she accepted Aneurin Bevan's dictum from the 1959 election that the trade unionist then had 'voted at the polls against the consequences of his own anarchy'.[111] The Wilson Government lived throughout in dread of embarrassingly irresponsible unofficial strikes that would undermine both their economic policies *and* their electoral credibility. During the 1964 campaign, Wilson's nervousness about strikes had come out in his unfounded allegations that an unofficial strike at Hardy Spicer, a Midlands motor accessory firm, had been deliberately provoked by friends of the Tory Party, and in the 1966 campaign, with Labour defending a precarious majority, the lead-up to the election was dominated by press and Tory Party attacks on 'shop steward anarchy' centring on the infamous 'noose trial' affair at Cowley.[112] Wilson attributed the government's being 'blown off course' in 1966 to the seamen's strike and felt that the dock strike in 1967 had forced him into devaluation.[113] Unofficial strikes were the most visible symptom of the weakness of Labour's authority and their inability to develop a sustained governmental relationship with the unions. The upshot was the Wilson–Castle strategy that the unions had to be made stronger and more responsible and better controlled in order to be a fit partner for a Labour Government. This was embodied in *In Place of Strife*. It must be emphasised that this was *not* a wholly anti-union document. On the one hand, it extended union rights to negotiate and organise and, notably, in proposing that the *status quo ante* should prevail during the negotiation of a dispute, it reversed the key longstanding provision of engineering procedure in favour of the unions. On the other hand, it imposed new legal obligations on unions to act constitutionally in the conduct of disputes and to discipline their membership.[114] The unions neither wanted nor felt themselves capable of exercising such a responsibility. The biggest unions had strongly resisted the devolution of power to the shop floor in the 1940s and 1950s. But cooperation with government in moderating free collective bargaining had only reinforced a shift to local bargaining where bigger increases were obtainable through deals with managements anxious for high output, high productivity and adequate supplies of labour in a market environment where wage costs could easily be passed on. The result was a decentralisation of bargaining into the hands of local lay officials, and by the 1960s this change was moderating the structures of the big unions too, symbolised by the changes from Deakin to Cousins or Carron to Scanlon. *In Place of Strife* was demanding a restoration of control by union leaderships over their members that they were not in a position to exert. In the motor industry at least it was not until the effects of changed bargaining structures with the consolidation of Measured Day Work along with replacement of degenerated multi-employer bargaining by new centralised and more highly coordinated management of British Leyland against the background of a deteriorating economic climate, that unions were prepared to move again in this direction under the next Labour Government.

The wide-ranging importance of the state to the shape of development of industrial relations in this industry, often looked on as the epitome of 'voluntarist' free collective bargaining in this period, suggests the need for a wider framework of looking at the state than that, for instance, used by Clegg in his classic chapter on 'The State and Industrial Relations' in *The Changing System of Industrial Relations*, where the state is analysed almost solely in terms of legal changes bearing on industrial relations.[115] The notion of 'abstention' which characterises Clegg's description of the state's role in fact evades most of the difficult substantive questions of how the state operates in this area and the actual influence that it exerts.

The preceding survey has shown how in the Second World War government action facilitated certain forms of union advance but also placed severe political constraints on its elaboration. During the post-war Labour Government the incorporation of the major unions into some form of partnership with the government inhibited their shop floor development and created a space for a revival of militant sectional bargaining and the emergence of a third motor industry union, thus laying the basis for the peculiar form of workplace multi-unionism that was to exist in the industry for almost the next 30 years. In the late 1950s when the motor employers made a crucial attempt to tighten their grip on the workplace through a coordinated managerial offensive, it was government policy that cemented the alliance of employers necessary for this purpose in the first place, and the withdrawal of government support that made such a hard line unthinkable in the decade or so that followed, forcing even the most recalcitrant motor employers like BMC and Ford to come to some sort of *modus vivendi* with unions against whom they could no longer organise coordinated resistance. In the 1960s, the motor employers turned to the government for assistance, if not in confrontation, at least in control of the workplace situation. In this they were able to achieve considerable success despite the rejection of their case by Donovan, because of wider political, electoral and economic developments bearing on the government – in which the shop floor situation in motors played a key symptomatic and symbolic part.

This account stresses the ways in which government policies and state actions continuously interact with the internal politics of employers and trade unions. The state played a crucial role on occasion in making it possible for divided and fragmented groups of employers to achieve a limited coherence in their political objectives and to create the preconditions for more far-reaching managerial strategies. But conversely, because the state responds to a much wider array of forces than simply the interests of employers, its erratic course made it an unreliable ally. Government interaction with the internal politics of the unions was similarly ambiguous. In so far as governments drew the unions into involvement in national political strategies, they also created the conditions for sharp conflicts with the shop floor interests of their members, or enabled unions to fulfil certain of their objectives at the expense of others. These ambiguities have had profound effects on the internal structures of the unions themselves, the forms of bargaining and on the pattern of union activities within the industry. In the context of a primarily voluntaristic system of industrial relations, fragmentary and partial legal regulation, and erratic and contingent government interventions produced a series of unintended and unpredictable consequences.

NOTES

Much of this paper is based on archive and interview material. The principal archival sources were the Ministry of Labour (LAB) files at the Public Records Office; the records of the Engineering Employers' Federation (EEF); the Minutes of the Amalgamated Engineering Union (AEU) Coventry District Committee in the AUEW Coventry offices; and the verbatim notes of Works and Local Conferences at the Modern Records Centre. In addition, the papers of Arthur Bate, Reg Taylor and Eric Wigham are in the possession of the author; the papers of Dick Etheridge and Les Gurl are deposited at the Modern Records Centre; and the diary of Reg Scott was consulted courtesy of Mr Scott. The interviews were conducted by the author except where otherwise stated and the transcripts of all interviews referred to are in the possession of the author. The videotapes of interviews conducted for the Channel 4 TV Series *Making Cars* are deposited in the TV History Workshop Archive, 42 Queen's Square, London WC1.

1 For this view see J. Zeitlin, 'The Emergence of Shop Steward Organisation and Job Control in the British Car Industry: A Review Essay', *History Workshop Journal* 10 (Autumn 1980) pp. 122–3; A. L. Friedman, *Industry and Labour* (London, 1977), ch. 14; R. Hyman and A. Elger, 'Job Controls, the Employers' Offensive and Alternative Strategies', *Capital and Class* 15 (Autumn 1981) pp. 133–4; P. J. S. Dunnett, *The Decline of the British Motor Industry: The Effects of Government Policy, 1945–79* (London, 1980), especially pp. 52–5, 82–5 and 108–14; R. Price, 'Rethinking Labour History: The Importance of Work', in J. E. Cronin and J. Schneer (eds.), *Social Conflict and the Political Order in Modern Britain* (London, 1982), p. 196; K. Middlemas, *Politics in Industrial Society* (London, 1979), p. 400. For earlier works from which this view in part derived see, S. Melman, *Decision-making and Productivity* (London, 1957); H. A. Turner, G. Clack and G. Roberts, *Labour Relations in the Motor Industry* (London, 1967).

2 S. Tolliday, 'Management Strategies and Shopfloor Organisation: Austin and Standard Motors, 1929–60', paper presented to the King's College, Cambridge, Seminar on Shop Floor Bargaining, Job Control and National Economic Performance, March 1982 (mimeo) presents some qualifications of the classic picture of Standard Motors.

3 These estimates and others given later in the paper are based on work in progress at the King's College Research Centre, Cambridge.

4 For an analysis of these issues see: S. Tolliday, 'Militancy and Organisation: Women Workers and Trade Unions in the Motor Trades in the 1930s', *Oral History* 11, 2 (Spring 1983).

5 T. J. Claydon in his thesis 'The Development of Trade Unionism Among British Automobile and Aircraft Workers, 1914–46' (Ph.D., University of Kent 1981) estimates union density in the motor industry, as a whole as 37.1% in 1946. But Claydon's figures are generally on the high side because he includes all the membership of certain union branches as 'motor' membership when in fact many of the members worked in other trades. See table 2.2, p. 133 and table 2.3, p. 134. The estimates for particular car firms' union density given in the text are my own.

6 R. P. Hastings, 'The Labour Movement in Birmingham, 1927–45' (M.A. Thesis, Birmingham University 1959), p. 87; see also, 'Memorandum by Mr Niness on Points Arising from the Austin Dispute', 15 September 1938, EEF A(1)51. Interviews with Les Ambrose and Dick Etheridge.

7 Interviews by Len Holden with Tom Adair and Harold Horne. Minutes of Luton Branch of National Union of Vehicle Builders, 1942–6.

8 R. Croucher, 'Communist Politics and Shop Stewards in Engineering, 1935–46' (Ph.D. Thesis, University of Warwick, 1978). Interviews by the author with Harold Taylor and Ernie Roberts. Coventry AEU District Committee Minutes, 8 September 1940.

9 E. Fairfax (pseud.), *Calling All Arms* (Oxford, 1948) pp. 29–75. Claydon, 'The Development of Trade Unionism', pp. 115–16. Interview by the author with Les Gurl. A. Exell, 'Morris Motors in the 1940s', *History Workshop Journal* 9 (Spring 1980), pp. 90–5.

10 Exell, 'Morris Motors', pp. 107–10. See also interviews with Norman Brown and Arthur Exell by Nina Fishman, and video interviews with them by Channel 4 TV, November 1982.

11 On the break-up of organisation at Austin see: 'The Report of the Recent Dispute at the Austin Motor Company, September 16th–20th 1944' by the Austin Shop Stewards' Committee, and Minutes of the Austin Shop Stewards' Committee, September 1944 to October 1945 (Arthur Bate Papers). Dick Etheridge, Daily Working Notes, 1944–5 (Etheridge Papers). Interviews with Arthur Bate, Dick Etheridge, Alf Allen and Albert Bennett (Austin) and Freda Nokes and Les Ambrose (Austin Aero).

12 Interviews by the author with Jack Jones and Reg Jenkins.

13 See the papers of Reg Taylor, a former shop steward who became an LSI. I am grateful to Mr Taylor's widow for letting me have these papers. Also interviews with Jack Jones.

14 Interview with Jack Jones.

15 See the weekly reports by the Midlands Region Conciliation Officer. PRO LAB 10/348–352.

16 See PRO LAB 10/348–352, and interview with Ernie Roberts. Roberts was sacked from at least seven firms in the course of the war: see Coventry AEU District Committee Minutes for details.

17 Interview with Jack Jones.

18 Interviews by the author with Harold Taylor and Reg Scott. See also

Reg Scott's diary entries for October 1939–February 1940. I am grateful to Mr Scott for letting me read this diary.
19 Standard Motors is a classic case in point. See, interviews with Harold Taylor, Kath Smith, Reg Scott, Jack Jones, Arthur Sterry. See also minutes of local conferences between Standard Motors and AEU and TGWU, 1939–45. Warwick MRC MSS 208 and EEF P(5)225, P(5)284.
20 Interview with Jack Jones. P. Inman, *Labour in the Munitions Industries* (London, 1952) pp. 377–90. Gen. Bayley, Sec. Coventry District Engineering Employers' Association, 'Notes on JPCs' 17 February 1942, AVIA 15/2539.
21 Both firms remained hard to organise in the postwar years. AEU District Committee Minutes, 29 April 1947 and 21 November 1950. On other recalcitrant firms during the war see J. Hinton, 'Coventry Communism: a study of factory politics in the Second World War', *History Workshop Journal* 10 (Autumn 1980) pp. 100–2.
22 Croucher, 'Communist Politics', pp. 234–53.
23 S. Melman, *Decision-making and Productivity* (London, 1957), gives a full account of Standard. See also S. Tolliday, 'Management strategies' for some critical comments on his views.
24 H. Friedman and S. Meredeen, *The Dynamics of Industrial Conflict: Lessons from Ford* (London, 1980), p. 24.
25 N. Fishman, 'Trade Unions at Dagenham, 1933–45', unpublished paper.
26 Friedman and Meredeen, *The Dynamics of Industrial Conflict*, pp. 23–4. Report of a Court of Inquiry (Doughty Report) Cmd 6284, 1941.
27 Edmund and Ruth Frow, *Engineering Struggles. Episodes in the Story of the Shop Stewards' Movement* (Manchester, 1982) pp. 158–9. Fishman, 'Trade Unions'.
28 Memorandum by Craven.
29 'Memo from Sir Frederick Leggett, 16 June 1943', LAB 10/274. R. Chambers (Secretary of Ford's Shop Stewards' Committee) to Industrial Relations Officer, 20 August 1943, LAB 10/274. Regional Industrial Relations Officer, *Weekly Reports* November–December 1943. LAB 10/354.
30 Fishman, 'Trade Unions'.
31 This account is based on documents in the TUC files on Ford, particularly reports by Vic Feather. See also *Catholic Worker*, February–July 1944.
32 Comments by Industrial Relations Officer, 21 April 1944, LAB 10/274.
33 A. Bullock, *The Life and Times of Ernest Bevin*, vol. 2. *Minister of Labour* (London, 1960). On the Wagner Act, see D. Brody, 'The Emergence of Mass Production Unionism' in J. Braeman *et al.* (eds.), *Continuity and Change in 20th Century America: The Thirties* (London, 1964); see also the chapter by Howell Harris in this volume.
34 Bullock, *Ernest Bevin*; see also Inman, *Labour in the Munitions Industries*, pp. 377–90, Middlemas, *Politics in Industrial Society*, ch.

10; P. Addison, *The Road to 1945. British Politics and the Second World War* (London, 1977).

35 Bevin was able to overcome the resistance of Tory backbenchers to the Catering Wages Act, but the Act itself provided for direct regulations of the industry through a Catering Commission and Wages Board of outside appointees and not for the establishment of collective bargaining relationships. Bullock, *Ernest Bevin*, pp. 220–4, 235–7.

36 Bullock, *Ernest Bevin*, chs. 6 and 8; M. W. Kirby, *The British Coalmining Industry, 1870–1946. A Political and Economic History* (London, 1977), p. 174.

37 R. Croucher, *Engineers at War, 1939–45* (London, 1982) p. 218. Middlemas, *Politics in Industrial Society*, pp. 266–307.

38 L. Panitch, *Social Democracy and Industrial Militancy: The Labour Party, the Trade Unions and Industrial Militancy, 1945–74* (London, 1976).

39 P. Weiler, 'British Labour and the Cold War: the London Dock Strike of 1949', in Cronin and Schneer, *Social Conflict*, pp. 146–78. See also the essay by Noel Whiteside in this volume.

40 Dick Etheridge Papers, MRC, Warwick University. Papers of Arthur Bate, one of the stewards involved.

41 Private information to the author.

42 H. Beynon, *Working for Ford*, pp. 43–65.

43 L. Holden, 'Think of me simply as the skipper: Industrial Relations at Vauxhall, 1920–50', *Oral History* 9, 2 (1981): Luton Branch NUVB Minute Books, 1942–56.

44 J. Corina, 'The British Experiment in Wage Restraint, with Special Reference to the Period 1948–50' (D.Phil. Thesis, Oxford University, 1961) p. 90.

45 AEU Journal, 1948–50. Membership figures for Birmingham from AEU District Office.

46 This compares with a national figure of less than 2% p.a. See H. A. Clegg and R. Adams, *The Employers' Challenge. A Study of the National Engineering and Shipbuilding Disputes of 1957* (Oxford, 1957).

47 NUVB *Quarterly Journal*, 1947–9.

48 *Ibid.*

49 *Ibid.*, and documents on these disputes in the EEF Archives.

50 On this agreement see Claydon, 'The Development of Trade Unionism', pp. 341–2 and NAT Award No. 899, 28 November 1946.

51 *Ibid.*

52 Interview with George Evans.

53 *Ibid.*, and Etheridge Papers.

54 Interview with George Evans.

55 For the diminishing returns on further NUVB claims, see: NAT Award No. 990, August 1947: NAT Award No. 1522, 21 September 1950: NAT Award No. 1635, 28 March 1951: NAT Award No. 1637, 29 March 1951.

56 Industrial Relations Department HQ to Birmingham Regional Industrial Relations Officer, 9 May 1946, LAB 10/353.
57 Colin Crouch, *The Politics of Industrial Relations* (London, 1979), ch. 1; Middlemas, *Politics in Industrial Society*.
58 A. Soldon, *Churchill's Indian Summer: the Conservative Government 1951–5* (London, 1982), p. 203.
59 *Ibid.*
60 H. Macmillan, *Tides of Fortune, 1954–55* (London, 1969), p. 490.
61 E. Wigham, *The Power to Manage: a History of the Engineering Employers' Federation* (London, 1973), p. 164.
62 *Ibid.*, pp. 165–74; E. Wigham, *Strikes and the Government, 1893–1974* (London, 1976), pp. 108–15.
63 P. J. S. Dunnett, *The Decline of the British Motor Industry; the Effects of Government Policy, 1945–79* (London, 1980), pp. 31–85.
64 J. C. R. Dow, *The Management of the Economy, 1954–60* (Cambridge, 1965).
65 Wigham, *Strikes*, p. 113.
66 Wigham, *Power*, p. 179.
67 Wigham, *Power*, pp. 178–82.
68 Wigham, *Power*, pp. 182–7.
69 *Ibid.*
70 G. Goodman, *The Awkward Warrior: a Biography of Frank Cousins* (London, 1979).
71 Quoted by Wigham, *Power*, p. 185.
72 'Informal meeting between a deputation from the Midlands Regional Committee and representatives of the Federation', 16 October 1967. Wigham Papers.
73 'Statement by deputation from Midlands Regional Committee', 16 October 1957 and the discussion in 'Informal meeting between a deputation from the Midlands Regional Committee and representatives of the Federation', 18 December 1957. Wigham Papers.
74 Wigham, *Power*, pp. 182–3.
75 EEF Records and Turner, Clack and Roberts, *Labour Relations*, p. 139.
76 Wigham, *Power*, pp. 198–202.
77 Minutes of Meeting of Birmingham District Association, 14 May, 1959.
78 Friedman, *Industry and Labour*, pp. 198–9.
79 On Standard's break away see Melman, *Decision-making* and EEF Archives.
80 Wigham, *Power*, pp. 202–5.
81 On the Coventry firms, see Friedman, *Industry and Labour*.
82 K. G. J. C. Knowles and T. P. Hill, 'The Structure of Engineering Earnings', *Bulletin of the Oxford Institute of Statistics* 16, 9 and 10, September–October 1954.
83 Beynon, *Working for Ford*; Friedman and Meredeen, *The Dynamics of Industrial Conflict*. On the absorption of Briggs, see *Report of a Court*

of *Inquiry* (Cameron Report), Cmd 131, 1957 and *Report of a Court of Inquiry* (Jack Report), Cmd 1949, 1963.

84 EEF s(9)62 on BMC dispute, 1956, especially 'Analysis of Austin Strike, 25th July 1956'.

85 J. R. Edwards, 'Notes on the McHugh Case', 6 February 1953, EEF D(3)248.

86 'Memorandum on BMC Redundancies, August 1956', EEF s(9)62.

87 'Report for EAENF Management Board on the BMC dispute, 27 August 1956', EEF s(9)62.

88 See Dick Etheridge Papers for Longbridge and Les Gurl Papers for Cowley.

89 Turner, Clack and Roberts, *Labour Relations*, pp. 58–67.

90 Dunnett, *The Decline of the British Motor Industry*, pp. 108–14.

91 Files on Horseman strike in EEF Archives.

92 'Statement by Employers and Trade Union Representatives on Industrial Relations in the Motor Industry, 19th April 1961'. Reprinted as an Appendix to Motor Industry Employers' Evidence to the Royal Commission on Trade Unions and Employers' Organisations.

93 W. E. J. McCarthy and B. A. Clifford, 'The Work of Industrial Courts of Inquiry', *British Journal of Industrial Relations* 4, 1, (March 1966), p. 44.

94 Minutes of a meeting of Birmingham District Engineering Employers' Association, 14 May 1959.

95 'Memorandum for J. R. Edwards on a Motor Section of the Federation, 30th May 1961'. Wigham Papers.

96 Turner, Clack and Roberts, *Labour Relations*, pp. 282–6. Steve Jeffereys, 'Pressed Steel, 1945–68', paper presented to the Car Workers Group Seminar at the LSE, March 1982. K. Weller, *The BLSP Dispute. The Story of the Strike* (London, 1962).

97 J. D. Edelstein and M. Warner, *Comparative Union Democracy. Organisation and Opposition in British and American Unions* (London, 1975), pp. 263–319.

98 Evidence of the AEU to the RC on trade unions, etc., 1966. Esp. pp. 968–9.

99 Crouch, *The Politics of Industrial Relations*, pp. 67–8.

100 Turner, Clack and Roberts, *Labour Relations*, ch. 1.

101 Dunnett, *The Decline of the British Motor Industry*, pp. 108–14.

102 Motor Industry Employers, Memorandum of Evidence to the Royal Commission on trade unions, etc., February 1966.

103 *The Times*, 1968 *passim*.

104 Motor Industry Employers, Memorandum to Royal Commission and Minutes of Motor Employers' Evidence, 15 February 1966.

105 George Woodcock, during examination of witnesses, 15 February 1966, pp. 898–902.

106 O. Kahn-Freund, *ibid.*, p. 905.

107 K. W. Wedderburn, *The Worker and the Law*, 2nd edn. (London, 1971), pp. 173–80; Lord Wedderburn, R. Lewis and J. Clark (eds.),

Labour Law and Industrial Relations: Building on Kahn-Freund (Oxford, 1983), pp. 44–5.
108 Crouch, *The Politics of Industrial Relations*, p. 68.
109 Report of the Royal Commission, 1968.
110 *In Place of Strife* (HMSO, 1969).
111 P. Jenkins, *The Battle of Downing Street* (London, 1970), p. 26.
112 See press reports in the weeks preceding the 1966 election.
113 Jenkins, *The Battle of Downing Street*, p. 29. Harold Wilson, *The Labour Government 1964–70: A Personal Record*, (London, 1971) pp. 623 and 641–55.
114 *In Place of Strife.*
115 H. A. Clegg, *The Changing System of Industrial Relations* (London, 1979), pp. 290–305.

5

The snares of liberalism? Politicians, bureaucrats, and the shaping of federal labour relations policy in the United States, ca. 1915–47

HOWELL HARRIS

Introduction

Between 1932 and 1947 the United States government adopted a fairly coherent set of policies encouraging the organisation of workers into unprecedentedly strong unions, independent of employer control. Under this dispensation they secured members, recognition, permanent bargaining relationships, and overall legitimacy. The regulation of industrial relations became primarily a federal rather than a state responsibility; and federal policy was articulated in a series of laws which were given force by powerful and autonomous administrative agencies. The higher federal courts, which had acted as positive creators of industrial-relations policy from the 1890s through the 1920s, played a relatively modest part in this process: for several years after 1937, in particular, they did little more than settle some marginal issues where legislative intent was unclear, or where administrative discretion had been exercised in ways clearly beyond the bounds of the developing political consensus on the proper role and behaviour of America's newly powerful unions.

Changes in the substance and processes of industrial-relations policy in this period were certainly dramatic enough to deserve the epithet 'revolutionary' – insofar as any policy changes in a sluggish, decentralised and consensual liberal democracy like the United States ever can. And the results were equally dramatic: aided by changes in public attitudes accompanying the Depression of 1929–40, and by the tight labour market during the hectic years of war mobilisation 1940–5, American labour unions increased in numbers, in membership (from less than three million to almost 15 million), in labour-force coverage, in bargaining power, and in

148

political influence. Industrial conflict also increased, reaching a high point, by one conventional measure, in the great reconversion strike wave of 1945–6. But that conflict was very different from what America had experienced before the New Deal. It was relatively peaceful, largely because local law-enforcement authorities maintained a surprisingly even-handed approach in policing picketing. Also, employers generally did not use the injunction weapon against strikers, even where they could, and made few attempts to maintain production or employ strikebreakers. The issues of industrial conflict involved the 'proper' subject-matter of collective bargaining – wages, hours, working conditions, job control, and the details of the unions' institutional status in the employment relationship. They did not, for the most part, raise fundamental questions about the very existence and essential practices of the labour movement – as, for example, the post-First-World-War strike wave had. America was on the way to acquiring the mature industrial-relations system, the institutionalised industrial conflict involving orderly, predictable mass strikes, for which it became famous – perhaps unjustly – among scholars in the 1950s, and the envy of some British labour relations 'reformers' in the 1960s.[1]

How are we to explain these developments? Two established traditions exist to provide us with much of our raw material, and our ways of looking at it. Conventional scholarship offers us lovingly detailed chronicles of the New Deal 'revolution' in public policy towards organised labour; but the impressive empirical research on the origins of that policy has not really been followed by close and critical analysis of its development and impact. Liberal historiography has not questioned the premises of New Deal labour policy – it has accepted them unequivocally. It has not accounted for the limits and peculiar biases of public policy; it has been written too much from the inside.[2]

In the last 15 years, however, a rival point of view has arisen within academe, represented in 'New-Left' historiography,[3] Marxisant political sociology,[4] and most recently 'critical legal studies'.[5] It serves the necessary purpose of encouraging us to caution in evaluating the motives and consequences of liberal reform, to moderation in celebrating the New Deal and its legacy. But the goal of revisionist scholarship is much more ambitious than that of balancing received interpretations; it seeks to supplant them.

Revisionist scholarship consists more of essays in reinterpretation than of primary source-based, original empirical research. Its practitioners tend to rely on the direct rehashing of conventional accounts for the 'facts' to which they supply an ideologically informed re-reading, or even on the faithful repetition of one another's interpretations as if they were accepted 'facts' themselves. This is all rather parasitic and incestuous, but it does mean that revisionist scholarship is actually far closer to liberal historiography than one might at first expect, and that it is sufficiently self-referential that we may fairly identify a common core of assumptions.

Liberal and left-revisionist accounts of the rise of the 'new' American labour movement in 1933–47, to which the new state policies undoubtedly made a necessary, though not sufficient, contribution, share many common conclusions, though differently expressed – that its revolutionary potential, if any, was easily contained; that it contributed to the legitimation of representative democracy and rationalisation of some aspects of capitalist enterprise (especially employment practices); that it resulted in an institutionalised form of industrial conflict and a narrowly economistic, politically neutralised labour movement.

The differences arise partly over the assessment of the outcome – should one applaud it, or simply take it for granted as the 'natural' tendency of modern industrial societies in general, and the United States, with its distinctive traditions, in particular? Or should one deplore it, as yet another example of the snuffing out of chances for radical social change, of the early abortion of a potentially revolutionary mass movement, which American capitalism in a decade-long crisis might and should have spawned? But the welcome, or otherwise, extended to the acknowledged result is not the end of the disagreement. Equally important is the argument over the nature and origins of liberal reformist state intervention itself.

Liberal historiography does not really have any very satisfying explanation of the bases of reformist initiatives, or the dynamics of state policy. As it is written from a position firmly within the New Deal camp, this absence of theory is scarcely surprising. 'Problems' arise for political solution, but how, why, and by whom are they defined and perceived *as* problems? It seems to be simply assumed that, at recurring intervals, liberal versions of the political agenda must come to the fore, placed there more or less mechanically by social change or economic crisis. Similarly, it is simply assumed that the United States has an open, democratic, pluralist polity, so that eventually and from time to time liberal definitions of the public interest must secure sufficient support to overcome the presumed entrenched opposition of conservatism and the business community. However belatedly, The People triumph over The Interests. Revisionist scholarship cannot be accused of any similar absence of an explicit theoretical base.

It starts with its conclusion, that liberal reform in twentieth-century America in general, and New Deal labour policy in particular, has been a sophisticated, far-sighted, and deliberate response by 'the state' and the 'power elite' to the threat or actuality of massive 'working-class' disaffection with 'democratic' capitalism. Liberal 'reform' has been devised and implemented, pre-emptively or reactively, by the intellectuals and politicians who are, necessarily, the servants of capital; but enlightened representatives of the business community and America's bourgeoisie have also played a *direct* part in getting legislation enacted and accepted. And such reforms have worked: the disaffected have been tamed, their revolutionary potential has been defused, channelled into tolerable, limited, institutionalised conflicts which sustain rather than threaten the system. There has been nothing of chance in this outcome: it has been awesomely intentional *and* structurally determined.

Labour unions and the state-regulated collective bargaining system, key inheritances of the New Deal era, are therefore seen not as a partial solution to the problem of the continuing exploitation and powerlessness of the working class, but as a major part of the problem itself. Grievance procedures, contracts, institutionalised 'solidarity', and National Labor Relations Board (NLRB) rulings are significant, but not because they confer some measure of security, some rights in the employment relationship, on the minority of organised workers lucky enough to have secured, and maintained, them. Instead, they detract from individuals' rights, infringe on unions' autonomy, and foreclose (usually unstated) alternative patterns of self-organisation offering more benefits within the system, and a greater likelihood of its ultimate overthrow.

The problem with this interpretation, in particular in its earlier and cruder versions, with their instrumentalist view of the state and determinist vision of the political process, is that it explains too much. Because the conclusions, rooted in contemporary intellectual fashion and political concerns, come first, the actual 'history' is simply selected, cut, and trimmed to produce a usable past, an ahistorical underpinning of one reading of present realities. The result is a failure to inquire too closely into what actually happened; an excess of preconceptions leads interpreters to ignore the abundant evidence in primary and secondary sources that the reality was much more interesting, much less straightforward, much more contingent. It deserves, and rewards, close analysis.

This essay is itself a synthesis, informed by both of the established interpretive traditions it seeks to criticise and build on. But it is not even-handed in its use and treatment of these two approaches. It starts from a position of respect for, and sympathy with, liberal scholarship; in particular, it insists that readers must accept that New Deal reformism was dramatic in its impact and extent. The New Deal constituted a change in public policy and organised class relations that deserves to be called radical, and certainly stretches any definition of liberal reform to the limit. The extent of the change can be appreciated only if the prehistory of government policies towards organised labour and industrial conflict are understood; only then can we proceed to examine the new departures of the 1930s in their proper light.

The state and labour before the New Deal

It is a mistake to look for too much coherence and consistency in government policies towards industrial relations before the New Deal. The key features of the American political system – in real as well as formal terms – were constitutionalism, separation and limitation of powers, federalism and local control. The United States' governmental system remained extraordinarily weak and fragmented well into the twentieth century, in the face of structures of private interest and economic power already comparatively well-integrated at the national level. Accordingly, in looking at relations between 'the state' and 'the working class', its organisations and self-activity in the pre-New Deal years, historians may confuse themselves and their readers by using the singular where, in both cases, the plural would be more appropriate.

The United States' polity throughout most of the nineteenth century was one of 'courts and parties'. The parties controlled both the powerful legislative and the starveling, dependent executive–administrative branches of government, at state and federal levels.

There they built, preserved, and balanced coalitions of voters and interest-groups by distributing public goods and devolving 'public' authority to 'private' interests. Courts created a legal framework to facilitate and stabilise a competitive, individualistic capitalism, and were accepted as an alternative locus of public policy making, setting bounds on the conduct of other agencies of government, and acting where the latter were unable or unwilling to regulate the behaviour of contending private parties. In the early twentieth century the United States began to build a centralised, regulatory administrative state. But that was a slow and uneven process.[6] Through the 1920s, the judiciary still had a far greater part to play than the executive or legislative branches of state and federal government in defining public policies towards organised labour. They exercised this role by adjudicating 'private' disputes in cases involving employers and workers, and by endorsing or, more commonly, constraining the policy initiatives and preferences of other branches of government.

The independent policy-making role of the American judiciary, especially its higher and federal courts, was one of the distinctive features of the American polity. In addition, given the highly politicised and class-biased nature of judicial appointments and decisions, it was impossible that the mystifying belief that judges were law-finders, not law-makers, could persist unchallenged in the United States. Between the 1880s and the 1920s, even the most 'conservative' spokesmen for organised labour in America came to an inescapable conclusion, the lesson of bitter experience, that the all-important judiciary played a role of contestant, rather than referee, in cases involving trade-union organisation and industrial conflict. Less important agencies of the state, by their actions, won the same general condemnation.[7]

Before the 1930s, most American industrial conflicts were inevitably local affairs, for most union organisation and bargaining was decentralised, and major national-market industries, apart from coal mining and the railroads, were citadels of the open shop. And local governmental power was usually to be found arrayed on the side of capital, particularly at such times of crisis.[8]

So when the organised working class looked at the judiciary, both state and federal, and at the local state, not surprisingly it conceived a deep suspicion of, and aversion towards, their intervention. The 'voluntarism' of the American Federation of Labor (AFL) was a craving for autonomy, some legitimate sphere of activity within which it would not be disturbed, that the state was unwilling to allow it.[9] Labour's only hope of deliverance lay in putting pressure on the most responsive branches of government. From local authorities, it could try to obtain police neutrality or abstention in times of conflict, and many other everyday advantages. Between the 1870s and 1920s, in areas with relatively mature industrial economies and organised, articulate working classes, state governments began to take a constructive interest in the 'labor problem', partly in response to industrial conflict, but also to labour's local political action. They collected statistics and investigated the facts about working conditions, established agencies for mediation and conciliation in industrial disputes, and on occasion attempted, ineffectually, to limit the powers of courts to intervene coercively in industrial disputes, and to outlaw some of the effective tactics of belligerent anti-union employers. More positively, state and local governments enacted laws under their police powers to regulate some conditions of employment for especially vulnerable classes of workers. Most dramatically of all, in the years before the First World War, state legislatures confronted the problem of compensation for America's appalling toll of industrial accidents, breaching the common-law defences that the judiciary had erected around employers' liability, and substituting a regulated, insurance-based system.[10]

The federal government was slow to be similarly active. It had no clear constitutional responsibility for employment relations other than those of its own civilian workers, and of employees indisputably engaged in inter-state and foreign commerce; and in any case most industrial conflicts were small-scale affairs that hardly attracted its attention. In addition, there was no nationally organised political articulation of working-class interests to compel its concern. When it did intervene, it was generally by sending in federal troops which, like the National Guard, 'restored order' in industrial disputes in a manner favouring employers.[11] The federal judiciary was much more innovative in the late nineteenth and early twentieth centuries, honing its tools of coercive intervention to new peaks of refinement, sharp and awfully blunt at the same time, and with the same general effect.

This situation began to change in the 1890s. The federal government was eventually compelled to take a positive interest in the 'labour problem' first by the formation of strong nationwide craft

Brotherhoods on the railroads – a federal responsibility under the inter-state commerce clause of the Constitution – and later by the emergence of large unions in other basic industries, especially coal mining, of vital importance to an increasingly urban population.

The federal government began to perform a mediatory role: *ad hoc* courts of inquiry into particularly large or bloody strikes were appointed; President Theodore Roosevelt himself intervened in the great anthracite strike of 1902, offering the government's good offices to bring about a compromise settlement. This set a new pattern of executive involvement, and signalled a new conception of the 'public interest' – in industrial peace, yes, but not at any price, and not necessarily on the employer's terms or in strict defence of the status quo. The federal government's new role was increasingly institutionalised: a permanent, if ineffective, system of mediation and conciliation in railroad labour disputes was developed by trial and error, and in 1913 the new Department of Labor was charged with providing impartial third parties to help settle strikes in other industries.

Public policy evolved alongside the institutions through which it was expressed and implemented. Official actions and pronouncements came to reflect a newly sophisticated understanding of the workings of the industrial relations system within a capitalist democracy, and promote social change to bring realities into line with the new model. Unions were to be given a useful and legitimate role within industry for collective bargaining over wages, hours, and conditions of employment, with the idea that this would lead to a more stable, peaceful and just relationship between management and workers; and the AFL was to be granted a recognised status as *the* political representative of America's wage earners, which it somewhat ambitiously claimed on the basis of having organised about 10% of them.[12]

Such recognition was first extended by a private organisation of enlightened capitalists, the National Civic Federation (NCF),[13] but the federal government soon followed suit. The necessity of collective organisation, the desirability of collective bargaining, the national interest in securing some kind of 'industrial democracy', became commonplaces of respectable and official rhetoric. And if Presidents or Congress wanted to talk to some 'responsible' representative of the organised working class – numerically small but politically significant for the Democratic Party after 1910 – they had little choice but to turn to Samuel Gompers and his AFL. In consequence, Gompers became a public figure, and the AFL acquired a certain legitimacy. Congress responded, however ineffectually, to some of its requests, notably for protection against anti-trust suits and other common forms of legal harassment, via the 1913 Clayton Act, and under the Wilson administration it acquired a seat in the cabinet.

The First World War: making America safe for 'industrial democracy'?

The nascent functional representation of the AFL and its ability to exact political and economic concessions were given a mighty push forward by the war emergency of 1916–19. That period was both a false dawn and a forcing-house for the ideas and institutions which shaped the development of the American industrial relations system in the 1930s and 1940s. The AFL, particularly its national leadership, played an important role in defending the Wilson administration's foreign policy to the working class, both at home and abroad; in tune with its new-found super-patriotism, it assisted the federal government – and some states – in their repressive activities directed against the anti-war section of the socialists and the Industrial Workers of the World (IWW). But this cooperation was not offered without calculation. The AFL aimed to free itself and its members from the taint of un-Americanism, and from unsympathetic state attentions; it expected immediate, concrete, economic and organisational gains; and it looked forward to a permanent alteration in the relations between unions and employers, the labour movement and the state, in the postwar world. It expected the public rhetoric about 'industrial democracy' in Progressive Era America to be turned into reality.[14]

The AFL succeeded in attaining most of its short-term objectives, but not the last and most important. Membership nearly doubled between 1916 and 1920 from 2.073 to 4.079 millions. Apart from a few important occasions in 1919–22, state repression did not affect it or its affiliates directly. Particular sections of the labour force – railroad workers and seamen – received dramatic improvements in their conditions of employment by federal laws enacted in response to astute and persistent lobbying and, in the former case, the real threat of an all-out national strike. The 'labor movement' as a whole

– meaning the 'legitimate' unions of the AFL and the Railroad
Brotherhoods – was granted representation on the advisory committees overseeing the mobilisation and preparedness effort, and on the
all-important committee which determined wartime labour-relations policy, as well as on the National War Labor Board (NWLB) of
1918–19 and subsidiary authorities in specific industries which
implemented it. This political recognition was symbolic of the
permanent status to which the AFL laid claim. Even more significant
was its immediate outcome.[15]
    The cardinal features of wartime federal policy were that there
should be no strikes or lock-outs, no interference with union-
organised shops, and no attempt by unions or workers to win new
formal recognition agreements, extend collective bargaining, or
increase membership by 'coercive measures'. Most significantly,
'[t]he right of workers to organise in trade unions and to bargain
collectively through chosen representatives [was] recognised and
affirmed'.[16]
    Obviously there were some unresolved inconsistencies here. While
this policy may have been, as David Bowman puts it, 'designed less to
protect the growth of unionization than to prevent any opportunistic
growth of labor organisation', it was still important in practice and
theory.[17] It represented a part of the state's response to a crisis of
manpower, inflation and industrial conflict which dictated a new
departure in public policy, amounting to an explicit recognition of
the unions' claim that their status as autonomous bargaining institutions should be protected against that ingrained and pervasive
employer hostility which the state had hitherto generally assisted. So
great were those obstacles, so comparatively weak the existing
labour organisations which it was now public policy to foster and
manipulate, so extreme the emergency, that the United States took
the course of basing its industrial-relations system on a framework of
positive rights and administrative intervention, rather than simply
extending legal immunities for trade-union organisation and
behaviour. In so doing, it decisively rejected the British, and the
AFL's normally preferred, model of voluntarism, and began to carve
out its very own distinctive path. When another national emergency
presented itself less than a generation later, the war experience
offered a persuasive model of how to meet it, and many helpful
precedents.
    In 16 months' activity the NWLB developed a number of pro-

cedures to give effect to its policies and resolve disputes coming before it. First, some common employer practices were prohibited – blacklisting, the imposition of individual non-union ('yellow-dog') contracts, espionage, interrogation, and surveillance aimed at hampering legitimate self-organisation. Secondly, effective remedies were devised for workers discriminated against because of legitimate union membership or activity – which might include a strike provoked by an employer's breach of contract; reinstatement with back pay (less any interim earnings) was the remedy for individuals. To enforce public policy, administratively supervised orders prohibited discriminatory discharges, demotions, or suspensions, and required that discharges be for 'just and sufficient' causes capable of standing up to impartial investigation. Arbitrary employment practices were further restricted by the imposition of the seniority principle in layoffs.

The Board could not compel companies to begin collective bargaining with unions 'as such'. But it could and did require them to maintain relationships already established, and to meet and negotiate with committees representing their employees. Firms could not compel membership of a company union, nor satisfy the requirement that they negotiate by 'bargaining' with one while refusing to deal with a representative workers' committee. In numerous cases the Board ordered the establishment of works committees in non-union plants, supervising secret-ballot elections for the purpose, and determining election districts and representation ratios. In these cases, to be sure, unions were not recognised 'as such'; and the machinery of representation and bargaining was not what the AFL and its affiliates preferred. But under an acceptable compromise formula, unions were assisted to establish themselves in practice as an important, even controlling, element in some of the works committees whose birth the NWLB oversaw. This was admittedly a temporary measure; but NWLB officers, AFL leaders, and businessmen foresaw that such novel arrangements among unskilled and semi-skilled workers, and in mass-production industries, for the most part previously unorganised, might well provide the basis for open collective bargaining with an 'outside union' once the no-strike rule was removed and employers were unprotected against labour militancy. The NWLB's *de facto* recognition of unions even went so far as to protect local officers' right to have time off to engage in union business outside the plant, without pay but without loss of job either.[18]

Managerial autonomy and its unilateral authority to determine employment policy were well and truly violated by NWLB orders. In the short run, given the necessity of industrial peace, the bargaining power and militancy of workers enjoying an unprecedentedly strong labour market, and the lack of cost constraints, employers were generally willing to go along with NWLB orders. Some even accepted that some form of 'collective dealing', possibly formalised via a 'trade agreement', had a real contribution to make to the improvement and stabilising of in-plant labour relations.

But few employers indeed were prepared to accept the AFL's claim that independent, outside unions represented, not just the best, but the only legitimate channel for collective bargaining. And fewer still were prepared to go along with the AFL's underlying vision of bilateral trade agreements covering wages, hours and other employment conditions at the level of the firm, or better, employers' association, as the basis for a co-determined collective control of the economy.[19]

The 1920s: managerial counter-offensives, conservative polity, private initiatives

The troubled postwar years 1919–22 saw first inflation, continuing over-full employment, and a sustained rise in union membership accompanied by massive, formal industrial conflict; then a frightened, repressive reaction by the propertied classes and the state, on the grounds that aliens and radicals were subverting American institutions, its private capitalist economy first of all; and finally, a short, dramatic recession, with massive unemployment in the short term, from which recovery was very patchy and slow in hitherto strongly unionised sectors. The recession brought wage cuts, and helped stimulate employer attacks on the gains in union membership, recognition and job controls, won in the hectic years 1916–20. This was no fitting context for the realisation of the collectivist dreams of the AFL and its liberal or social democratic allies.

Instead, it nourished an impressive and successful reactionary movement. As America moved into peacetime, the extraordinary powers of the federal government, which had underpinned the NWLB's success, lapsed, and the first National Industrial Conference called by President Wilson in 1919 to resolve the causes of industrial unrest quickly reached a deadlock. Industry would not accept organised labour's claim to the exclusive right of representation of workers' interests: instead, large firms moved to convert works councils into company unions, or to install the latter themselves to forestall outside unionisation; while trade associations orchestrated a nationwide drive against union organisation in the name of the 'open shop', the 'American Plan', and the 'right to work'. In the great coal and railroad strikes, the Wilson and Harding administrations initiated anti-union actions; the state and federal judiciary developed extreme doctrines to further restrict picketing, prevent union organisation, and penalise strikes, boycotts, or sympathetic actions. The United States reverted to its anti-union normalcy.[20] Unions were confined to sick industries, like coal, railroads, and textiles; to some competitive local-market industries, including construction and the needle trades; to their craft bastions, for example, printing; and to employees of some public utilities and branches of government service.

Labour's dreams of 1917–19 were easily, and utterly, dashed. It made no difference whether the unionised minority worked for nationalisation of basic industries, establishment of a labour party, or achievement of employer recognition by the promise of cooperation. In the 1920s, all roads led to failure, except for the railroad operating crafts, entrenched in a major industry under federal supervision, and with a uniquely well-developed national political machine for mobilising congressional support. The railroad unions gained a measure of legal protection by the 1926 Railroad Labor Act, but at a price. Collective bargaining as a means to settle disputes and ensure industrial peace was endorsed, and employer interference with employees' freedom of association condemned. But the unions were enmeshed in a complex and unsatisfactory *federal* procedure governing contract negotiation, which provided for temporary prohibitions against strikes, and were saddled with a grievance-handling system in which company unions might still find a place.[21]

This thoroughly interventionist law did not offer a model capable of general application. Even if it had been otherwise attractive or acceptable, the constitutional obstacles to an active federal policy covering the bulk of extractive, manufacturing and processing, and local-market industries seemed insuperable. Instead, the AFL and its allies still hoped to import into the United States the principles of

British labour law, to establish and protect an arena for collective action and voluntarist, adversarial labour relations free from judicial meddling. The role the AFL and its friends wished the state to play was one that would be passive and even-handed. They neither wished nor expected the federal government actively to promote unionisation in peacetime by extending aspects of railroad labour policy to all industry, or by permanent intervention along the lines the NWLB had mapped out.

In one important respect, however, the 1920s was a decade of preparation for the New Deal 'revolution'. This period saw the consolidation of the infant discipline of industrial relations in the universities and the emergence of influential streams of ideas such as those associated with John R. Commons' circle at the University of Wisconsin. Groups such as these, were destined to play a key role in New Deal policy-making and to provide the Roosevelt administration with legislative draughtsmen, advocates and administrators. In the 1920s they perfected their ideas about what sort of industrial relations system they wanted. Collective bargaining would be an essential component of a system of industrial peace, social justice, economic progress and political stability. They found their blueprint for this system in microcosm in the responsible industrial unionism of the needle trades.[22]

In some metropolitan markets of the needle trades, employer acceptance of unionisation as a fact, perhaps even a business asset, was an established fact by the 1920s. The industry itself was desperately competitive, chronically unstable, and had relatively few large firms, so unionisation seemed to offer employers a great deal. Inclusive organisation of employers and workers across an entire labour and product market promised to reduce the variability of wage costs in a labour-intensive industry, taking some of the pressure off high-cost producers. A plethora of piece-rates, informal and arbitrary employment practices, and considerable workgroup solidarity, often along lines of ethnicity or craft, had resulted in chaotic labour relations and frequent 'job actions'. The unions offered the stability of a fixed-term contract, a non-strike pledge backed up by union *and* employer discipline, and a formalised grievance procedure. In return for recognition and the security of a written contract, plus the very real benefits expected to accrue to their members from the industry's stabilisation, they offered to reduce personnel problems, share responsibility for what remained, and even provide credit, design, and industrial engineering skills to which entrepreneurs in an industry whose units typically had limited managerial resources did not have easy access. Leaders of the main unions, and some employer representatives, had a real commitment to using voluntarist, collectivist bargaining institutions to try to rationalise and stabilise the industry as a whole, not just its employment practices.

In many respects their achievement was disappointing. They could not overcome weaknesses intrinsic to the industry's structure, especially given the uncontrollable competition of the large non-union sector. But in one respect, it was important and lasting. They developed the institution of the 'Impartial Chairman' or permanent arbitrator, sitting at the end of the grievance procedure, empowered to settle 'disputes of right' arising under the terms, and during the life, of a contract, without the costs and uncertainty to both sides of industrial conflict.[23]

Arbitration was not confined to the needle trades, even in the 1920s, nor had it originated there. But it was their example, and the men and precedents their experience developed, which was to be most influential in the long run. It was a decentralised, voluntarist mechanism for the settlement of disputes, promoting peace and order in industry, but not at the expense of 'justice', or of the right to strike in the last resort. It offered labour-relations academics jobs and a satisfying policy-making role in association with some of America's most progressive industrial unions. Early arbitrators used the 'governmental' analogy of collective bargaining as the American way to 'industrial democracy' so common in the aftermath of the First World War. Unionisation introduced 'constitutional government' into industry via the trade-agreement mechanism. And they were to be that constitution's judges.

Arbitrators were committed to making the parties' bargaining behaviour more civilised and rational, instructing inexperienced managers and union representatives in their 'responsibilities'. They breathed life into loosely worded contracts by their rulings in particular cases. They exercised an equitable jurisdiction, developed standards of 'due process' in employment relations, built up a common law, case by case, and codified it into new agreements and understandings.[24] They helped lay a firm foundation of ideology and practice on which they and those they trained or influenced would help build a larger, more progressive, but 'responsible' American labour movement.[25] Before this could happen, however, a revolution in public policy, informed by historical experience, but developed in response to immediate pressures, would be needed.

1932: voluntarism ascendant

Organised labour and its liberal allies had responded to the judiciary's perfection, and employers' increasing use, of the injunction weapon in the 1920s with a counterattack involving persistent lobbying and propaganda. In 1932, all that effort finally bore fruit. The progressive elimination of right-wing Republicans at the polls – and the consequent reduction of Congressional sensitivity to business pressures – which began in 1930, and continued for the next three elections, gave them their opportunity. The Supreme Court had already declared that, on the railroads, the state had the power to make company unions and other forms of employer interference with workers' rights to free self-organisation unlawful. But that was no green light for a generally interventionist federal labour relations policy, given the same court's restrictive interpretation of the Constitution's 'commerce clause'. In any case, the AFL desired nothing of the sort. Three reformist lawyers, a counsel for the railroad brotherhoods, and a Wisconsin School labour-relations specialist, drafted a law which the AFL supported, and Congress endorsed – the Norris–La Guardia Act, which raised so many procedural barriers and safeguards that labour injunctions would henceforth be hard to obtain, and much less useful to employers. In addition, yellow-dog contracts were specifically declared contrary to public policy, unprotected and unenforceable.[26]

Norris–La Guardia was the almost perfect expression of the AFL's attitude towards the role of the 'law' (i.e. the courts) in labour-relations: that there should scarcely be one. Eventually, the courts themselves seemed to agree, extending the Act's protection of union organisation and practices – including concerted refusals to work or patronise, inducements to strike or boycott, and picketing, regardless of objectives – from injunctive restraint, to include immunity against civil actions for damages and, in large measure, criminal prosecution. But the belated triumph of voluntarism in American labour law took years to achieve: in 1932, Norris–La Guardia's importance was chiefly symbolic. It only applied to federal courts, and was not, in any event, upheld as constitutional by the Supreme Court until 1938.[27]

By that time, the United States had rejected such thoroughgoing voluntarism as the basis for its labour-relations policy, and put continuous administrative intervention and deliberate institution-building in its place. For a few years, the courts were busy scrapping one traditional set of restraints on unions, while the NLRB was busy inventing another, with those same courts' active encouragement and passive consent.

1933–1935: voluntarism transcended

The radical transformation in public policy, and partial opening of the floodgates to a surge of unionisation, which occurred with the enactment of Section 7(a) of the National Industrial Recovery Act (NIRA) in summer 1933, was so largely the unintended result of an incredibly confused legislative process that it is still difficult, 50 years on, to explain quite how or why it happened.

But it is clear that the initiative for including what became 7(a) came from the AFL, not from any section of organised business or the administration; and that the subsequent beefing-up of 7(a) in committee similarly owed nothing to administration support, which was conspicuously absent, and occurred over the desperate opposition of the National Association of Manufacturers (NAM) and other weak and disunited business groups.

At the beginning of that legislative process, organised business thought 7(a) an acceptable bargain – in return for federal sanction of its preferred scheme of economic stabilisation, involving devolution of some of the state's regulatory power to trade associations under loose government supervision, there would be a vague, unthreatening declaration of principle favouring workers' self-organisation. The original 7(a) was tamer than the relevant provision of the NWLB's code of 1918; but when the Act finally emerged, it had had the language of Norris–La Guardia grafted on, and explicitly prohibited employers from denying workers their rights through the mechanism of company unionism.[28]

In the NIRA's corporatist scheme, Section 7 explicitly recognised organised labour as a part of the 'social compact' it envisaged; it provided for the possibility of labour representation on the industry authorities designated to draw up codes of 'fair competition', includ-

ing labour standards. And in addition, of course, it seemed to
endorse the spread of free trade unionism and collective bargaining
as instruments and objectives of public policy. But the business
community was determined to exploit its advantages – including the
wavering resolve of the Roosevelt administration, the lack of any
real enforcement mechanism, and the weakness of the labour movement – to make sure 7(a) did not have the effects that some of its
draughtsmen intended. The administration seemed to expect that in
return for this grant of rights the labour movement would peacefully
participate in the work of economic reconstruction, without
acknowledging that encouraging union organisation in an environment of employer hostility and chronic economic stagnation must
inevitably result in increased industrial conflict – at least in the short
term, though in the longer run one might reasonably anticipate a
restoration of industrial peace within the newly democratised
employment relationship. And the labour movement and its liberal
allies had great hopes that 7(a) really meant what they thought it
said, giving labour that voice in economic planning at the level of the
workplace, industry and nation that they had claimed for a generation, with the objective of redressing the skewed balance of social
power and income distribution which they thought explained
America's economic collapse and political malaise.

The NIRA was not, however, self-enforcing. Given the
preponderant economic power of organised business, and the
administration's major commitment towards using the NIRA for
economic stabilisation and recovery, not power redistribution, the
way the Act worked bitterly disappointed the AFL and its liberal
allies, notably Senator Robert Wagner, a New York democrat. In
particular, under the 'Blue Eagle' business managed to increase the
numbers of employees covered by company unionism faster than
resurgent independent unions added to their membership.

Though workers were mostly unable to form viable unions and
establish bargaining relationships in 1933–4, there was nothing to
stop them trying. The resulting strikes troubled an administration set
on building national unity and a synthetic social harmony across the
lines of party, class and interest, with uninterrupted economic
recovery its primary objective. It had to find some way of defusing
industrial conflict, policing and enforcing NIRA's labour provisions,
and thereby allaying criticism from its own lib–lab supporters.

Accordingly, a National Labor Board (NLB) with no clear policies, uncertain authority, and no independent enforcement powers, was established in August 1933, with Senator Wagner at its head. It was tripartite in membership, at both the national and local level; its major purpose was the speedy restoration of 'industrial peace' through mediation and conciliation. But the most intractable strike issues were organisation and recognition. Employers were belligerent and imaginative in their defence of the 'open shop', denounced the Board and resisted its proposed settlements; the administration and the courts failed to support it. Still, the NLB did have some achievements. It began the business of recruiting and training a federal labour relations bureaucracy, and it completed the education of Senator Wagner in the realities of American industrial relations and employer behaviour.

The NLB devised a formula for ending strikes which drew on the experience of the NWLB, Railroad Labor Board, and private dispute-settlement. Strikers were to return to work without discrimination, bargaining on wages and hours was to begin, representatives were to be selected by secret ballot under NLB auspices, and any unresolved matters or disputes over interpretation of resulting agreements were to be settled by NLB arbitration. All the 'Reading Formula' needed to become effective was employer acceptance, or administration and judicial support. It had neither in adequate measure. By summer 1934, the NLB was a busted flush.

Through 1935 Wagner, his few congressional allies, the AFL, and his corps of NLB-experienced advisers, accordingly tried to win some independent legislative mandate for the NLB to develop and enforce what they thought national policy was, or should be. But the Roosevelt administration resisted. It was only willing to go so far as to create a somewhat stronger, quasi-judicial NLRB, in 1934. Congress accepted this reform of the NLB's structural weaknesses – the new Board was administratively autonomous, staffed exclusively with impartial 'experts' – which had not addressed the basic problems of jurisdiction and power. Congress and the administration acted in this way to stave off an impending national steel strike, and to satisfy the Democratic Party's pro-labour supporters before the 1934 elections.

What the history of labour relations policy in the early New Deal clearly shows is that it was not developed by the Roosevelt administration, but independent of and almost in spite of it. Nor was it developed with any assistance from the business community, but in unequivocal opposition to its actions and forcefully declared wishes. It was developed in consultation with the AFL; but, for the most part, it resulted from the frustrating, but educative, encounters Wagner, his aides, and the federal labour-relations bureaucrats had with the administration, business, and the judiciary. The legislative history of the Wagner Act, the most radical of the few structural reforms enacted in the term of office of America's most vaunted 'liberal' president, demonstrates that any crudely instrumentalist view of the development of state policy is notably unhelpful. The most consistent pressure for a clear declaration of federal policy came from the NLB and first NLRB themselves. Ignoring their agencies' marginal status and wavering official support, the Boards' pro-labour and liberal pluralist staff members acted as if they were empowered to be vigorously innovative policy-makers and enforcers. They fleshed out vague words of the 7(a) and gave them practical meaning: with more conviction than helpful precedent, they tried to restrict employers' ability to form or dominate company unions, and to protect workers' right to organise from other employer interference. They determined that the choice of the *majority* of employees voting in a Board-supervised election should be the exclusive bargaining representative of *all*; and they began to define, procedurally and substantively, what such bargaining would amount to – including the presumption that it would result in a written, fixed-term contract covering the major issues of union recognition, wages, hours and working conditions.[29]

This surely was a case of bureaucratic audacity, scarcely comprehensible if one neglects the prior experience and beliefs of the New Deal's 'experts', which told them what kind of labour-relations system America had to have, and that they must intervene creatively to build it. They were able to get away with this audacity, though not to see their policy preferences enacted until 1935, or enforced until after 1937, only because of the extraordinary openness and confusion of the policy-making and administrative process in the mid-1930s. Roosevelt himself had no great interest in the organisation of labour, but was, for the most part, benignly indifferent to the Wagner camp's initiatives, as he was to workers' self-help activities. The business community had committed everything to a strategy of obstruction and reaction. From 1934 to 1937, this did not pay off because it relied for success on the declining Republican Party, whose right wing was nearing extinction, and did not impress the new, uncommitted or pro-labour Democrats. The organised labour movement supported its bureaucratic and congressional friends' legislative proposals, but played little part in determining what they were, and scarcely understood their detailed implications.

Wagner, almost singlehandedly, and against the odds, sustained the campaign for federal labour law reform in 1934 and 1935. When it finally received the administration's belated and half-hearted endorsement, it was largely because the Supreme Court's vetoes had created a policy vacuum, and because Wagner had made it clear that he was going to force the issue to a vote, and that he had sufficient support in Congress to get it through, with or without the administration's help. In a pre-election period, the administration saw no harm in gaining some credit for a piece of legislation for which it deserved none, with which it would never completely sympathise, and whose political benefit to the Democratic Party neither it, nor Wagner, ever envisaged. The fact and manner of the Wagner Act's passage in 1935 may have been quite accidental, but the *content* of the Act was quite otherwise, because it had the benefit of two years' detailed experience of the problems of employer opposition to independent unionism, and because it was unusually cleverly drafted to give a carefully established bureaucracy a broad discretionary power to implement a clearly declared public policy. The Act was as proof against judicial meddling and attack as its draughtsmen could make it, and the new NLRB it created set about its business in September 1935 with care and confidence.[30]

The Wagner Act: meaning and impact, 1935–1941

As far as the Wagner Act's draughtsmen were concerned, the NLRB could now eliminate employer obstruction, by intervening, with the support of a changed public opinion, and hopefully of the courts, to strike down and prevent the recurrence of specified 'unfair labor practices'. This would remove one particularly frequent source of bitter industrial conflict, the recognition dispute. The NLRB's powers to determine appropriate bargaining units, to hold elections, or in other ways discover the wishes of the majority of workers in such a unit, as to which organisation, if any, should represent them all, would help shape the emerging structure of labour organisation in collaboration with the initiatives of workers and their unions. Such designated representatives would have a clear status when they came to the bargaining table, and the legitimacy which derived from serving a clear public interest: the 'equalisation' of bargaining power in industry and the redistribution of income in such a way as to satisfy institutional economists' prescription for regenerating and then stabilising the economy.

The net result of workers' initiatives, employers' concessions, and state sponsorship would be a 'democratic' form of 'industrial government' resting on representation, due process, compromise, and the development of industrial codes governing, in the first instance, wages, hours and working conditions. All of this would be conducive to industrial peace, as grievances about employer autocracy would be removed, and permanent institutions established to resolve the remainder, which were much more amenable to settlement by negotiation, compromise and third-party mediation or conciliation.[31]

The Wagner Act was not without ambiguity of language and inconsistency of purpose, but its main lines were clear. Whatever modern 'legal revisionist' scholars like Karl Klare may suggest, it was not, even potentially, a charter for *participatory* democracy in industry. It should be read in the light of the ideology and intentions of the 'experts' who drew it up and administered it, and of what they had already done on the NLB/NLRB. There could be little 'deradicalisation' where there was no radical intent. The Supreme Court cannot be blamed for obstructing a course of policy development which none of the Act's draughtsmen, few of its early administrators, and very few indeed of its clients and beneficiaries in the labour movement had any conception of, or interest in.[32]

This is not to deny, however, that the Wagner Act's progenitors had some semi-utopian objectives, and that it was somewhat denatured in practice. But the area in which this occurred was not the one Klare identified, but rather in the hopes and expectations of the collectivist labour 'experts'. Building on their limited experience with collective bargaining in labour-intensive, decentralised, disorderly industries, whose undercapitalised firms lacked managerial resources, they expected similar 'beneficial results' as collective bargaining 'matured' in the core firms of basic manufacturing industry. There would be 'progress' towards an increase in the scale of the bargaining unit – from the plant to the firm, to the entire industry – and in the scope of bargaining, going beyond immediate job regulation to include some kind of union–management cooperation in productivity improvement and economic planning. This was, they thought, a logical evolution, conducive to the appearance of responsible labour leadership and stable industrial relations, as well as to real efficiency gains.

This collectivist vision appealed to some managerial progressives, Catholic corporatists, and numerous labour activists who had moved within the orbit of the Socialist Party and/or League for Industrial Democracy.[33] But it had no constituency to compare with that of the plant- or firm-based, narrowly job-conscious unionism that the 1930s and 1940s actually encouraged. There was little practical interest in the labour movement in working towards any such vision, no comparable political consensus to support such a revolution in America's economic structure as existed for the Wagner Act's more modest and immediate objectives, and unremitting employer hostility to any such entrenchment of labour in the strategic decision-making heart of the enterprise, where it had no right to exist and could make no useful contribution. America's core firms had existed before the regulatory machinery of an administrative state; their growth strategies had been fiercely autonomous, insulating themselves from market vagaries and political intervention, asserting control over their raw material sources, suppliers, investment capital, employees, distribution networks, customers' buying preferences, and even over the development of new products and technologies. They had neither received nor sought much direct help from the state; their preference had always been for unilateral authority; and they had sufficient managerial resources to believe they had nothing to gain, and a lot to lose, by allowing any 'outside' agency, such as a union, a trade association, or a bilateral industry-wide body, to intervene in the holy-of-holies of strategic managerial decision-making. They had no liking for 'political capitalism', pace Kolko and Weinstein, certainly saw no place for co-determination, nor even for the milder industry-wide determination of basic conditions of employment. Any such agreement would have hindered firms' abilities as multi-plant units, to take advantage of significant differences in labour cost in the variety of labour markets which made up the United States, and to insulate themselves against 'labor problems' in parts of their empires.[34] There were some businessmen, notably Gerard Swope and Owen D. Young of General Electric, who were attracted to some form of business-dominated bi- or tri-lateral corporatist scheme in the early 1930s; but, after the disappointing experience of the NIRA years, only those industries, like soft coal, whose managements could not look after themselves, continued to turn to the federal government and the labour unions as partners in economic stabilisation.[35] For the most part, business reverted to its long-standing commitment to unilateralism – a commitment from which it has scarcely wavered since, and certainly not in the area of labour relations.

So one of the visions of labour law reformers was destined to be frustrated. But, in the event, the transformation which actually occurred in American labour relations in 1935–47 was sufficient to convince them that they had wrought well, and achieved everything of importance.[36]

What actually happened was that, in a way exceeding the most optimistic forecasts of the NLRB's lawyers, the Supreme Court in 1937, acting under severe political pressure, removed the constitutional uncertainty which had made the law something of a dead letter in the two years since its passage – the two years which saw the formation of the Committee for Industrial Organisation (CIO) and the breakthroughs in union organisation and recognition in the steel, automotive, rubber, electrical and other core sectors of the economy. Those breakthroughs owed little to the NLRB's direct assistance – until 1937, it could do nothing against an employer determined to obstruct or delay in his compliance with the law. Afterwards, it could do more, but only slowly, uncertainly, and retroactively. More important was the uniquely favourable political context created by the ability and willingness of workers to help themselves, the structural capacity of unions to assist them, and the support or complaisance of public opinion and agencies of the local state, responsible to the electoral strength of workers remaking the Democratic Party into a close approximation to a labour party in numerous industrial districts. To this conjuncture of forces must be added the effects of the 'boomlet' of 1936–7 on workers' ability to strike, and employers' willingness to concede direct wages-and-hours benefits, in addition to limited union recognition and bargaining rights, as the price of resumed production and the *promise* of industrial peace.[37]

The NLRB became much more important after the Supreme Court unshackled it in 1937 and, in surely the most extraordinary *volte-face* in its long history, went on to give the Board fairly consistent support. Indeed, in many instances the Court abstained altogether and allowed the NRLB's policy-making to proceed unhindered.

Simultaneously, the Court extended the meaning of the Norris–La Guardia Act far beyond what its sponsors had dared hope, and went so far as to determine that picketing was 'free speech', and thus protected against local prohibitions and regulations by the full force of the Bill of Rights.

What happened in the field of public policy, then, was a somewhat contradictory set of developments. As conservatives began to regain power at the state level in and after 1938, federal law became the chief defence of workers' and unions' rights. The higher federal judiciary cleared away many of the most important legal restraints on industrial conflict, whatever its purposes and methods, that they and their predecessors had painstakingly fashioned over generations. And the NLRB, implementing the Wagner Act with unsurpassed vigour, began to modify the behaviour of employers in relation to unions at the same time as it began to show unions that federal aid did not come without strings. Even as the courts were freeing the labour movement from the burden of hostile local and judicial regulation which had been voluntarism's target, the Board was developing a much more thoroughgoing regulation of the structure and functions of collective bargaining, and of the organisational and conflictual behaviour of workers and their unions. The AFL's leadership had not bargained on this when they pressed hard for the Wagner Act's passage, and was understandably miffed. Organised labour supported the Democratic cause in the 1936 election and lobbied Congress intensively for adequate funds to enable the NLRB to handle the massive caseload that almost swamped it in 1937–9. But the Board did not respond by behaving as the labour movement's grateful client. Instead, it acted more like a patron, confident that it alone had the strategic vision and the public responsibility to shape the labour movement to fit in with the requirements of its conception of the national interest.[38]

Modification of employer behaviour *vis-à-vis* unionisation struggles, recognition disputes, and the establishment of routine collective bargaining was much the greater part of the NLRB's achievement. It would be a mistake to play down this essential fact, as some contemporary 'critical legal theorists' appear to do. Especially after the return to economic recession and stagnation in the summer of 1937, and the recovery of conservative strength in local and state politics which followed, the NLRB offered the safest route to bargaining status for fledgling unions, particularly in the mass production industries. The NLRB was a vigorous and dedicated agency, certainly a partisan of the labour movement, and perhaps preferred its newer and weaker organisations in the CIO which actively besought its aid and fitted its model of the kind of labour unions large-scale industry 'needed'. The La Follette Committee of the Senate gave sterling service in revealing the most discreditable and violent aspects of the employers' anti-union tactics, creating a public opinion hostile to them and a disinclination on the part of many firms to use such crude and overt modes of anti-unionism. The NLRB backed that work up, ordering reinstatement of individuals dismissed for union membership or activity, with appropriate restitution for lesser discrimination, dis-establishing company unions and voiding 'sweetheart' contracts negotiated between AFL unions and employers which ignored workers' wishes. Employers were required to 'cease and desist' from a wide range of anti-union behaviour, and to post notices around their plants admitting their guilt and promising not to misbehave in future. They were required to negotiate with unions in 'good faith', which the Board proceeded to define, on a range of mandatory issues, which it determined in developing case law. And they were obliged to formalise their agreements in written, fixed-term contracts, to confine their recognition and negotiations *exclusively* to a certified majority representative, and in effect to obey a code of positively acceptable labour practices which the Board developed and the judiciary, with relatively few exceptions, endorsed.[39]

So much for the good news. Before proceeding to the less good, or positively bad, it is worth emphasising that even during the peak years 1937–9 when the NLRB was providing ' "the outstanding instance during the present century of an aggressive programme sustained over powerful opposition of regulated parties" (and) "the most high powered and effective law enforcement in our history" ', and when it was dealing with a massive caseload both in unfair labour practice and representation cases, its work was not entirely successful, even by its own standards. Delays created by a burgeoning load which grew faster than staff could be recruited and trained, exacerbated by the need to take decisions ignored or appealed by employers to successive stages of the judicial system for review and enforcement, reduced the effectiveness of NLRB intervention. Employers *could* perfectly well ignore and obstruct NLRB orders if they chose. The cost was high in legal fees and possibly in back pay, and could result in workers who were dissatisfied with the rewards of following orderly procedures deciding to strike to try and win recognition or effective bargaining rights. But those were costs many firms were willing to incur, because the course seemed *right* and because the rewards of weakening and demoralising a union unable to win anything for its new, imperfectly attached members, or to strike with equanimity in a stagnant economy, looked worthwhile. Growth in union membership still depended on organising initiatives, grass-roots militancy, good tactics and strategy, and persistence, as much as on the NLRB. And, as the years 1940–5 were to prove, it was far more responsive to the course of economic recovery and re-employment than it was to a favourable turn in federal policy after 1937. Perhaps the most that can be said for the NLRB's work in its heroic period, 1937–9, is that the NLRB prevented too severe a fall-off, and facilitated slight recovery in union membership after the shock of the 1937–8 recession when worker militancy, and union activists' *élan*, visibly diminished, along with public tolerance of the most effective organisational tools – especially the sit-down strike – deployed to such effect in 1936–7.[40]

The end of voluntarism and the tightening of controls

And now for the really bad news. The Wagner Act, by making policy-making in labour relations a matter of continuous administrative regulation, progressively denied unions the autonomy they had long cherished. From 1937 onwards, they discovered that the decisive turn away from voluntarism meant that their *own* institutional prerogatives were open to NLRB and judicial challenge as well as those of the employers who were the Act's prime – and, in their eyes, exclusive – targets. The AFL, in particular, as Christopher Tomlins has reminded us, was horrified to discover that, by order of a Board it had played a large part in creating and nurturing, some of its customary organising tactics (e.g. signing up with employers rather than, or before, enrolling workers into membership) were outlawed, and the resulting contracts, sometimes containing valuable closed-shop provisions, declared null and void. In the name of protecting the individual employee's right to choose, the Board denied AFL unions full freedom to exploit employer preference for them over those of the novel and less respectable CIO as a shortcut to the unions' institutional objectives – expanded membership, however recruited, and bargaining rights, however unfavourable the terms of those bargains might be to the workers' concerned. The NLRB went beyond this. It used its exclusive power to determine what was an appropriate unit for collective bargaining *and fulfilling the purposes of the Act* – increasingly defined as industrial peace and stabilised, efficient labour relations – in order to establish the structure of collective bargaining, whether on a single or multi-plant basis, employing industrial or craft units. It did this in a way which ignored established AFL unions' pretensions to define their own jurisdictions, and to suit their bargaining structure to their own best estimates of what suited each situation. The NLRB's unit determinations could favour one union over another in a competition for members and exclusive bargaining rights. They even came to define the conditions under which craftsmen (or those the AFL was ready to call such) would be granted, at the Board's entire discretion, the privilege of an election to determine whether they wanted to be separately represented or not. Increasingly, NLRB policies dictated an appropriate structure for union organisation and collective bargaining responsive to 'experts'' readings of what public policy required rather than workers' or unions' attempts to follow their ingrained traditions and the dictates of their own interests. Simultaneously, NLRB decisions, judicial rulings, and limitations on strike activity imposed by the economic stagnation of 1937–9 and the unions' wartime no-strike pledge of 1941–5, blocked off the possibility that unions might ignore NLRB rulings and escape their impact by using the age-old techniques of the recognition strike, boycott, or secondary action. Even before Taft–Hartley was enacted in 1947, unions were finding themselves increasingly entrapped within a formal and legalistic structure of rules, which declared orderly resort to NLRB machinery and acceptance of Board decisions, however unpalatable, to be the only way to win the valuable status of legitimate, legally protected, collective bargaining representative.

NLRB policy, increasingly influenced by the Supreme Court after 1939, became positively unhelpful in certain areas. Definition of subjects where collective bargaining was mandatory showed employers where they need not even go through the forms of negotiation on union demands on non-mandatory issues, since any attempt to enforce them would not enjoy the law's protection. 'Economic' strikers' right to strike was in practice restricted by permitting employers permanently to replace them, and giving them no right to be rehired. Even before Taft–Hartley specified unfair labour practices that workers and unions might commit, thereby running in to legal penalites, the Board and the courts had already written some of them into case law – even though the Wagner Act had been silent on this and had, indeed, stated that none of its provisions were to be so interpreted as to infringe upon the right to strike. That did not stop the Board identifying certain kinds of strike whose methods or objects disqualified the strikers from the Act's protections. The unluckiest workers of all were those, like foremen and supervisors, whom the Board and the courts decided were not 'workers' at all, when it came to enjoying Wagner Act protection; their self-organisational efforts were fully exposed to employer hostility.[41]

This picture of the complex reality of federal labour law in the 1940s is one with which critical legal historians like Tomlins and Klare would probably not disagree – which, indeed, they helped construct. But how are we to explain the course of development that law and public policy followed? Scholarship like theirs, or James Atleson's, which concentrates on the words and rationales of judicial and administrative decisions, taking legal and bureaucratic processes, and judges' and bureaucrats' ideological preferences as the primary determinants of the reign of rules, misses a great deal of the truth.

A more satisfying account must be based on a broader awareness of the political context in which rulemakers' opinions were formed, and of the institutional pressures to which they were subjected. Nor should we neglect the larger forces – of members' expectations, unions' institutional structures and goals, and employers' policies and objectives – which pushed all immediately interested parties to work towards, and ultimately accept, the collective bargaining model of limited, responsible, economistic 'industrial pluralism'. The role of the law was important, but it was neither the exclusive, nor even the primary, determinant of what happened. The law was, after all, often irrelevant to everyday outcomes, and always itself more determined than determining.

The course of administrative and, to some extent, judicial decision-making is explained partly by the fact that the Wagner Act gave the Board wide discretion to implement a policy some of whose premises were contradictory. The Board, prodded by the courts, had to resolve them. Thus, for example, employees' exercise of their right to self-organisation, unfettered by employer actions *but under NLRB supervision*, was supposed to lead more or less automatically towards the establishment of satisfactory collective bargaining relationships, industrial peace, etc. As time went on, the NLRB increasingly ruled that employee self-organisation was only the *means*; orderly collective bargaining (enshrined in ongoing contractual relations) was the Act's major objective. What if employees exercising their free choice should want to break away from an existing bargaining unit unsatisfactory to them, or seek a new union to represent them while an existing union had a valid contract? In such a situation, the Board came to rule that order and stability came first: breakaway unionism threatened bargaining structures it had deemed satisfactory to effect the purposes of the Act, and the institution of the fixed-term contract. Accordingly, the Board would only allow craft or professional groups the privilege of separation from an existing unit if they met stringent conditions and the Board judged that the situation merited it; and would deny any dissidents the opportunity to challenge an existing duly-certified representative for a year after a Board certification, or up to two years if a valid contract ran that long. The Congress made it even harder for changes of representative to take place; and the NLRB and the courts devised sanctions to protect NLRB certifications and established contractual relationships from disturbance by 'direct action'.

But why did the Board, the courts, and Congress, decide these difficult and ambiguous questions as they did? The answer is that the Wagner Act irreversibly politicised industrial relations. Disputes between managers and workers, employers and unions, unions and unions, unions and the NLRB, were not finally resolved by the NLRB's ambitious bureaucrats, even when the federal judiciary upheld its decisions rather than, as on occasion, overturning them or pushing them in new and 'safe' directions. The theory of administrative regulation was that the Board was impartial, expert, autonomous. But in practice it was not perceived as such by contending parties; and in truth it was far from autonomous. From 1935–9 the NLRB ignored rising opposition to its policies from employers, the press, conservative politicians and finally the disillusioned AFL, much the stronger of the rival labour organisations. It did not enjoy the Roosevelt administration's favour – indeed, it was treated as a political liability. The NLRB achieved four years of autonomy, acted as if it were invulnerable, did not trim its policies to accommodate presidential unease, AFL grievances, or business and conservative hostility. It neglected the vital task of winning itself a constituency – it did nothing to attempt to counter its bad press, built no political bridges. This was dangerous folly: it made the NLRB an unnecessarily easy target for its enemies, at the same time as alienating friends or neutrals.

An administrative agency can be harassed by elected branches of government, responsive to insistent lobbyists, in a number of ways. The President nominated Board members; the Senate had to approve them; the House had to appropriate sufficient funds for it *each year*. In 1939 a conservative House of Representatives, revitalised by Republican rightists elected in 1938 in the wake of the Roosevelt recession, dominated by a coalition of Republicans and Southern Democrats from low-wage, newly industrialising states determined to preserve the advantage freedom from unionisation gave them, subjected the Board to a debilitating and prolonged investigation. Out of that investigation came a set of proposed Wagner Act 'amendments' which the AFL and organised business, for their different purposes, supported, and which later formed the basis of the Taft–Hartley Act. Roosevelt responded to this pressure by failing to reappoint Board members discredited for enforcing the Act too vigorously and independently, and thereby saved himself from future political embarrassment by pushing Board policies in the direction of 'order and stability'. Even after the Board's policies 'moderated', and its personnel had been 'cleansed' of politically suspect characters – communists or outright partisans of industrial unionism – the NLRB remained vulnerable, however accommodating it tried to be. The AFL, by getting its friends to tag a 'rider' onto successive appropriations bills, was able to deny the NLRB power to revoke closed shop contracts secured by an unrepresentative, minority union – often through collusion with the employer. Organised business, by getting its conservative congressional friends to propose swingeing restrictive legislation, succeeded in persuading the NLRB to change its mind and deny mass-production supervisors the Wagner Act's protection.[42]

The simple fact is that, once labour relations had become politicised, the NLRB found itself with only one constituency to which to appeal for protection, the organised labour movement. By its own policies it had succeeded in alienating the AFL, the most significant part of the movement. And when it came to the crunch, the NLRB was dependent on the actions of a Congress where rural districts were flagrantly over-represented and where there were far more legislators responsive to the dominant economic interests of their constituencies as reflected by the anti-union local elites who provided party finance and organisation, than there were from the metropolitan and industrial districts where the Democratic Party had turned into an approximation of the British Labour Party. In such a situation, there was only one way the heavily politicised federal labour policy could develop, and that was in the direction of promoting order, stability, efficiency, and industrial 'peace' – and even then that proved insufficient to fend off the business/conservative attack which eventuated in Taft–Hartley.[43]

The pressures of war, 1941–1945

There is a further important reason for the conservative, institution-building turn clearly taken by federal labour relations policy after 1940. That is, quite simply, the demands of wartime economic mobilisation for freedom from 'unpatriotic disruption' (as strikes were generally perceived) and from destabilising wage inflation. Those great pressures led to the creation of two more temporary, but vastly important, federal labour relations bureaucracies which took over the primary responsibility for shaping and controlling the American labour movement.

The National Defense Mediation Board (NDMB) of March–November 1941, and its stronger successor, the National War Labor Board (NWLB) of January 1942–August 1945 (which actually kept operating until 1946, but with only a shadow of its former authority after V–J Day), were much more powerful than the NLRB had ever been. They did not have to worry about judicial review, though a heavy caseload led to long delays for the NWLB in 1943 in particular. They had full authority, as a result of executive orders under the war powers of the presidency, to settle any labour dispute by conciliation, mediation, or compulsory arbitration. They were supposed to act in conformity with relevant federal statutes (particularly the Wagner Act), and generally did so; and their autonomy in setting wage policy was increasingly restricted as the war progressed. Nevertheless, the NDMB and, even more, NWLB enjoyed a wide-ranging freedom that the NLRB never possessed, and they had a full panoply of enforcement devices at their disposal – from persuasion and horse-trading, through moral blackmail, up to and including denial of union security and revocation of favourable contract terms (for labour), and federal seizure and operation of plants (for management).

They were tripartite in structure, so that 'voluntarism' was in theory preserved by moving bargaining from the level of the plant or firm to that of the industry commission, or the regional or national board, in each of which organised business and labour were represented. But, in practice, voluntarism came to mean simply the right to participate, to be informed, to share responsibility for Board decisions *and for their acceptance* by the interested parties' 'constituents'. The Boards worked, in that they produced 'practical', conservative, compromise solutions, more or less acceptable to both sides and to the federal government. Industrial production was rarely inconvenienced by strikes; the lid was kept on increases in workers' basic rates of pay; the 'national interest' was served.[44]

NDMB/NWLB experience pointed the way towards continued federal intervention to determine the outcome of important collective bargains in peacetime – via 'fact-finding' boards in 1945–7, Taft–Hartley's emergency disputes provisions, or successive counter-inflation policies. In the short term, they perfected the decentralised, 'private' institutions for controlled industrial conflict developed under state sponsorship since 1933. They were far stronger than the NLRB: it could not determine the terms of a collective agreement, but simply state that on certain subjects bargaining in good faith was obligatory on management (and, increasingly, on labour too); it could push both sides to negotiate and observe written, fixed-term contracts, but could not order them to establish machinery to guarantee observance.

The NDMB and NWLB operated under no such limitations. As representatives of labour and management were opposed on all the most important issues coming before them, it was the *public members* of the Boards who came to occupy the balance of power. They had a continuous, expert presence; they had significant prior experience, and a 'received wisdom' to guide them in their institution-building task. While the NLRB continued with the important business of operating its machinery for unions to win recognition, even against employer hostility, without the dangers of a strike, and policing the conduct of both sides in routine collective bargaining, the NWLB had a much more interesting job. Accordingly, many NLRB staffers migrated to the rival agency with the free-wheeling style, higher salaries, and draft exemptions. It selected the most useful and acceptable precedents of 'mature collective bargaining' in prewar industry, and imposed its model of labour relations on unions and employers over their strong protests. It *generalised* certain characteristics of America's relatively few stable labour relations systems, applying them to the industrial unions and core firms in the durable goods industries; these lay at the vital heart of the war economy and had no indigenous bargaining history to speak of at all.[45]

The NWLB made important contributions to several critical developments. It established institutionally secure unions, constrained to behave 'responsibly' as the price of acceptance by employers, and tolerance or support from the state. It further defined the scope and area of collective bargaining, confining it to matters of wages, hours and working conditions, for the most part at the level of the plant, firm, or community, rather than region or industry. It developed orderly grievance procedures, in which the union's role was strictly reactive, and there was little room for fractional bargaining and 'enhancement' of the contract by pressure and 'interpretation', by imposing a legalistic system of arbitration. It more or less completed the process of training and establishing an interrelated labour relations 'profession' and federal bureaucracy which had begun in 1933: in effect, it created a massive short-term demand for manpower (especially lawyers and economists) on its own staff and in firms and unions bringing cases before it, and a longer-term demand resulting from the specialised expertise – of arbitrators, labour lawyers, job analysts, fringe-benefit and payment-systems consultants, etc. – they needed to operate the complex bargaining systems it bequeathed. The NWLB acted as a 'transmission belt' for the received wisdom of the fathers of America's academic industrial-relations business, relaying it, but without any of the radical implications it had had in their younger days, as occupational ideology and institutional inheritance into the postwar world.[46]

Conclusions

By the end of the war, as a result of the combined efforts of the NLRB and NWLB, the American labour movement was unprecedentedly strong, at least as measured by statistics of membership, contractual relationships, closed shop, union shop, maintenance of membership, or dues checkoff agreements, and other conventional indices. But it was also unprecedentedly dependent on the federal government, trapped in a situation where it was defenceless against intervention from new 'friends' (the NLRB) as well as familiar old antagonists – unsympathetic courts, actively hostile state and federal legislatures, recovering their power and reactionary self-confidence.

During the 1930s, the labour movement had actively sought federal assistance for the straightforward purpose of weakening or even neutralising the power of its opponents. In those terms, the Norris–La Guardia and Wagner Acts had been unqualified successes. What the labour movement had not generally seen (but could have) was that, once the unions became agents of public policy – whether its objectives were the defence of employee rights, the 'equalisation' of their bargaining power, the redistribution of income, the elimination of violent and potentially destabilising industrial conflict, or any other of the Wagner Act's liberal purposes – they were undeniably 'affected with a public interest'. They owed a substantial measure of their power, if not their existence, to the state. Accordingly, they could expect continuous interference from it, and had no credible intellectual defences, nor sufficient independent political strength, to set against that unwanted development.[47]

Even before Taft–Hartley, the NLRB, NWLB, judiciary and Congress had shown what this might mean. The Supreme Court, for example, had begun to develop a 'duty of fair representation' which meant that unions enjoying exclusive bargaining rights and closed-shop contracts under the law could not discriminate *themselves* against members, potential members, or non-members on grounds of race. Unions were no longer voluntary associations, in the eyes of the law: they were quasi-public institutions, and could expect to be treated as such. Congress agreed, and began to require financial reports from unions under the provisions of the (misnamed) War Labor Disputes Act of 1943. This development led directly to Taft–Hartley's and Landrum–Griffin's many and more serious limitations on unions' membership requirements, internal disciplinary procedures, financial administration, and freedom to elect or select their own office-holders in their own way.[48]

Labour's dilemma was real, and was probably inevitable. In politics, it had nowhere to go but the Democratic Party, however unreliable a friend that proved to be. In labour relations matters, against persistent employer opposition, in a situation where the direct action alternative to NLRB and NWLB procedures was uncertain at best, dangerous at worst, it had to use the channels the federal government provided, however constricting. And, by and large, it *chose* to. For the simple fact is that 'responsible unionism' *paid off*. During the war, unions observing the no-strike pledge, not pressing their members' economic demands with the full weight of their bargaining power, obtained institutional security of income and membership, a recognised status in the plant or firm, liberal fringe benefits, some extensions of joint consultation and even bargaining, and arbitration-terminated grievance systems which denied employer demands for unilateral authority *at the same time* as they confined unions and their members within the language of contract and the time-consuming, legalistic procedures. It is not self-evident that 'irresponsible' unionism would have secured more than this, given the willingness and ability of Congress and the administration to strike at non-complying unions in a variety of harmful ways.[49]

Similarly, the NLRB denied some workgroups the ability to choose, or change their bargaining representative, or narrowly specified the conditions under which that might be done. It became less vigorous and effective in resisting employer unfair labour practices, especially as the latter became more technical and sophisticated, though no less effective (e.g. anti-union propaganda which the Supreme Court defended as 'free speech'). And it defined certain categories of strikers – those attempting to change a contract before its term, acting in violation of a contract, employing illegitimate force, attempting to overthrow or ignore a ruling of the NLRB or some other federal agency, etc. – as unprotected by the Act against the full weight of an employer's power to hire and fire. But the unions evidently still found the Board useful and necessary, as witnessed by their heavy reliance on its machinery and protections, their attempt to defend it in 1946–7, and the desperation of new, weak organisations, like the Foremen's Association of America, to get in under its leaky umbrella as the *best* protection against active employer hostility, otherwise utterly unrestrained.[50]

Federal labour relations policy from 1932 to 1947 simultaneously strengthened the unions as institutions and circumscribed their role. The unions were fortunate indeed that a liberal, but not a very interested or sympathetic, administration was brought to do this in probably the only set of circumstances when American public policy *could* have taken such a dramatic deviation from its past courses. Only the collapse and chronic stagnation of the economy, the desperate search for answers and palliatives, the massive turnover of state and federal politicians, the partial 'revolution' in the balance and social bases of the two main parties' support, and the accompanying erosion of the political influence of the business community, could have created an opportunity for something like the Wagner Act. Only the advent of full employment in a time of war, when the state had to intervene directly and continuously in industrial relations to preserve a working social harmony, guarantee uninterrupted production, and maintain economic equilibrium, could have provided such a favourable environment for the new unions of the 1930s to become entrenched, and continue to grow. They did so under the auspices of a relatively liberal regime that preferred to rely on manipulation in its management of the clash of domestic class interests, and which was itself probably saved by the war from the full effects of the conservative reaction already setting-in in 1937–8.

In this conjuncture, America's labour movement enjoyed 15 years when, at different times, the political climate, the tightness of the labour market, the spontaneous militancy (*or* organisability) of its potential membership, all favoured it. And America's budding labour relations experts had unprecedented opportunities for employment, on-the-job training, and real creative influence on that 'responsible' labour movement and pluralistic, rational industrial relations system they were dedicated to building. From 1932 to 1947 both the labour movement and its nurturing, confining, nanny-like bureaucracy enjoyed an extended period of extraordinary freedom to develop a new industrial relations system which may well have come to serve a system-sustaining function, but which was created only over the strenuous, but unsuccessful opposition of a business community displaying an unusual degree of unity in its hostility, of a press which served as its mouth-piece, and of a conservative political establishment only temporarily weakened by economic collapse and political disorder.

Given the American labour movement's pre-New Deal weakness – its ideological subordination, political dependence, marginal legal status, organisational impotence – it is scarcely possible to conceive of the creation and entrenchment of what was, for all its glaring deficiencies, the nearest thing to a dynamic, inclusive, mass movement that the American industrial working class has ever managed to put together, without the transformation in public policy after 1932. The resulting labour movement certainly has benefited *non*-members, as many employers desirous of keeping their workforces nonunion have felt compelled to extend the same kinds of benefits, but without the influence over working practices and the right to challenge management's personnel policy decisions, to groups of employees potentially vulnerable to organisation efforts. The labour movement has also been, until relatively recently, one of the few substantial nationally organised constituencies for broadly egalitarian and welfarist causes in the United States.

This achievement may not impress contemporary critics who emphasise the confinement of the dwindling labour movement within the web of rules liberal 'experts' helped spin. But what were the alternatives? Given the political outlook and industrial relations policies of the American business community, and the means of domination it commands, now and in the past; given the ideological resilience of capitalism, and its broad mass appeal, even during the New Deal years; given the limited and instrumental attitude of most industrial workers towards the employment relationship and their unions, and the ability of the system to satisfy or contain them from that day to this: what better thing was on offer than liberal reform and a somewhat rationalised, civilised capitalism? What else had a mass constituency, or any hopes of realisation? What was achieved, against the odds, as a result of a wildly unlikely sequence and conjuncture of circumstances, surely looks quite impressive.[51]

NOTES

1 On American labour in the 1940s, see David Brody, 'The Uses of Power. I: Industrial Battleground', in Brody, *Workers in Industrial America* (New York, 1980); for industrial conflict, see Paul K. Edwards, *Strikes in the United States, 1881–1974* (Oxford, 1981).

2 Irving Bernstein, *The New Deal Collective Bargaining Policy* (Berkeley and Los Angeles, 1950); Sidney Fine, *The Automobile Under the Blue Eagle* (Ann Arbor, 1963); James A. Gross, *The Making of the National Labor Relations Board* (Albany, NY, 1974); J. Joseph Huthmacher, *Senator Robert F. Wagner and the Rise of Urban Liberalism* (New York, 1968), especially ch. 10 – for examples of the genre.

3 See Stanley Aronwitz, *False Promises: the Shaping of American Working Class Consciousness* (New York, 1973); Barton J. Bernstein, 'The New Deal: the Conservative Achievements of Liberal Reform', in *idem* (ed.), *Towards a New Past* (New York, 1978), especially pp. 269, 273–6; Jeremy Brecher, *Strike!* (Boston, 1975), especially ch. 5; Gabriel Kolko, *Main Currents in Modern American History* (New York, 1976); Frances F. Piven and Richard Cloward, *Poor People's Movements: Why They Succeed, How They Fail* (New York, 1977), ch. 3; Ronald Radosh, 'The Corporate Ideology of American Labor Leaders from Gompers to Hillman', *Studies on the Left* 6, part 6 (November–December 1966), pp. 66–88 – all examples of New Left history and analysis, seen at its worst in G. William Domhoff, *The Higher Circles: the Governing Class in America* (New York, 1970), ch. 6, and Rick Hurd's ludicrous 'New Deal Labor Policy and the Containment of Radical Union Activity', *Review of Radical Political Economics* 8 (Fall 1976), pp. 32–43.

4 The most satisfying political analysis is offered by Fred Block, in 'The Ruling Class Does Not Rule: Notes on the Marxist Theory of the State', *Socialist Revolution* 33 (1977), pp. 6–28, and his critic Theda Skocpol, 'Political Response to Capitalist Crisis: Neo-Marxist Theories of the State and the Case of New Deal', *Politics and Society* 10 (1980), pp. 155–201.

5 For 'critical legal studies', see especially Karl Klare, 'Judicial Deradicalization of the Wagner Act and the Origins of Modern Legal Consciousness, 1937–1941', *Minnesota Law Review* 62 (1978), pp. 265–339, and *idem*, 'Labor Law as Ideology: Toward a New Historiography of Collective Bargaining Law', *Industrial Relations Law Journal* 4 (1981), pp. 450–82, with its comprehensive bibliography. More satisfying are James B. Atleson, *Values and Assumptions in American Labor Law* (Amherst, Mass., 1983), and Christopher L. Tomlins, 'The State and the Unions: Federal Labor Relations Policy and the Organized Labor Movement in America, 1933–55' (Ph.D. diss., Johns Hopkins, 1980).

6 Richard P. McCormick, 'The Party Period and Public Policy: An Explanatory Hypothesis', *Journal of American History* 66 (1979), pp. 279–98; Stephen L. Skowronek, *Building a New American State: The Expansion of National Administrative Capacities, 1877–1920* (Cambridge, 1982), ch. 2.

7 For the social background to judicial policy making, see Jerold Auerbach, *Unequal Justice: Lawyers and Social Change in Modern America* (New York, 1976); Arnold M. Paul, *Conservative Crisis and the Rule of Law: Attitudes of Bar and Bench, 1887–1895* (Ithaca, NY, 1960); and

on voluntarism, Haggai Hurvitz, 'The Meaning of Industrial Conflict in Some Ideologies of the Early 1920s: The AFL, Organized Employers, and Herbert Hoover' (Ph.D. diss., Columbia University, 1971), esp. ch. 4.

8 On the community dimension in industrial conflict, see especially Delbert C. Miller and William H. Form, *Industry, Labor, and Community* (New York, 1960); and for 'law-enforcement', see Howard M. Gitelman, 'Perspectives on American Industrial Violence', *Business History Review* 47 (1973), pp. 1–23, and Robert J. Goldstein, *Political Repression in Modern America: from 1870 to the Present* (Cambridge, Mass. and New York, 1978).

9 Hurvitz, 'Meaning of Industrial Conflict', ch. 4; Tomlins, 'State and the Unions', especially ch. 2.

10 Edwin E. Witte, *The Government in Labor Disputes* (New York, 1932), ch. 11.

11 Jerry Cooper, *The Army and Civil Disorders: Federal Military Intervention in Labor Disputes, 1877–1900* (Westport, Conn., 1980).

12 Edward Berman, *Labor Disputes and the President of the United States* (New York, 1924); Robert H. Wiebe, 'The Anthracite Strike of 1902: A Record of Confusion', *Mississippi Valley Historical Review* 48 (1961), pp. 229–51; Gerald G. Eggert, *Railroad Labor Disputes: The Beginnings of Federal Strike Policy* (Ann Arbor, Michigan, 1967) – for the development of federal mediation; on industrial relations more broadly, see John Lombardi, *Labor's Voice in the Cabinet: A History of the Department of Labor from Its Origins to 1921* (New York, 1942); John S. Smith, 'Organized Labor and Government in the Wilson Era: Some Conclusions', *Labor History* 3 (1962), pp. 265–86; and Melvyn Dubofsky, 'Abortive Reform: The Wilson Administration and Organized Labor', in James E. Cronin and Carmen Sirianni (eds.), *Work, Community and Power: The Experience of Labor in Europe and America, 1900–1925* (Philadelphia, Pa, 1983).

13 On the NCF, the best and most recent source is Bruno Ramirez, *When Workers Fight: The Politics of Industrial Relations in the Progressive Era* (Westport, Conn., 1978), especially ch. 4.

14 Dubofsky, 'Abortive Reform'; Simeon Larson, *Labor and Foreign Policy: Gompers, the AFL, and the First World War, 1914–1918* (Rutherford, NJ, 1975); for the effectiveness of repression, see especially William Preston, *Aliens and Dissenters: Federal Suppression of Radicals, 1903–1933* (Cambridge, Mass., 1963).

15 US Bureau of the Census, *Historical Statistics of the United States* (Washington, DC, 1960), Table D–735, p. 97. Lewis Lorwin, *The American Federation of Labor* (Washington, DC, 1933), part 3: Lombardi, *Labor's Voice*, part 3; Hurvitz, 'Meaning of Industrial Conflict', chs. 1–3.

16 For the full statement, see W. Jett Lauck and Claude S. Watts, *The Industrial Code* (New York, 1922), pp. 267–73.

17 David O. Bowman, *Public Control of Labor Relations: A Study of the National Labor Relations Board* (New York, 1942), p. 10.

18 For the NWLB, see Valerie J. Conner, *The National War Labor Board*

(Chapel Hill, NC, 1983); near-contemporary accounts are in some respects more satisfactory – see Alexander M. Bing, *Wartime Strikes and Their Adjustment* (New York, 1921); Gordon S. Watkins, *Labor Problems and Labor Administration in the United States During the World War* (Urbana, Ill., 1920); and Frank J. Warne, *The Workers at War* (New York, 1920), especially chs. 9–11. See also, for detail, NLRB, Division of Economic Research, *Bulletin* No. 1 (August 1936), 'Governmental Protection of Labor's Right to Organize' (Washington, DC, 1936), especially pp. 130–41.

19 Hurvitz, 'Meaning of Industrial Conflict', especially chs. 2–3. For a telling example of the limits to managerial 'war liberalism', see Gerald G. Eggert, *Steelmasters and Labor Reform, 1886–1923* (Pittsburgh, Pa, 1981), ch. 5.

20 David Brody, *Labor in Crisis: The Steel Strike of 1919* (Philadelphia, 1965), remains the best overview of this period, but see also Haggai Hurvitz, 'Ideology and Industrial Conflict: President Wilson's First Industrial Conference of October 1919', *Labor History* 18 (1977), pp. 509–24. On employee representation plans, see Daniel Nelson, 'The Company Union Movement, 1900–1937: A Reexamination', *Business History Review* 56 (1982), pp. 335–57; on belligerent anti-unionism, see Allen M. Wakstein, 'The Open Shop Movement, 1919–1933' (Ph.D. diss., University of Illinois, 1961); and for the 1920s, Irving Bernstein, *The Lean Years: A History of the American Worker 1920–1933* (Boston, Mass., 1960), chs. 1–4.

21 Erik Olssen, 'The Making of a Political Machine: The Railroad Unions Enter Politics', *Labor History* 19 (1978), pp. 373–96; Robert H. Zeiger, *Republicans and Labor 1919–29* (Lexington, Ky, 1969), ch. 9.

22 See Paul J. McNulty, *The Origins and Development of Labor Economics* (Cambridge, Mass., 1980), especially chs. 6–7; Milton Derber, *The American Idea of Industrial Democracy 1865–1965* (Urbana, Ill., 1970), sections 1–3. For studies of the fathers of the labour relations profession, see J. Michael Eisner, *William Morris Leiserson: A Biography* (Madison, Wisconsin, 1967), especially chs. 2, 4; Theron F. Schlabach, *Edwin E. Witte: Cautious Reformer* (Madison, Wisconsin, 1969), pp. 21–31, ch. 10; Edward B. Shils *et al.*, *Industrial Peacemaker: George W. Taylor's Contributions to Collective Bargaining* (Philadelphia, Pa, 1979), especially pp. 6, 10, 17, and ch. 3.

23 Jesse T. Carpenter, *Competition and Collective Bargaining in the Needle Trades, 1910–1967* (Ithaca NY, 1972); Steve Fraser, 'Rehearsal for the New Deal: Shop-Floor Insurgents, Political Elites, and Industrial Democracy in the Amalgamated Clothing Workers', in Michael H. Frisch and Daniel J. Walkowitz (eds.), *Working-Class America: Essays on Labor, Community, and American Society* (Urbana, Ill., 1983), pp. 212–55, is a good recent study; Julius H. Cohen, *Law and Order in Industry: Five Years' Experience* (New York, 1916), an important contemporary account from the employer's side.

24 William M. Leiserson, 'Constitutional Government in American Industries', *American Economic Review* 12 (1922), *Supplement*, pp.

56–79; Eisner, *Leiserson*, ch. 5; Shils, *et al.*, *Industrial Peacemaker*, ch. 2. For later influence of this model, see George B. Heliker, 'Grievance Arbitration in the Automobile Industry: A Comparative Analysis of Its History and Results in the Big Three' (Ph.D. diss., University of Michigan, 1954).

25 For the conventional wisdom of labour relations academics, see NLRB, Division of Economic Research, *Bulletin* No. 1, and No. 4, (November 1939), 'Written Trade Agreements in Collective Bargaining' (Washington, DC, 1940), with Ordway Tead and Henry C. Metcalf, *Labor Relations Under the Recovery Act* (New York, 1933).

26 I. Bernstein, *Lean Years*, especially ch. 11; Schlabach, *Witte*, ch. 4; Tomlins, 'State and the Unions', pp. 135–6.

27 Charles O. Gregory, *Labor and the Law* (New York, 1946), chs. 10, 12; Irving Bernstein, *The Turbulent Years: A History of the American Worker, 1933–1941* (Boston, Mass., 1970), ch. 13; Archibald Cox, *Law and the National Labor Policy* (Berkeley, CA, 1960), pp. 4–6.

28 I. Bernstein, *New Deal Collective Bargaining Policy*, ch. 3; Bowman, *Public Control*, pp. 20–8; Grant N. Farr, *The Origins of Recent Labor Policy* (Boulder, Colorado, 1959); Louis Galambos, *Competition and Coercion: The Emergence of a National Trade Association* (Baltimore, Md, 1966), especially ch. 8; Robert F. Himmelberg, *The Origins of the National Recovery Administration* (New York, 1976), ch. 10, especially pp. 207–9.

29 For the NIRA period see, in addition to sources cited in n. 2, Lewis L. Lorwin and Arthur Wubnig, *Labor Relations Boards: the Regulation of Collective Bargaining Under the NIRA* (Washington, DC, 1935), and Leverett Lyons (ed.), *The National Recovery Administration: An Analysis and Appraisal* (Washington, DC, 1935).

30 On the passage of the Wagner Act, good recent accounts are Daniel A. Sipe, 'A Moment of the State: the Enactment of the National Labor Relations Act, 1935' (Ph.D. diss., University of Pennsylvania, 1981), especially chs. 5–6, and Peter H. Irons, *The New Deal Lawyers* (Princeton, NJ, 1982), Section 3, especially chs. 10–13.

31 NLRB, Division of Economic Research, 'Governmental Protection of Labor's Right to Organize', especially part 1; Huthmacher, *Wagner*, especially ch. 10.

32 Klare, 'Judicial Deradicalization'. For a comparable refutation see Anon., 'Comment: The Radical Potential of the Wagner Act: The Duty to Bargain Collectively', *University of Pennsylvania Law Review* 129 (1981), pp. 1392–426.

33 For this view, see Tead and Metcalf, *Labor Relations Under the Recovery Act*, especially chs. 1, 5, 7–8; NLRB Division of Economic Research, 'Governmental Protection of Labor's Right to Organize', especially pp. 18, 27–31; Clinton S. Golden and Harold J. Ruttenberg, *The Dynamics of Industrial Democracy* (New York, 1942); and Morris L. Cooke and Philip Murray, *Organized Labor and Production* (New York, 1940).

34 See James A. Ward, 'Image and Reality: The Railway Corporate-State

Metaphor', *Business History Review* 55 (1981), pp. 491–516; Rowland Berthoff, 'The "Freedom to Control" in American Business History', in David H. Pinkney and Theodore Ropp (eds.), *A Festschrift for Frederick B. Artz* (Durham, NC, 1964), pp. 158–80; David J. Vogel, 'Why Businessmen Distrust Their State: The Political Consciousness of American Corporate Executives', *British Journal of Political Science* 8 (1978), pp. 45–78; Howell J. Harris, *The Right to Manage: Industrial Relations Policies of American Business in the 1940s* (Madison, Wisconsin, 1982), ch. 3; and, of course, Alfred D. Chandler, *The Visible Hand* (Cambridge, Mass., 1977).

35 Ellis W. Hawley, *The New Deal and the Problem of Monopoly* (Princeton, NJ, 1966); Galambos, *Competition and Coercion*; James P. Johnson, *The Politics of Soft Coal: The Bituminous Industry from World War I Through the New Deal* (Urbana, Ill., 1979).

36 Harris, *Right to Manage*, pp. 49–50; Derber, *American Idea of Industrial Democracy*, Sec. 5.

37 Brody's 'The Emergence of Mass-Production Unionism', in Brody, *Workers in Industrial America*, and his 'The Expansion of the American Labor Movement: Institutional Sources of Stimulus and Restraint', in Stephen E. Ambrose (ed.), *Institutions in Modern America: Innovations in Structure and Process* (Baltimore, MD, 1967), pp. 11–36, are essential reading, as is Stanley Vittoz, 'The Economic Foundations of Industrial Politics in the United States and the Emerging Structural Theory of the State in Capitalist Society: The Case of New Deal Labor Policy', *Amerikastudien/American Studies* 27 (1982), pp. 365–412, especially pp. 393–404 on G.M. and U.S. Steel. On the limits to NLRB effectiveness, see Harris, *Right to Manage*, p. 215, n. 19; and for the continuing importance of militant action, see Robert H. Zieger, 'The Union Comes to Covington: Virginia Papermakers Organize, 1933–1952', *Proceedings of the American Philosophical Society* 126, part 1 (1982), pp. 51–89.

38 Tomlins, 'State and the Unions', especially chs. 5–6.

39 Bowman, *Public Control*, part 2; Robert R. R. Brooks, *Unions of Their Own Choosing* (New Haven, Conn. 1939); James Gross, *The Reshaping of the National Labor Relations Board, 1937–1947* (Baltimore, Md, 1981).

40 Kenneth C. Davis, *Administrative Law Text* (St Paul, Minn., 1959), p. 8; and Louis L. Jaffe, *Administrative Law* (New York, 1953), pp. 79–80, quoted in Gross, *Making of the NLRB*, p. 1. Harris, *Right to Manage*, especially pp. 23–32; sources cited in n. 35.

41 Harry A. Millis and Emily Clark Brown, *From the Wagner Act to Taft–Hartley: A Study of National Labor Policy and Labor Relations* (Chicago, Ill., 1950), part 1, remains the most thorough study of NLRB policies, 1935–47. On the effective limitation of the 'right to strike' see Atleson, *Values and Assumptions*, especially ch. 1.

42 Tomlins, 'State and the Unions', chs. 5–6; Fred Witney, *Wartime Experiences of the National Labor Relations Board 1941–1945* (Urbana, Ill., 1949), especially chs 2, 7, 9, 13, for policy development;

Harris, *Right to Manage*, p. 82, on policy changes in the face of legislative pressure.
43 For inbuilt anti-labour bias, especially in the House, see R. Alton Lee, *Truman and Taft–Hartley: A Question of Mandate* (Lexington, Ky, 1966), and Seymour Z. Mann, 'Congressional Behavior and National Labor Policy – Structural Determinants of the Taft–Hartley Act' (Ph.D. diss., University of Chicago, 1951). See also Billy H. Wyche, 'Southern Industrialists View Organized Labor in the New Deal Years, 1933–1941', *Southern Studies* 19 (1980), pp. 157–71, to understand the sentiments and interests that Southern Democrats represented.
44 W. Ellison Chalmers *et al.*, 'Problems and Policies of Dispute Settlement and Wage Stabilization During World War II', US Department of Labor Bureau of Labor Statistics *Bulletin* No. 1009 (Washington, DC, 1950); Harris, *Right to Manage*, ch. 2.
45 Witney, *Wartime Experiences*, especially ch. 7, charts NLRB–NDMB–NWLB conflicts.
46 Harris, *Right to Manage*, especially pp. 47–58; Shils *et al.*, *Industrial Peacemaker*, on NWLB Vice-chairman and Chairman Taylor's work.
47 Tomlins, 'State and the Unions', especially ch. 7; Joseph Shister *et al.* (eds.), *Public Policy and Collective Bargaining* (New York, 1962), especially chs 1, 7.
48 Aaron Levenstein, *Labor Today and Tomorrow* (New York, 1946), ch. 5.
49 Joshua Freeman, 'Delivering the Goods: Industrial Unionism During World War II', *Labor History* 19 (1978), pp. 570–93; Nelson Lichtenstein, *Labor's War at Home: The CIO in World War II* (Cambridge, 1982), is not so pessimistic.
50 On supervisory unionism, see Harris, *Right to Manage*, especially pp. 78–87; Witney, *Wartime Experiences*, ch. 10.
51 Historians have begun to ask, and answer, the important, hard questions about the meaning, value, and potential of militancy in the 1930s. See David Brody, 'Radical Labor History and Rank-and-File Militancy', in Brody, *Workers in Industrial America*, pp. 146–57; Melvyn Dubofsky, 'Not so "Turbulent Years": Another Look at the American 1930s', *Amerikastudien/American Studies* 24 (1979), pp. 5–20; Ronald Schatz, 'American Electrical Workers: Work, Struggles, Aspirations, 1930–1950' (Ph.D. diss., University of Pittsburgh, 1977); Robert H. Zieger, 'The Limits of Militancy: Organizing Paper Workers, 1933–1935', *Journal of American History* 63 (1976), pp. 638–53.

6

Politics, law and shop floor bargaining in postwar Italy

GIOVANNI CONTINI

Introduction

When shop floor bargaining emerged in the late 1960s and early 1970s, it produced a crisis in Italian industrial relations. It was seen as something completely new; but a survey of the long-term trends shows that the traditional structure of industrial relations was reconstituting itself during this period of crisis. From the fascist period until the late 1960s, job control by Italian workers had been confined to limited informal bargaining, while industrial relations in general had been dominated by broader political interests. This supremacy of politics was to reappear in the late 1970s when the trade unions again became more and more concerned with their relations with the political system and saw the development of shop floor bargaining as something which threatened their control over their members.

But contemporary interpretations of the emergence of shop floor bargaining were dominated by the impression that they were dealing with a totally new situation, and most of them tended to attribute the change to a permanent structural modification of the workforce, or to major internal developments of trade union strategy and structure.

The leftist interpretation, which stretched from the far left groups across certain sections of the Communist Party to the *sinistra sindacale* (an influential left-wing current running through the principal unions) explained it as the behaviour of a totally new type of worker, the *operaio massa* (mass worker), a product of mass production and repetition work. This type of production undermined any work ethic, and the new worker was extremely mobile in the labour market, intelligent and revolutionary. This interpretation was influential in key sections of the trade unions in the early 1970s, although later many who had held this view completely reversed their positions.[1]

A second interpretation, which has become particularly common among the official historians of the unions, interpreted the changes as a result of a shift in the strategy of the unions in response to the repressive attitudes of employers in the 1950s and 1960s. The union leadership is seen as correcting past errors and initiating a new strategy at the top which was communicated to the shop floor.[2] A closely related account can be found in the writings of legal scholars, many of whom were personally involved in the transformation of Italian labour law. In this case, however, the emphasis falls primarily on the consolidation of workers' shop floor gains by the legal system through a formal recognition of newly acquired rights.[3]

Up to the end of the 1960s, economists tended to see the movement of the labour market as a simple reflection of wider macro-economic trends. In this period it seemed that deflationary policies had been able to restrain wage settlements, and some economists tried to apply Keynesian models based on the Phillips curve to explain swings in industrial conflict.[4] But the 'Hot Autumn' of 1969 and the continuing wave of strikes despite rising unemployment, clearly demanded an alternative explanation. In this vein, Paci showed that a segmented labour market did not respond mechanically to macro-economic trends and argued that the militancy of strong groups such as young, semi-skilled workers in large factories was unaffected by the deteriorating position of weaker groups such as women, older workers, and those employed in small firms.[5] Following this analysis, economists such as Salvati have emphasised the importance of legal and political institutions in the regulation of the labour market, tracing the links between the political system, legal reform and the emergence of new patterns of industrial conflict.[6]

Perhaps the most promising interpretation of the strike wave of 1968–72 is that produced by a group of sociologists led by Pizzorno. In this view, the key to understanding the struggles of this period lies in two distinctive features of Italian trade unions: their historical subordination to the political parties and their lack of effective organisation on the shop floor. The key figures in the strike wave were the new group of semi-skilled workers in the large factories of the north, who were not represented within the existing bargaining system and sought to take advantage of their favourable position in the labour market through direct and often unofficial action. But in order to make their struggles effective, the semi-skilled workers were soon forced to turn to the unions with their superior bargaining experience and organisational resources, and the latter took control of the movement and guided it into traditional institutional channels. By the middle of the 1970s, therefore, the wheel had come full circle and the historical subordination of Italian industrial relations to the political system was reaffirmed.[7]

Fruitful though this interpretation has been, two central difficulties emerge. On the one hand, little real weight is given to the empirical motives and demands of the strikers themselves, while on the other, the ultimate outcome of the strike wave appears more as a product of the general immobility of the Italian political system than of specific historical contingencies. Thus the aims of the strikers are deduced from the results of the struggles without a close analysis of their changing outlook and relationship to other social groups. As a consequence, the emergence of a new collective identity appears inexplicable and irrational, and workers' behaviour a mere passive adaptation to the strategic calculations of the unions and other institutions.[8] And as we shall see, the overall emphasis on the coherence and stability of the political system neglects the ways in which legal and political changes in the 1950s and 1960s themselves helped to undermine the established system of industrial relations, and overstates the inevitability of the eventual outcome.

With these objections in mind, this essay traces the evolution of shop floor bargaining in Italy from the fascist period through the 1980s, focussing in particular on the turning point of the late 1960s. The central emphasis throughout falls on the importance of legal and political change for the development of workplace industrial relations.

Two points need to be investigated in greater depth: first, the importance of 'cultural' changes within the working class; secondly, the importance of links between the political and legal system and the emergence of shop floor bargaining and its ensuing crisis. Elsewhere, I have looked more closely at the 'cultural' changes (see note 33). In this paper I focus on the second point and especially on the importance of the legal system.

Workers and the state under Fascism

The Fascists came to power in Italy in 1922 after two years of fierce and violent struggle against the labour movement. Many *Camere del Lavoro* (local bodies similar to trades councils) had their head-quarters vandalised and destroyed; as did the PSI (Italian Socialist Party). But the fascist movement did not consist of violent repression alone. Edmondo Rossoni, a former anarcho-syndicalist, had established a fascist trade union movement which for some years after the seizure of power tried to win support and build up membership among the workers by opposing the 'subversive trade unionism of the reds'. This new fascist trade unionism was to be 'constructive' rather than 'destructive'; but it remained a trade union, organised strikes when necessary and even proposed 'integral trade unionism' as the future model for the whole of fascist society.[9]

Historians have observed that the 1920s witnessed a transformation of Italian Fascism. Until 1925 the two components of Fascism, the 'movement' and the 'regime', worked in harmony; but from the middle of the decade the latter rapidly eclipsed the former. Under pressure from Mussolini Fascism became increasingly identified with the state. The Fascist Party itself was progressively weakened and deprived of any real political function. In this process, it was the fascist trade union which suffered most, since it had been the heart of Fascism as a movement, of that 'fascism of the left' which had proposed to abolish private property in favour of 'social' or 'corporate' property.[10]

At first it had seemed as if Fascism intended to increase the importance of its own union. The *Confindustria* (Confederation of Italian Employers) preferred to negotiate with the *commissioni interne* (elected works bodies which had been established during the First World War), which it regarded as more representative than the fascist unions. But in 1925 the *Confindustria* was compelled to enter into an agreement which recognised the Fascist Trade Union Federation as its sole bargaining partner. The *commissioni interne* were simultaneously abolished, and such shop floor bargaining as had been conducted under its auspices was eliminated. In 1927 the labour legislation known as the *Carta del Lavoro* or Labour Charter was enacted, which represented an enormously increased role for the state in collective bargaining and in industrial relations more broadly. The following year the Confederation of Fascist Corporations was divided into six separate organisations, and in 1929 the final attempt of the fascist trade union movement to play an independent role was defeated. The *fiduciari di fabbrica*, the representatives of the fascist unions on the shop floor who were responsible for supervising the implementation of collective agreements were abolished; and the fascist unions thus lost all semblance of autonomy and became a mere organ of the regime.

But at the same time, the Fascist state was moving explicitly towards an extension of its role in industrial relations: collective agreements became legally enforceable and their application was guaranteed by a special labour magistracy created specifically for that purpose. Collective agreements were even extended into sectors where they had previously been unknown. Holidays and welfare provisions were improved while the new Penal Code of 1930 further reinforced the centralised role of the state by making strikes and lockouts illegal.

Thus for 20 years, the working class remained without direct influence at the shop floor level, where national agreements between the fascist unions and the employers were simply imposed from above. But despite this position of near absolute powerlessness, the Fascist regime's need to maintain some semblance of popular consensus, however passive and qualified, seems to have ensured that the new structure of industrial relations offered some protection for workers' material interests. Beyond the improvements they secured in holidays and welfare benefits, the fascist unions were able to exert a real control over two key areas of factory life: piece rates and grading were decided by paritary joint boards of employers and fascist unionists. The results of this bargaining, according to Giugni, were quite satisfactory for the work force; speed up was limited, and in these areas, Italian unions, like their British counterparts, though to a lesser degree, showed some ability to impose restrictive practices which limited managerial freedom of action in the workplace.[11] Such constraints, interestingly enough, were related to the rearmament programme, when demand for labour increased and problems of costs and productivity appear to have become less pressing.[12] It is striking that these controls were exercised without the direct participation of the workers on the shop floor.

Postwar reconstruction

The long years of Fascist rule marked a dramatic break in the history of the Italian labour movement as it had developed prior to 1922. While some trade union leaders continued their activities in exile, others made their peace with the Fascist regime, and the prewar unions retained little influence in the factories after the mid-1920s. When the CGIL (General Confederation of Italian Labour) was resurrected in 1943, it was as a direct result of an agreement between representatives of the various political parties cooperating within the framework of the resistance, and the new union confederation retained its heavy dependence on these parties throughout the period of postwar reconstruction. Up until 1947 the anti-fascist parties from Christian Democrats (DC) to Communists (PCI) formed a series of coalition governments, and the left-wing parties exercised a powerful pressure on their representatives within the CGIL. These political groupings were among the best organised and most influential in the union confederation, and sought to control the wave of strikes which broke out in the factories in 1944–5, and which were creating difficulties for their parties within the coalition.

This subordination of industrial to political objectives in part explains the CGIL's adoption of a highly centralised bargaining strategy which denied any autonomy not only to the shop floor but also to the industrial federations, reserving all negotiating powers for the leaders of the Confederation. But there is another reason why the CGIL tended to adopt a highly centralised bargaining strategy. Because it had been created from above by the political parties, the Confederation had inherited none of the fascist unions' bureaucratic machinery, and was consequently ill-equipped to work within the complex and inegalitarian fascist system of collective agreements which remained officially in force. Thus, for example, the industrial category of 'Textiles and Clothing' at the end of the 1930s was regulated by 15 national agreements divided into numerous sections and sub-sections, as well as by another 300 provincial agreements.[13] The strike wave of 1944–5, precisely because it generated plant bargaining based on the fascist experience, tended to increase differentials in wage rates existing between each industry and region. The egalitarian orientation of the CGIL, together with its emerging institutional interests, therefore led it to conclude a series of agreements with the *Confindustria* in 1945–6 which concentrated all bargaining activities at the centre, thus reducing wage differentials at the cost of abandoning the plant level.

The joint boards which had controlled piece rates and grading were buried with the fascist unions, and these bodies were not replaced by a direct union presence on the shop floor. The consequences of this loss of direct control over piece rates and grading remained hidden during the immediate postwar years, since a very strong political mobilisation and the presence of left-wing parties in the government were able to protect workers' material conditions in the factories. In this period, national agreements prevented dismissals and workers' purchasing power was maintained by the *scala mobile*, a system of escalator clauses introduced in 1945 which automatically raised wages as the cost of living increased. As we have already noted, this national system of wage determination was specifically designed by unions, employers, and political parties to contain the tendencies towards shop floor bargaining which had begun to appear after the Liberation.

With the onset of the Cold War in 1947, however, the Italian political situation changed radically. De Gasperi, the leader of the Christian Democrats, decided to form a new government which for the first time excluded the Communists and Socialists and won a sweeping victory in the first postwar legislative elections in June 1948. But the left-wing parties had no real alternative strategy: for many years they simply hoped to be readmitted to power and therefore hesitated to inaugurate an aggressive policy. Thus after the attempt on Togliatti's life in July 1948, the Communist leadership was forced to call off the mini-insurrections launched by its supporters in many northern industrial centres, dispelling the myth that its parliamentary strategy was a screen for revolutionary preparations. These events highlighted the political tensions within the CGIL and provided the occasion for the Catholic and Social Democratic factions within the union to break away and form their own Confederations, the CISL (Confederation of Italian Workers' Unions) and UIL (Union of Italian Workers). The CGIL's continuing reliance on a parliamentary strategy even after the split can be seen in its 1950 proposals for the *Piano del Lavoro*, a mildly Keynesian proposal for managing the Italian economy which it submitted to the government. But given the new government's commitment to economic liberalism and to the Western Alliance, there was little scope for such proposals, and the CGIL and its allies were pushed to the margin of Italian political life.

Einaudi, the new Treasury Minister, launched a draconian deflationary policy which soon cut into working-class living standards.
Dismissals became more and more frequent, and Scelba, the new
Minister of the Interior, began to set the police against demonstra-
tions by the unions and the leftist parties. In this deteriorating
situation, the labour movement had no legal or institutional defence
on which it could fall back. The new Italian Constitution, though
very democratic in theory, consisted of a series of principles whose
implementation remained to be defined.[14] The old fascist legal codes,
both civil and criminal, remained in force, and the Prefects, having
been trained under the fascist regime, interpreted them to the
disadvantage of the workers. Similarly, the decisions of the
magistrates and judges pushed the interpretation of the fascist penal
code towards more severe sanctions against strikers. Until the
establishment of the Constitutional Court (*Corte Costituzionale*) at
the end of the 1950s, it was, moreover, impossible to revise the
fascist codes, since there was no body empowered to rule existing
statutes unconstitutional. In this context the factories became a sort
of no man's land in the eyes of the law. Collective agreements were
no longer legally enforceable, and many employers, particularly
small firms in the south, left the *Confindustria* to escape any
responsibility for implementing bargains reached with the unions at
the national level.[15] At the same time, the labour market shifted more
and more in favour of the employers, and the labour movement was
further weakened by the split between its Communist and Catholic
wings. But precisely at this moment, a series of parallel processes
were set in motion which would ultimately overturn the balance of
forces between workers and employers which prevailed through the
1950s and early 1960s.

*The 1950s on the shop floor: political unionism and informal
bargaining*

As we have seen, Italian trade unions chose not to develop a plant-
level organisation after the liberation. But it was in the factories that
the employers launched an attack on workers' low productivity: the
key issue in the resulting struggle became control over piece rates.
During the Fascist period, as we have noted, the existing institutions
ensured some control over speed up, even if from above. Now these
structures were no longer available, though the popular memory of
their operation was still vibrant in the immediate postwar years. In

the euphoria of the liberation, piece rates were abolished, and even when they were reintroduced some months later, the political mobilisation which protected workers against redundancies also guarded them against speed ups.

But when the employers' offensive accelerated after 1947, workers found themselves without an organisation on the shop floor. Nevertheless, the Civil Code still retained certain clauses regulating piece rates. The law authorised changes in piece rates only where there were 'changes in the conditions of execution of the work'.[16] Moreover, when piece rates were modified or introduced for the first time, a trial period was obligatory; and the Code required employers to communicate to the workers beforehand the basis on which the rates were calculated, the precise nature and quantity of the work to be performed, and the exact price for each piece or time unit.

Hence resistance to speed up could base itself not merely on the memory of the past, but more effectively on the Civil Code: the absence of the unions from the factories and the existence of a specific law theoretically protecting workers against rate cuts together produced the informal shop floor bargaining characteristic of postwar Italy. Although possible in principle, an appeal to the courts over piece-rate payment was very difficult in practice. As a result, workers were pressed to find some structure in the factory which could enforce their legal rights, and the commissioni interne and Communist factory cells already in existence came to assume this role. The commissioni interne, re-established during the war, were formally empowered to supervise the implementation of collective agreements in the factory but not to engage in any direct bargaining. The legal code regulating piece rates gave them a basis on which to contest managerial decisions, and soon began to generate a lively process of informal bargaining over its interpretation.[17] Similarly, in 1955, a judgement by a lower magistrate's court in Naples which gave a worker monetary compensation for his firm's failure to provide a canteen triggered off a vast spontaneous movement involving thousands of workers all over the country who rushed to claim their newly established legal rights.[18] Thus the law, which had previously been supported by the Fascist bureaucracy, now tended to stimulate new bargaining structures. And these structures, particularly when they involved the Communist cells, in turn tended to give a strong political stamp to the emerging shop floor bargaining.

As I have tried to show elsewhere, the battle over piece rates during the 1950s was largely unsuccessful. In many cases these disputes ended with increases in wages rather than an end to speed up, since the low basic wage rates generated a pressure for the monetarisation of grievances, while such restraints on the pace of work as existed resulted from the traditional informal mechanisms of job control.[19] But the experience of these struggles shaped the consciousness of a new generation of union officials, and so laid the foundations for future transformations. The radicalism of Italian unions in the late 1960s clearly had its origins in the resistance to what was called in militant jargon the 'superexploitation' of the 1950s.

At the same time, the Catholic trade union confederation CISL was turning towards the factories in an effort to carve out an independent institutional space. In contrast to the CGIL, which defined itself as a centralised, class conscious, political union, the CISL decided to become (relatively) autonomous of the Christian Democratic Party, and to establish itself as an associational union firmly based on the shop floor. Thus in 1953, when the CGIL remained committed to a highly centralised bargaining strategy, the General Council of the CISL, influenced by American ideas, launched a new policy of plant bargaining in which each worker's wage would be linked to the productivity of his or her own firm. Since the working class was extremely weak, this proposal remained purely theoretical for many years. Moreover, it must be noted that the CISL intended this plant bargaining to be closely linked to centralised negotiations, while the union's general approach was very far from the conflictual factory negotiations of the late 1960s: following its Catholic ideology, the CISL aimed at the integration of the workers within the enterprise and saw conflict as a last resort to be used only when all efforts at peaceful mediation had failed.[20] But even if these were the views of the union's founders, new officials were trained in the 1950s, and when the employers' aggressive behaviour showed cooperation to be futile, the latter were prepared to push plant bargaining beyond the prior collaborative framework.[21]

Party politics and employer solidarity

Beginning in the early 1950s, a series of interrelated developments in the political and legal spheres were set in motion whose ultimate effect was to undermine the absolute hegemony which the employers had established in the factories at the end of the previous decade. With the waning of the Cold War, the grip of the Christian Democratic Party (DC) on the Italian political system began to loosen, and pluralistic tendencies began to reassert themselves even within its own ranks. In 1953 the DC sought to consolidate its political position by introducing a system of majority voting which would have greatly reduced the representation of the opposition parties. This initiative, known as the *legge truffa*, or legal swindle, was defeated, and the centrist political formula was thrown into a period of crisis. During the second half of the 1950s, therefore, state policy towards the workers also changed, and since the Christian Democratic regime was a highly contradictory structure,[22] some of its components began to adopt a more conciliatory stance towards the labour movement.

Certain factions of the DC, particularly those linked to the CISL and more generally concerned with social problems, were pushed in this direction not only by the political crisis, but also by the growing sensitivity of public opinion to the disquieting condition of the working class itself. An inquiry conducted by ACLI (the Catholic Association of Italian Workers) in 1952, and a more general investigation undertaken some years later by a parliamentary commission, called attention to Italian employers' manipulation of factory elections and victimisation of union activists, and to the deteriorating material conditions of the workers themselves.[23] As a consequence, pressure was building up against the continued membership of state-controlled enterprises (*partecipazioni statali*) in the *Confindustria*; the CISL MPs were the most active in pushing the *partecipazioni statali* to leave the private employers' association. At the end of 1956, a new law excluded the state sector from further participation in *Confindustria*.[24] This law was also weclomed by CISL activists, particularly those who had come to recognise that it was impossible for the moment to reconstruct the union on the shop floor simply by taking over piece-rate bargaining after its catastrophic defeats in *commissioni interne* elections at FIAT and other major factories in 1955.

By the end of the 1950s, the political situation was changing very rapidly, as the declining electoral performance of the Christian Democrats forced its leaders to search for a new governmental formula, resulting in the establishment of a centre–left coalition in

1962. In this context, the state firms began to assert their independence of the private employers, and in 1960, for the first time, they signed an agreement with the electromechanical section of the metalworkers' union which provided some facilities for shop floor bargaining.[25] Two years later, the *partecipazioni statali* again broke the employers' front, signing a second agreement covering all metalworkers which established a more decentralised bargaining framework articulated at the sectoral and plant levels. Although this clause provided only for bargaining over the implementation of national agreements rather than over substantive issues, it was nonetheless the first step in the direction of a complete acceptance of shop floor bargaining, and the *Confindustria* was forced to follow suit a few months later. These concessions revived the unions' flagging morale and played a major role in the dramatic upsurge of industrial militancy during the 1960–2 boom.[26]

Judicial debate and legal reform

The growing thaw in the political system also prepared the ground for a progressive liberalisation in the legal framework governing industrial relations. First, the long awaited Constitutional Court came into being and began to strike down certain clauses of the Fascist legal codes; secondly, the magistrates began to interpret existing laws more favourably, a tendency which in turn was confirmed by new legislation; and finally, certain influential jurists began to work towards the reconstruction of labour law as a whole.

The 'negative initiatives' of the Constitutional Court were particularly effective in abolishing restrictive labour legislation. Thus in 1960 the Court removed criminal penalties for strikes and lockouts in pursuit of bargaining objectives (political strikes and boycotts remained illegal). At the same time, it ruled unconstitutional the 'law against urbanism' of 1939, which forbade people from changing their place of residence unless they already had a job in the town to which they intended to migrate. While this law had remained in force, migrants had a semi-illegal status which greatly weakened their position on the labour market. The migrants' position was also improved by new laws enacted in the early 1960s which formalised a series of prior decisions by the magistracy, prohibited labour-only subcontracting and limited temporary employment contracts, practices which had been quite common during the 1950s. In these years, migrants working in large factories and building sites had often formally been employed by subcontractors; as a result their wages, working conditions, job security and benefits were often much worse than those of their northern workmates. Their relation to management and unions were likewise different: blackmailed by their weak position, these workers were more deferential to management and less active in the unions.[27] More broadly, the *erga omnes* law of 1959 extended the coverage of collective agreements to all workers in a particular industry, irrespective of whether their employers belonged to *Confindustria*;[28] new protection was introduced for working mothers; and, after a protracted parliamentary struggle, a law was finally passed in 1966 which stipulated that employers had to demonstrate 'just cause' as a basis for dismissals.

While the courts, the magistrates, and the legislators were slowly shifting the framework of labour law in favour of the workers, influential jurists were working towards the formulation of a comprehensive labour code, which ultimately became the *Statuto dei Diritti dei Lavoratori* or Charter of Workers' Rights. The juridical debate was polarised between two different lines. A first group, Marxists and members of left-wing parties, sought to resolve the legal vacuum in the plant by the introduction of workplace democracy, what they called 'the Constitution in the factory'. In their view, the rules which guaranteed the individual's freedom should apply not only to the relation between citizen and state, but also to the relation between private individuals, where one party is much more powerful than the other. The second and more heterogeneous group thought it better to construct a legislative framework which would strengthen the position of the union as an institution rather than to fight for the abstract rights of individuals; here they were deeply influenced by the Wagner Act in the US and the system of industrial relations created by the New Deal.[29]

When this debate began in the 1950s, it had no immediate practical effect since the unions were still too weak. But its culmination in the enactment of the *Statuto dei Diritti dei Lavoratori* coincided with the strike wave of the late 1960s, the largest in postwar Europe. To be sure, these strikes, which we will examine in more detail below, acted as a catalyst to force the long-debated legislation through the slow and rigid Italian legal system; but without the preceding judicial evolution its terms would have been much different, with unpredictable consequences for the outcome of the strike wave itself.

Migration, full employment and cultural change

Thus as we have seen, a series of legal and political forces were converging in the late 1950s and early 1960s to promote a revival of shop floor bargaining. These tendencies were accompanied by a remarkable transformation of the labour market during the 1960s. The 'economic miracle' of 1958–63 had begun to exhaust the reservoirs of underemployed southern labour, and employers who had adapted their production processes to the remarkable physical endurance of the young male migrants could not easily fill the gap by reintegrating the weaker groups such as women and older workers expelled from the labour market during this period.[30] Even if some unemployment remained, it was no longer the massive phenomenon of the 1950s, and by the beginning of the 1960s there were signs that the Italian economy was approaching full employment. The credit restrictions of 1964, which followed the first major wage increases in postwar Italy, temporarily reversed this trend and provoked a resurgence of unemployment: though productivity fell for only one year, the employment trend was more deeply affected and did not recover until 1966.[31]

But as we have suggested, by the late 1960s the segmentation of the labour market tended to make such unemployment as remained ineffective, since different occupational groups were no longer competing directly with one another.[32] During the recession of 1964–6, employers increased productivity through a sharp intensification of work loads rather than through new investment. As in the 1950s, rate cuts and speed up again became a normal part of everyday work experience. But now the workers' position was stronger, and the southern migrants began to use their indigenous traditions of solidarity and struggle to disrupt the tacit bargain which had been struck in the 1950s between northern workers and employers over the skill hierarchy and factory discipline.

The migrants' conflictual behaviour resulted both from their historical experience of popular struggles in the south and from the unintended consequences of state intervention. The Italian state had launched a far-reaching campaign of development and welfare policy for the south after the Second World War. In the 1950s, the *Cassa per il Mezzogiorno* was established to promote industrial take-off through a massive injection of funds. But within a few years it became clear that the main consequence was instead to reinforce the traditional patronage networks which had historically blocked the development of the region. The resulting shift in state policy and the decision to abolish general subsidies for inefficient small farms produced a dramatic crisis of traditional southern society, whose most important expression was an enormous migration to the industrial areas of northern Italy and Western Europe.

Up until the mid-1960s, the character of the migration remained quite traditional: it was seen as a temporary phenomenon, a means of acquiring funds to improve one's position in the village. But later on the increasing cultural and material crisis of traditional southern society gave rise to a new type of migrant, who rejected southern society as such and sought his future in the north. But the migrants' experience of northern society gave rise to a disillusionment as intense as the original expectations. Poor housing, social services, schools and brutal working conditions together fuelled the migrants' anger at the betrayal of their previous hopes, and help to explain their massive participation in the struggles of 1969 and after.[33]

The 'Hot Autumn' and the Statuto dei Lavoratori

The favourable trend in the labour market and the growing militancy on the shop floor coincided with a gradual *rapprochement* between the Catholic and Communist wings of the labour movement and an increased willingness on the part of the unions to support the emergence of new bargaining structures in the factories. Thus the CISL began to abandon its Catholic organicism in the face of the strikes of 1962–3 which undermined a consensual interpretation of plant bargaining. Similarly, the recession of 1964, which rolled back much of the ground gained during the previous two years, demonstrated to the CGIL the urgency of a direct union presence in the factory, and the union began to moderate its hypercentralised bargaining strategy, while maintaining its previous radicalism. The project of establishing union sections in the plant remained theoretical through most of the 1960s, and the old *commissioni interne* continued to serve as the basic structure of worker representation in the factory. But despite the relative immobility of the leadership, the new union officials and the *commissioni interne* were collaborating more and more. This fusion of Catholic and Communist unionism became progressively more evident in the industrial conflicts of 1967–8; and finally the explosive strike wave of 1969 known as the

'Hot Autumn' brought to fruition this movement towards shop floor bargaining.

If the strength of the 1969 strike wave resulted from a series of social and economic causes, the permanence of the changes it produced requires some additional explanation. The wage increases of 1962–3 were followed by a recession which halted the revival of the labour movement. By contrast, the Hot Autumn of 1969 produced a much more durable transformation of Italian industrial relations. Shop floor bargaining, previously a rather marginal phenomenon, now moved to centre stage; and both unions and workers consolidated their positions more deeply. Italian industry suffered a productivity crisis lasting more than three years; even when this trend was reversed, it did not return the working class to its previous position of weakness.

The explanation for the remarkable scope and durability of the gains won in the 1969 strike wave lies primarily in the combination of the centre–left government's growing sensitivity to political pressure from the unions with the longer-term movement towards institutional reform which we have already traced. The government's concern to propitiate the unions ensured that it would respond to the strike wave with a policy of benevolent neutrality; the strikes served as the catalyst for the enactment of the long-delayed reform of labour law; and the new legal framework, once in place, served as a guarantee of the strikers' gains against a subsequent resurgence of employer power.

The centre–left government had been conceived as a government of reform, but its sole achievement had been the nationalisation of electricity. Subsequently, the reform programme remained an objective to which successive governments made constant reference, but in practice no reforms were carried out. The trade unions, including the CGIL, were at first quite prepared to support an incomes policy, but the government responded to the recession of 1964 with a return to traditional deflationary policy, demonstrating the effective non-existence of its capacity for reform. As a result, both the Catholics in the CISL and the Socialist faction within the CGIL increasingly lost faith in their parties in government, and any kind of political change seemed ever more remote.

For the Socialist Party the late 1960s were years of increasing frustration. The clientelistic Christian Democratic state demonstrated itself to be incapable of reform, because it was composed of a series of interest groups which were 'very diverse . . . very organised . . . lacking any proper hierarchy'.[34] The entrenchment of the two, posed insuperable obstacles to any programme of political reform. By 1968 the Communist Party was continuously gaining ground at the expense of the Socialist Party, which had reached a state of crisis, and was ready to exploit the ever-increasing leftward drift of Italian society to improve its position within the coalition government. At the same time, those sections of the Christian Democrats which were linked to the CISL transmitted to the party as a whole the union's dissatisfaction, and tended to move in the same direction as the Socialists.

One of the first results of this double pressure from within and without the coalition was the reform of the pension system. This was the outcome of the first united general strike since the 1940s, and gave great encouragement to the emerging radical movement since it seemed to demonstrate that class struggle paid immediate dividends. A second result was the favourable mediation during the strikes of the Hot Autumn of the Christian Democratic Minister of Labour, a former CISL official, who restrained the full force of employer reaction and helped to extend the range of concessions. Finally, and most crucially, the coalition passed the *Statuto dei Lavoratori*, drafted by a socialist lawyer with the backing of a socialist Minister of Labour, which played a key role in consolidating the gains of the strike wave. This law, enacted in 1970, was a comprehensive labour code, consisting of two parts, each of which reflected the influence of the two conflicting judicial currents to which we referred earlier. The first part consisted of a series of articles guaranteeing the freedom of the worker as a citizen. Freedom of thought and expression in the factory was guaranteed; the role of security guards and supervisors was strictly limited; television could no longer be used for surveillance; disciplinary sanctions were restrained by a detailed framework; and employers were forbidden from sending doctors to check on the absences of sick workers. Job security was ensured; employers were obliged to assign workers to jobs in line with their formal qualifications; and mobility from job to job within the plant was permitted only if it did not involve downgrading. The second part of the law provided direct institutional guarantees for the unions. Black lists, discrimination, and the victimisation of union activists were prohibited; and the rights of association and union participation were affirmed. Moreover, the law now authorised unions to constitute their own structures on the shop floor, and permitted workers to hold assemblies and referendums in the plant; union officials now had the right to paid leave, to a meeting room, and to collect dues in the factory.

In 1969–70, when the reform of labour law was entering its final stages, the growing wave of strikes was giving rise to an extremely radical movement in the factories. In 1969, rank and file workers encouraged by left-wing students set up in some firms a new type of structure known as the *Comitato Unitario di Base* (Unitary Committees of the Rank and File), whose aims and organisation conflicted directly with those of the official unions: thus they were 'unitary' in the sense that their members ignored the divisions among the three union confederations. At this point, the new labour law, which was still under discussion, was termed polemically by some as a charter of *union* rather than *worker* rights.[35] But by the spring of 1970 the spontaneous structures created by the workers had begun to evolve, shop stewards (*delegati*) were elected, hostility to the official unions diminished, and the leftist groups progressively lost their influence over the rank and file. When the law finally came into force in May 1970, the unions had succeeded in re-establishing themselves within the plants, and the articles of the *Statuto dei Lavoratori* provided the framework for the final institutionalisation of the spontaneous movement.

The new act had a highly ambiguous impact on the shop floor bargaining which had emerged from the 1969 struggles. At first, some observers saw it as a straitjacket for the spontaneous workers' movement; and a key article stipulated that workers' representatives could only be elected from either '(a) the unions associated with the confederations most representative at the national level; or (b) the unions not associated with the confederations mentioned above, but which are signatories to national or local collective agreements applied in the plant' (trans. by Silvana Sciarra). It is evident that this article was extremely instrumental in enabling the unions to win control of the rank and file movement from their opponents in the left-wing groups, and this was recognised at the time by the authors of the law. As Giugni, who was intimately involved in its drafting, has subsequently written: 'The policy underlying the so-called legislation of "support" for the union, in that specific historical moment, was connected also to the reasonable preoccupation with helping the union to overcome the crisis due to the pressure of spontaneous initiatives from certain groups of workers who accused it of bureaucratisation and refused to follow its lead.'[36] It helped, moreover, the process which ultimately produced a 'coincidence of the informal and official organisations',[37] in that the shop stewards' council became the union structure in the factory, even if the act did not devote even a single word to this body.[38]

At the same time, however, the unions by no means acquired complete control over the new factory councils: in contrast to the plant sections which they had sought to establish in the 1950s and 1960s, the shop stewards were elected by all the workers in the factory and not only union members. Furthermore, despite their incorporation within the official structures, the shop stewards' councils maintained considerable bargaining autonomy, and for a long time continued to pursue individual negotiating strategies which were not reducible to those of the national unions.[39]

Even if the Statuto helped the more moderate wing of the movement against the more radical one, a different role became more evident when the strike wave of the late 1960s and early 1970s ebbed, leaving the Act as a sort of protective barrier. If the Hot Autumn permanently changed the character of Italian industrial relations, this was largely the result of the new legal framework, without which the following period might have resembled more closely the recession of the mid-1960s, during which the gains of the preceding upsurge of industrial militancy were quickly rolled back, and workers' social position again deteriorated. But now, it was extremely difficult for employers to discriminate against the unions: employed workers were in a strong position, dismissals were extremely difficult, and downgrading was no longer permitted. The day-to-day life of the factory was radically transformed: piece rates, which had been central to the economic development of the 1950s and 1960s, lost their crucial function with the growth of shop floor bargaining and the emergence of wage drift; piece payment shifted from a variable to a quasi-fixed component of the wage, as did merit bonuses, which had previously been used by managers as an anti-strike premium. The lower magistrates were often prepared to give a radical interpretation of these issues, following the spirit of the new law: previously 'anomalous' types of conflict behaviour were now seen as normal, such as lightning stoppages or rolling strikes, and strikes without notice, while the lockout instead became illegal.[40] Since the magistrates' activity follows political trends, this orientation cannot be considered permanent; but the new law and its application, without being the sole cause, goes a long way towards explaining why the shop floor struggles and resulting productivity crisis persisted so long into the 1970s.

Conclusion: The 1970s and 1980s

The relationship between the unions and the political system is crucial for any understanding of the evolution of Italian industrial relations since 1969. As we have seen, in 1969–70 it was only with the greatest difficulty that the unions were able to assert their control over the enormous wave of strikes and to organise the emerging militancy. The experience of pension reform, which appeared to be the consequence solely of pressure from below, became for the union leadership a model for all future strategy.[41] A struggle for reforms, proposed directly by the unions, would be able to mobilise the rank and file in pursuit of a general political objective. And this in turn would enable the union leadership to regain control of the shop stewards, who had traditionally been engaged in a struggle to improve working conditions in the plants.

But the new union strategy failed to take adequate account of the structure of the political system at which it was directed. Despite appearances, the pension reforms had, in fact, *only* been possible because of the presence of a centre–left coalition with strong left leanings; and the same was true for the reform of labour law. But in the early 1970s, when the unions launched their 'struggle for reforms', the period of centre–left government was already coming to an end. At the same time, the economic crisis triggered off by the oil shortage, together with the escalation of labour costs after the Hot Autumn helped to make any further reforms impossible.

With the failure of the unions' independent struggle for reform, the demand for radical social change shifted directly to the political level. Thus in 1975–6 the Communist Party made enormous electoral gains, and the increase in the number of their deputies brought them to the threshold of governmental power: for the first time since 1947 a coalition was formed which was supported by the PCI (though the Communists were still excluded from the cabinet), and officially described as a 'government of national unity'. Thus, as in the 1940s, the 'transmission belt' mechanism linking the PCI and the CGIL seemed again to be acting as a brake upon the wider social movement. In 1978, the CGIL launched a new line reversing the unions' former strategy: for the first time the importance of market and competitive criteria was acknowledged, and the CGIL's traditional defence of employment was relaxed. This new strategy, known as the 'EUR line' after the Roman exhibition grounds at which it was adopted, was presented as a policy of necessary sacrifice for the workers in the interests of economic revival and investments in the underdeveloped southern region of the country.[42] But as has been demonstrated by those scholars who have studied the relationship between union leadership and rank and file during the 1970s, the new line remained principally at the programmatic level, with few practical achievements to its credit.

If the leadership of the unions became politicised during the 1970s, first through the struggle for reforms and then through the campaign for investment in the south, so too did the activists in the factories, but often in a different direction. In Italy the struggle at plant level has traditionally been imbued with a political dimension, being regarded as a struggle within the process of exploitation and therefore as the anti-capitalist struggle *par excellence*. This conception, already visible in the 1950s, came to the fore in the theoretical discussions within the emerging new left of the 1960s,[43] and in the early 1970s it entered the factories through the activities of the extraparliamentary left and captured a much wider audience than the membership of the groups themselves. This emphasis on the factory as the privileged site of anti-capitalist struggle became in turn more prevalent during the mid-1970s among shop stewards and lowerranking union officials as the failure of the leadership to win any real gains through its efforts at political exchange.

As a result, the level of industrial conflict remained relatively high in Italy throughout the 1970s, since the partial measure of control which the union leadership had secured over the rank and file was unable to contain 'the explosion of particularist claims, the sectorialisation of conflict, and the logic of imitation and pursuit'[44] emanating from below. At the same time, the widening gap between the orientation of the union leadership and the more militant shop stewards and workers promoted a growing sympathy among the latter for the wave of political terrorism which was another consequence of the blockage of reform and disenchantment at the prospect of a 'historic compromise' between the PCI and DC which appeared on the cards in the mid-1970s.

Thus the *Statuto dei Lavoratori*, aimed at recasting Italian industrial relations in a purportedly apolitical Anglo-Saxon mould, had very different consequences when inserted into the highly politicised Italian context, with its strong links between trade unions and the party system. Thus the provisions which had been intended to contain conflict tended in practice rather to facilitate conflict without controlling it.

The failure of successive strategies left the unions heavily dependent on the system of institutional guarantees which had emerged in haphazard fashion during the early and mid-1970s. Thus that section of the *Statuto dei Lavoratori* which made dismissals extremely difficult was reinforced by a law which raised the supplementary unemployment benefit paid by the *Cassa Integrazione Guadagni* (a governmental fund aimed at reconciling security of employment with a more open labour market) to 92% of the worker's previous wage. Thus industry, which paid only a small percentage of this socially financed wage, was relieved of its superfluous manpower whose cost would now be borne by the state. Similarly, the *scala mobile*, originally agreed in the 1940s, came to form an increasingly important component of workers' wage packets with the acceleration of inflation, and so tended to reduce the necessity of maintaining a militant struggle in the plants.

While the institutional defences raised at the beginning of the 1970s ensured that the unions would not easily revert to their weakness of the 1950s and 1960s, they were insufficient in themselves to protect the unions from a resurgence of hostility from the employers. Thus in the course of the 1970s Italian industrialists evolved new strategies which enabled them to evade, at least in part, the legal and contractual guarantees which workers had established in the large factories. Thus employers launched a campaign of productive decentralisation, subcontracting work to small workshops in which the *Statuto dei Lavoratori* was not legally enforceable; automation, restrictions on hiring, and internal mobility were used to re-establish managerial authority and destabilise the shop steward organisation in the plants. Even the *Cassa Integrazione* was used against the workers, as employees made idle by a strike in another part of the production process were sent home and paid by the state.

Thus the most powerful section of the workforce, that protected by legislation and by union organisation, found itself progressively isolated. The unions failed to extend their authority over the growing black labour market, nor to find a place within the mushrooming small factories which were in part the result of the large firms' subcontracting policies. At the same time, the unions opposed the dissolution of the numerous public sector firms which were no longer productive, but which were legally financed by the state to an unlimited extent, thereby constituting an important source of inflation.

Thus at the beginning of the 1980s, the unions found themselves in a dangerous impasse. The various attempts by the leadership to strike a neo-corporatist bargain within the political system have yielded no durable results. At the same time, the union structures at plant level have gradually lost their capacity for mass mobilisation. The decline of factory militancy is a consequence in part of the increasing aggressiveness of management, and in part of the determined efforts of the union leadership to shift conflict from the shop floor to the political arena. But it is also the product of a deep-seated ideological crisis among the shop stewards themselves, resulting from the failure of the highly politicised struggle over work organisation to bear practical fruits of either a revolutionary or reformist variety. Experiments with new forms of industrial organisation such as the assembly 'islands' introduced at FIAT brought disappointing results, and it proved impossible to found a new strategy of 'workers' control' on the struggle against the capitalist organisation of work. Thus a recent inquiry shows that bargaining over technological innovation has proved of little significance, while shop floor negotiations have concentrated on the work environment and the reduction of working hours; instead a *de facto* collaboration is emerging between workers and management in the form of an 'integration of the workforce into the decision-making process of the factory'.[45]

These developments have greatly weakened the hold of the unions over their members, and made them vulnerable for the first time since the late 1960s to a determined attack from the employers. The most dramatic sign of this changing tide came in the FIAT strike of autumn 1980, in which the unions were forced to call off their struggle against redundancies as a result of the 'march of the 40,000', an enormous back-to-work movement led by foremen and white-collar workers, but supported by a startling number of production workers as well. In the wake of this defeat, the disarray of the shop steward organisation has enabled the FIAT management to regain much of the undisputed control over the administration of production which it had lost during the previous decade. Elsewhere the situation is less grim, though Italian industry has given notice that it is no longer prepared to accept the implicit settlement of the 1970s by unilaterally renouncing the *scala mobile* over the protests of the unions and of a revived centre–left coalition government.

In January 1983 a new concordat was signed between the government, the unions and the national employers' confederation which promised to transform Italian industrial relations. Wage indexation was reduced, together with the importance of shop floor bargaining, and the national structure of the unions regained its prominence. A portion of employers' social obligations was transferred to the state; new controls on absenteeism were established; and the employers agreed in principle to open negotiations for a shorter working week. For its part, the state was supposed to reform the legal regulation of the labour market, legalising part-time work, and setting limits to claims on the *Cassa Integrazione*.

In the wake of the agreement there was much talk of a new 'social contract', of 'neo-corporatism', and even in some circles of a convergence between Italian and Swedish industrial relations.[46] But the agreement merely recorded the momentary intentions of the bargaining partners and soon began to disintegrate in the wake of mounting disagreements over its interpretation. The employers soon refused to negotiate over a reduction in working hours, and the unions in return rejected any further cuts in the *scala mobile*. As the industrial climate deteriorated, the employers, led by FIAT, launched a new offensive against the unions; the centre–left government sought to extricate themselves from their commitment to the support of ailing firms; and the unions were pushed back to their traditional reliance on the political parties.

At this point, no one can say how the renewed wave of conflict between Italian employers and trade unions will be resolved. But one thing seems certain: the future of shop floor bargaining in Italy, like its past, will continue to be intimately bound up with the ambivalent and unstable relationship between the unions and the political system.

NOTES

1 The 'mass worker' theory was developed in the 1960s and 1970s in various leftist journals, namely *Quaderni Rossi*, *Classe Operaia*, *Contropiano*, *Primo Maggio*, *Classe*; on the influence of this interpretation among union officials, see the article by Sergio Garavini, 'Qualifiche e ... composizione della forza lavoro', in *Quaderni di Rassequa Sindacale*, 30 (1971).

2 See S. Turone, *Storia del sindacato in Italia 1943–1969* (Bari, 1973); *Quaderni di Rassequa Sindacale*, 31–2 (July–October 1971); A. Accornero (ed.), *Problemi del movimento sindacale in Italia 1943–1973*, *Annali della Fondazione G. G. Feltrinelli*, 16 (Milano, 1976).

3 G. Giugni, *Diritto sindacale* (Bari, 1980); G. F. Mancini and U. Romagnoli (eds.), *Il diritto sindacale* (Bologna, 1971); U. Romagnoli and T. Treu, *I sindacati in Italia: Storia di una strategia* (Bologna, 1977).

4 F. Modigliani and E. Tarantelli, 'Curva di Phillips, sottosviluppo e disoccupazione strutturale', *Quaderni Storici*, 9 (1971); P. Sylos Labini, *Sindacati, inflazione, produttivita* (Bari, 1971).

5 M. Paci, 'Internal Migrations and the Capitalist Labour Market' in D. Pinto (ed.), *Contemporary Italian Sociology* (Cambridge, 1981); M. Paci, *Mercato del lavoro e classi sociali in Italia* (Bologna, 1973); S. Bruno, 'The Industrial Reserve Army, Segmentation and the Italian Labour Market', *Cambridge Journal of Economics*, 3 (1979).

6 M. Salvati, *Il sistema economico italiano: Analisi di una crisi* (Bologna, 1975); M. Salvati, *Alle origini dell'inflazione italiana* (Bologna, 1980); A. Gigliobianco and M. Salvati, *Il maggio francese e l'autunno caldo italiano: La risposta di due borghesie* (Bologna, 1980); M. Salvati, 'May 1968 and the Hot Autumn of 1969; The Responses of Two Ruling Classes', in S. Berger (ed.), *Organizing Interests in Western Europe* (Cambridge, 1981).

7 A. Pizzorno, *I soggetti del pluralismo* (Bologna, 1980); A. Pizzorno (ed.), *Lotte operaie e sindacato in Italia (1968–1972)*, 6 vols. (Bologna, 1974–8), especially the final volume, namely A. Pizzorno, E. Reyneri and M. Regini, *I. Regalia, Lotte operaie e sindacato: Il ciclo 1968–1972*, in *Italia* (Bologna, 1978); I. Regalia, M. Regini and E. Reyneri, 'Labour Conflicts and Industrial Relations in Italy', and A. Pizzorno, 'Political Exchange and Collective Identity in Industrial Conflict', both in C. Crouch and A. Pizzorno (eds.), *The Resurgence of Class Conflict in Western Europe since 1968*, 2 vols. (London, 1978); M. Regini, 'Labour Unions, Industrial Action and Politics', *West European Politics* (February, 1979); E. Reyneri, 'The Trade Union Movement, Social and Economic Crisis and Historical Compromise', in D. Pinto (ed.), *Contemporary Italian Sociology*.

8 Cf. the discussion in C. Sabel, *Work and Politics* (Cambridge, 1982), pp. 7–8.

9 A. Acquarone, *L'organizzazione dello stato totalitario*, 2 vols. (Torino, 1965); F. De Felice, *Mussolini il fascista* (Torino, 1966) vol. 1, pp. 404,

557, 666, 667; F. De Felice, *Mussolini il fascista* (Torino, 1968) vol. 2, pp. 274, 275, 287, 288; P. Melograni, *Gli industriali e Mussolini* (Milano, 1980), pp. 223–40; C. Shwarzenberg, *Il sindacalismo fascista* (Milano, 1972–3), pp. 18, 19, 25, 26, 40, 41.

10   F. De Felice, *Intervista sul fascismo* (Bari, 1975), pp. 27–46.

11   G. Giugni, 'Esperienze corporative e postocorporative nei rapporti collettivi di lavoro in Italia', *Il Mulino*, 1–2 (1956), pp. 3–17; G. Jocteau, 'La contrattazione collettiva. Aspetti legislativi e istituzionali 1926–1934', in G. Sapelli (ed.), *La classe operaia durante il fascismo*, Annali della Fondazione G. G. Feltrinelli, 20 (Milano, 1981), pp. 91–168.

12   M. Abrate, *Lavoro e lavoratori nell'Italia contemporanea* (Milano, 1977), p. 78.

13   Romagnoli and Treu, *I sindacati in Italia*, p. 197.

14   R. Romanelli, 'Apparati statali, ceti burocratici e modo di governo', in V. Castronovo (ed.), *L'Italia contemporanea (1945–1975)* (Torino, 1976), pp. 145–90.

15   *Documenti della Commissione Parlamentare d'inchiesta sulle condizioni dei lavoratori in Italia* (Roma, 1958–60) vol. 4, ch. 6, pp. 277–8.

16   *Codice Civile*, Libro 5, Capo 1, Sez. 3, art. 2101.

17   See, for instance, the contribution of S. Leonardi to the *Convegno nazionale di studio sulle condizioni del lavoratore nell'impresa industriale* (Milano, 1954), pp. 104–12. The CGIL journal *Notiziario CGIL (Rassegna sindacale* after 1955), had a special legal section, where one of the main subjects was the problem of piece rates considered from a legal point of view.

18   V. Foa, *Sindacati e lotte operaie 1943–1973* (Torino, 1975), pp. 113–14.

19   G. Contini, 'Le lotte operaie contro il taglio dei tempi e la svolta nella politica rivendicativa della Fiom (1955–1956)', *Classe*, 16 (1978).

20   T. Treu, 'La CISL degli anni '50 e le ideologie giuridiche dominanti', in G. Tarello (ed.), *Dottrine giuridiche e ideologie sindacali* (Bologna, 1973), pp. 269–396.

21   M. Sclavi, *Lotta di classe e organizzazione operaia, Pirelli-Bicocca Milano ('68–'69), OM-Fiat Brescia ('54–'72)* (Milano, 1974), pt 2, ch. 4; see also, P. Lange and M. Vannicelli, 'Strategy under Stress: The Italian Union Movement and the Italian Crisis in Development Perspective', in P. Lange, G. Ross and M. Vannicelli (eds.), *Unions, Change and Crisis: French and Italian Union Strategy and the Political Economy 1945–80* (London, 1982), pp. 114–15.

22   A. Gigliobianco and M. Salvati, *Il maggio francese.*

23   *Relazioni della Commissione Parlamentare d'inchiesta sulle condizioni dei lavoratori in Italia*, 16 vols. (Roma, 1958–1960); *Documenti della Commissione Parlamentare d'inchiesta sulle condizioni dei lavoratori in Italia*, 12 vols. (Roma, 1958–1960).

24   A. Collidà, 'L'Intersind', in A. Collidà, L. De Carlini, G. Mossetto, and R. Stefanelli (eds.), *La politica del padronato italiano dalla ricostruzione all' 'autunno caldo'* (Bari, 1972).

25 B. Bezza, S. Datola and R. Gallessi, *Le lotte degli elettromeccanici* (Milano, 1981).
26 F. Sabbatucci, 'Il livello aziendale' in *Quaderni di Rassegna Sindacale*, 35 (1971), pp. 26–54; Turone, *Storia del sindacato*, pp. 349–65; Romagnoli and Treu, *I sindacati in Italia*, pp. 222–5; see also, the bibliography in Mancini and Romagnoli, *Il diritto sindacale*, pp. 506–7.
27 G. Fofi, *L'immigrazione meridionale a Torino* (Milano, 1976), pp. 121–31.
28 On the debate on the *erga omnes* law, see the contributions of F. Santoro-Passarelli, U. Prosperetti, G. Giugni, V. Carello, T. Ascorelli, G. F. Mancini in Mancini and Romagnoli, *Il diritto sindacale*, pp. 437–53.
29 G. F. Mancini, 'Un apprezzamento positivo', in Mancini and Romagnoli, *Il diritto sindacale*, pp. 437–53.
30 M. Paci, 'Internal Migrations'.
31 M. Salvati, *Il sistema economico italiano*, pp. 40–50.
32 M. Paci, 'Internal Migrations'.
33 G. Contini, 'Southern Society, State Intervention and Migration: Prolegomenon to a Research Project on Workers' Struggles in Turin in the 1960s and 70s', working paper (Cambridge, March 1983).
34 Gigliobianco and Salvati, *Il maggio francese*, p. 42.
35 Mancini, 'Un apprezzamento positivo', p. 444.
36 Giugni, *Diritto sindacale*, p. 90.
37 Mancini, 'Un apprezzamento positivo', p. 450.
38 Giugni, *Diritto sindacale*, p. 21.
39 M. Regini, *I dilemmi del sindacato* (Bologna, 1981), pp. 106, 107, 162, 182; Gigliobianco and Salvati, *Il maggio francese*, pp. 75–7; Pizzorno, *I soggetti del pluralismo*, pp. 240–1.
40 Giugni, *Diritto sindacale*, pp. 233–53.
41 On the pension reform, see Regini, *I dilemmi del sindacato*, ch. 4.
42 On the EUR line, see Regini, *I dilemmi del sindacato*, pp. 52–4; see also Lange and Vannicelli, 'Strategy under Stress', pp. 165–80.
43 The most important journal which developed this theoretical perspective was *Quaderni Rossi*, edited by R. Panzieri, A. Negri, R. Alquati, A. Asor Rosa and others. Although not influential when it came out, this journal shaped the leaders of the *operaisti* groups; a reprint at the beginning of the 1970s became for some years a best seller.
44 Regini, *I dilemmi del sindacato*, p. 155.
45 See G. Giugni's introduction to F. Chiaromonte, A. M. Canfora, L. Circcarelli, F. Fiorelli and S. Iovenitti, *La contrattazione aziendale dell'organizzazione del lavoro 1976–1979*, p. iv.
46 G. Baglioni, 'Un triangolo che ci porta sulle orme della Svezia', *Il Sole 24 ore*, 2, 2, (1983). For an earlier comparison between Italian and Swedish industrial relations, see M. Regini and G. Esping-Andersen, 'Trade Union Strategies and Social Policy in Italy and Sweden', *West European Politics*, 3, 1 (1980).

7

Controlling production on the shop floor: the role of state administration and regulation in the British and American aerospace industries[1]

BRYN JONES

Introduction

Recent political and economic changes have probably moved state regulation of labour relations and industrial affairs in Britain closer to American practice than at any time this century. The Thatcher government's legal curbs on trade union activity and an explicit (if limited) retreat from state administration of industrial processes towards 'market forces' resembles (and may in some respects have been inspired by) American patterns.

An important element in these changes, and in the related political debates of both right and left, has been shifts in the balance of control over jobs and work between managements and unions as national differences in industrial efficiency and productivity have become unavoidably obvious. In this context comparisons of previous experiences of state influence upon industrial development and the control and organisation of jobs and production work ought to help clarify debates over present and future trends and the relevance of theoretical perspectives.[2]

Our understanding of the conflicts and bargains carried out over the control of production work is shaped by conceptions of the economic processes within which they take place. Whether these are thought of as efficiency-inducing market mechanisms, or as the exploitative imperatives of the reproduction of capital, it is frequently presumed that workers' collective controls over the allocation of labour to production tasks will tend (or ought) to yield to the more powerful pressures of underlying economic processes. The precision of these theories is of particular importance for the British economy. Lack of cost competitiveness and low output levels have been perennially associated with trade union controls over wage bargaining, labour mobility and production levels. Attention has focussed especially upon the relationship between this syndrome and the structure of the bargaining process. A peculiarly British pattern of devolved plant-level bargaining rooted in 'unofficial' union controls over the execution of jobs has been shown to be resistant to both long-term changes in the British economy and to the efforts of employers and the state.[3]

The nature and desirability of different forms of worker or management control over work processes is conditioned, on the one hand by the pattern of industrial organisation and production methods, and on the other by the institutions through which managements and organised labour contest and negotiate their conflicting objectives. The precise modification of both spheres by legislation or administrative intervention may best be understood through cross-national comparisons. Comparing Britain and America may be specially instructive because of the previous contrasts of state involvement in the sphere both of industrial organisation and of labour–management relations, arising from the different political traditions of the countries. Aerospace is a suitable case study because it illustrates these contrasts even though products and processes are essentially similar.

Intellectually what seems to be required is a better understanding of the conditions which make such controls significant. Politically divergent theories often assume that the economic and political environments have not worked, or cannot work together to make the institutions of shop floor bargaining effective. Left-wing and especially Marxist perspectives often see workplace controls as refuges of proto-democratic economic influence in an otherwise hostile environment.[4] Clustering at the other end of the political spectrum, and based upon various aspects of neo-classical economic theory, are interpretations of workplace trade unionism as an unfortunate, if perhaps partially tolerable, excrescence on a (potentially) freely regulating market system. The problem that has to be faced concerns the functions and effects of the state on the possible forms of economic regulation of labour affairs. On its own terms the market-economics viewpoint is consistent on this point. The involvement of the state in an industrial capitalist economy is acceptable in practical exigencies but produces the distortions which favour enhanced trade union powers in the workplace. Incomes policies breed localised and sectional resentment on which shop floor bargaining thrives. Nationalisation and public ownership replace market mechanisms of resource allocation only with interest bargaining and subsidised support for inefficient workplace practices.[5]

One of the key assumptions which leads leftist critics to attack similar targets to the orthodox proponents of the market system is the former camp's functionalist view of modern capitalism. Since the economy is almost always in 'crisis' (and the British economy is by extension the crisis economy *par excellence*) state intervention can have but one major aim and effect which is to support the economic system by restraining sectional interests, consuming the surplus, incorporating the working class through welfarism, mediating between finance and industrial capital, and so on.[6]

But the linkages between various state measures and objectives on the one hand and politically influenced institutions of the economy on the other are by no means express routes down which intentions and goals can arrive simply to be unpacked. These linkages are, moreover, heterogeneous. Ideology and legislation may develop inconsistently in the legislation and agencies which are their source. Conflict and incompatibilities may arise; now one interest, now another may be best served by their interactions. To understand the economic environment of workplace conflicts, and their resulting patterns of control requires some appreciation of state administration in the private economy which avoids the polar and abstract notions of its structure and process considered above.

Some of the difficulties and inadequacies stem from exaggerating the primacy of one sphere over the other. Radical commentators, especially those drawing their inspiration from Marxist ideas, tend to emphasise the autonomous force of the demands of production organisation and related management techniques as limiting the degree of workers' direct control over their work and generating the attendant conflicts over authority and reward with management. In consequence, legal regulation of the bargaining sphere can at best merely modify the expression of the fundamental conflict of interests and (because under capitalism it is thought to be inevitable that the legal impetus must reflect the basic economic interests of the dominant classes) will tend to stifle worker protests over the organisation and control of production. The centre and right of the spectrum of political values, however, has frequently given rise to claims about the gains from legal (or centralised quasi-legal) regulation of local labour–management contests in terms of harmony, equity and enhanced industrial efficiency.[7]

Marxist analyses are based either explicitly upon the concept of the 'labour process', or upon related assumptions about the technical and organisational imperatives that follow from it. In the strongest versions of the labour process perspective, late-twentieth-century industries are manifesting immanent tendencies towards the simplification and fragmentation of workers' tasks and a corresponding centralisation or consolidation of management command and control of all the constituents of the production processes. Either the logic of surplus-value extraction, or the broader dictates of capitalist rationality, together with an inherent recalcitrance by the workforce, require some form of Taylorist systems of management administration and automation on the basis of Fordist or computerised technologies.

The accompanying emphasis on deskilling and centralised managerial control as the organisational cement of production has been widely invoked by Marxist 'labour-process' theorists such as Braverman and Zimbalist, and in a less deterministic form by Marxist-inspired theorists of labour-market segmentation such as Edwards, Gordon and Reich.[8] In so far as these theories associate underlying trends with the endogenous imperatives of the labour process, however, they face the major problem that much of modern industry does not exhibit the expected features of standardised production and deskilling. Such cases are then disregarded as deviant or backward, and Taylorist or Fordist forms have become inflated out of all proportion to their actual significance in many industries.

The limitations of the explanatory models of both Marxists and neo-classical economists are further highlighted by their handling of the division of labour and the pursuit of collective interests in politically strategic industries.[9] Neo-classical economists treat such features as a political contamination of an otherwise rational essence. Despite their broader range, Marxists tend to characterise them as secondary or 'superstructural' consequences of universal processes of accumulation and production. In terms of numbers employed, capital expenditure, and export sales, aerospace is a dominant industry in both Britain and the United States: Boeing, for example, is America's leading direct exporter. Yet, like other sectors, its industrial structure, enterprise organisation and division of labour do not match what one would be led to expect by Marxist and neo-classical theories. For Marxists it is almost axiomatic to see large-scale mass-production units of monopolistic corporations as epitomising the development tendencies of capitalist economies. And despite the admitted weaknesses of neo-classical theory in relation to industrial concentration and non-competitive market structures, this has not prevented economists from applying the conventional categories of profit-seeking, relative factor prices and cost-optimising rationalisation to growth in the scale of production and technical innovation.[10]

Yet behind the particular capitalist processes of making and selling aircraft lies a whole structure of industrial and political institutions which have highly significant effects. These are largely ignored by mainstream economics. Marxism does not disregard the centrality of state influence on modern economic organisation; but it does presume that the outcome of these influences will be consistent with the logic of capitalist accumulation and the hegemony of the ruling class. The analysis which follows calls both views into question.

It might be argued that state involvement in aerospace is a special case because of such factors as political concern for national capacity in armaments manufacture. In a sense this is true: the political influences to which many industries are subject are, by their very nature, all 'special'. Yet their impact is nonetheless widespread. In both Britain and America the transportation, agriculture, pharmaceutical and other 'defence' industries have their product markets and production conditions shaped by state policy – even where there is no direct instance of intervention in the production sphere itself.

The first section below analyses the conditioning of industry structure and product markets in aerospace by state administration and procurement policies. In both countries the state provides a safety-net for the enterprises by means of its demand for military products. Yet the division of production facilities between development projects, military production and commercial aircraft leads (in both nations) to divergent and seemingly contradictory policies for the employment and organisation of labour. Substitution and simplification of labour skills by process technologies presumed by Marxists (and recommended by some industrial economists) are consequently limited because state policies bias managerial and technological efforts towards sophistication and quality in *product* technologies and piecemeal sub-contracting of production work.

Differences between the United States of America and the United Kingdom in the forms of administration of the aerospace firms' markets and industrial organisation make little effective difference to the organisation of production and employment of labour. It therefore appears that neither direct state intervention (UK) nor indirect administrative controls necessarily effect rationalisation in the labour process.

In the second section the general effects of legally *versus* voluntarily regulated labour management relations as between the two countries are reviewed. The secondary evidence suggests that radical writers have probably overestimated the extent to which judicial powers, legally enforceable contracts and the bureaucratisation of grievance procedures has blunted the scope for American plant-level unions' maintenance of job-control over management objectives.[11]

The interaction of national state administration of market and enterprise structure and local-management contests over job controls is brought together in the final section. Here documentary evidence plus the results of fieldwork in both Britain and the United States suggests that similar patterns of production organisation and degrees of job control have arisen in both countries' aerospace plants as indirect results of the interaction of state industrial policies within different national traditions of labour regulation.

The transcendental economics of aerospace

'You can forget all about aerospace. They are not in the real world like everyone else.' This was the response I received from the senior production engineer of a motor car components machining plant in the United Kingdom when I mentioned engineering decisions that I had learnt about from aircraft manufacturers. This contemptuous manager was referring to the priority for high-precision standards dictated by air-safety considerations and to the ubiquitous government financial support; both of which limited the pressure of commercial constraints on production methods.

On the latter point many industry analysts would agree with my shop manager, since the financial and market environment of even (nay, especially) the largest air-vehicle manufacturers is dominated by the decisions and policies of governments and state agencies in the provision of finance and contracts to production projects. The situation of aero-manufacturing enterprises which are single divisions of conglomerates and other diversified firms differs quantitatively but not qualitatively in these respects.

It is not possible to understand fully the production organisation and managerial employment priorities without outlining first the nature of product lines and product markets. These in turn cannot be understood without identification of the underlying influences by state bodies in purchasing military goods, provision of investment funds and administration of enterprise structures. The political dimension helps to explain why a seemingly 'unreal' mixture of high-technology products, under-resourced methods and units of production, and limited production runs possesses a very real logic of self-reproduction.

The interaction of a state-administered industry with the more usual business constraints of large-scale corporate organisation explains why financial security remains problematic and why production capital cannot develop the mass-production characteristics (of returns to scale) favoured by neo-classical economics and presumed as typical of 'monopoly capital' by Marxists. The state's involvement in the shaping of the product markets also explains why managers in different parts of the industry may deflect commercial pressures onto the workforce in some instances yet shelter them from the full force of economic risk in others. The underlying problems and processes of the industry remain substantially the same even though the national administrative frameworks that have come to be applied are, in some respects, at opposite poles of the possible political responses.

In the United States of America the principal commercial and military contracts are divided up between a handful of extremely large corporations, which are strictly too many for the available product demand, and a 'tail' of several thousand medium and small sub-contracting firms. The mixture of political and economic factors which brought about this pattern and continues to sustain it can be shown first of all by considering the differing role of the state in influencing the legal, product market, and capital-investment conditions of the industry in each country. Then the resulting production strategies adopted in response by the corporate managers can be outlined.

The United States

The present configuration of the aerospace industries (in both the United States and Britain) arose in the early 1960s as missiles replaced aircraft as the primary strike weapons. This switch meant large-scale reductions in the production capacity of an industry that had previously been geared to production of large numbers of conventional fighter and bomber planes. Missiles have simpler airframe requirements than manned aircraft and therefore allow different production techniques. But the relative simplification of the construction of the product did not lead decisively towards large-batch streamlined production methods. There remained a continuing demand for more specialised military aircraft. Moreover, missile production, with its intimate dependence on avionics (electronic guidance and control systems), entailed higher 'overhead' costs in the form of increased research and development expenditure.

It was this escalation of unit costs in the direction of high research and development and limited output which changed both the enterprise structure and production character of the industry. In the 1950s, and partly because of the Korean War, both Britain and the United States had supported multiple independent aircraft manufacturers turning out relatively large numbers of fighters and bombers.[12] The considerable spare capacity amongst the airframe manufacturers that resulted at the end of the Korean conflict and the switch to missile procurement led to several changes in the United States. Some firms simply went out of business; others either looked for new customers for aircraft in the foreign arms or civil airline markets, or they sought a measure of security in horizontal mergers with other aerospace producers. The numbers of major independent civil and military airframe manufacturing companies fell from 20 in 1954 to seven in 1967. Lay-offs and plant closures cut total industry employment from 882,000 in 1954 to 605,000 in 1964.[13]

Vietnam modified this trend slightly but it still meant that average production runs fell compared to the Korean War period.[14] The further relevance of this switch for production requirements is that the basic airframe requirements of missiles are less complex than aircraft (thus reducing difficult machining and assembly of wings, etc.) but the electronic and electro-mechanical features are more sophisticated and more technological expertise in production and more complex 'job work' machining is required. Indeed in the late

1950s the airframe manufacturers were ill-equipped to handle the new forms of precision work and the majority of missile orders went to metal-alloy working and electronics firms. However, the engineering design manpower of the major aircraft producers proved adaptable to the new technology and these firms had the decisive experience of established credibility in fulfilling the military's contract expectations: 'The importance of this factor in procuring contracts cannot be overestimated.'[15]

This conjunction of technological and economic factors meant that the industry's enterprise structure became more concentrated at the same time as the methods of production were becoming less susceptible to organisation on large-scale, volume sites of the 'Fordist' type. Other assembly-engineering industries also have to bring together a range of diverse parts into the sale of a final product. But in the following account it should be borne in mind that in aerospace consolidation of the establishment structure is limited by three factors: legal, product market, and finance-capital and by the direct strategies in each of these areas by government and state agencies toward the industry as a whole.

Governmental measures in the United States have shaped both the enterprise structure and product specialisms of the industry. In the early 1930s legislation (the Air Mail and Vinson–Trammel Acts of 1934) prohibited the existing integration of air transport, airframe and aero-engines companies and also had the effect of splitting the ownership of engine from airframe production operations. (Pratt and Whitney, now one of the world's 'big three' engine producers, was part of Boeing up until 1934.) Between 1938 and 1978, production orders for civil aircraft were also influenced by the Civil Aeronautics Board which regulated market entry and pricing policies for United States airlines. This system favoured a supply of aircraft for the more lucrative long-distance route operators (and therefore jet-engined, high-capacity planes) and erratic and prestige-conscious ordering of novel passenger-plane designs by the airlines.[16]

Enforced separation of airframe and aero-engine production limits the opportunities for technical and enterprise integration. The incentive to take over or merge with parts suppliers is also limited by the lack of continuity of demand between the different product types, as instanced by civil airline purchasing policies, just mentioned, and similar discontinuities in military demand. A subsequent failure to gain further contracts for the same type of production could leave a major company with the acquisition debts and redundant capacity of a suddenly unproductive supplier.[17]

Since 1970 the separate manufacturing policies of the engine and airframe makers have been accentuated by the airlines' practice of independently specifying the engine type they prefer for a given new model of aircraft. In addition a trend towards cross-national collaboration on research and development (especially to offset the enormous research and development costs of jet-propulsion technology) amongst the engine manufacturers has further limited any potential for national collaboration between airframe and engine firms. A similar dichotomy has prevailed in Britain despite the (separate) nationalisation of both sectors.

Despite regular and mammoth supplies of working capital from the defence contracting procedures the major companies have only weak long-term capital resources. Although determined separately, these problems stem from the highly cyclical demand patterns in both the commercial and defence markets. A vicious circle operates in which the enormous cost outlays for the development phase of a new aircraft or aero-engine leads to the 'bet your company' strategy of staking almost all available capital on a single project in the hope of cornering the market for a particular type of aircraft. On the civil side this can lead, and has led, to near-disasters if a competitor pre-empts demand by early marketing or if the airlines cut back investment in response to recession. Both Lockheed and McDonnell–Douglas lost out this way in the early 1970s move to wide-bodied jets.

In general this leaves the financial institutions averse to long-term credit supply and saddles the firms with short-term borrowings. The finance businesses are likewise unimpressed with the different kinds of risk involved in defence contracting. Political pressure or military unpredictability can curtail or defeat a project in unexpected ways: another reason why credit ratings, and therefore access to commercial sources for borrowing, remain limited. There is then an extra temptation to get overcommitted on the possibility of military fixes and thus effectively to abandon strategies for marketing civil products (Grumman, Rockwell, Vought and General Dynamics have become almost exclusively makers of military equipment). It is this market relationship which has led to the root cause of the industry's financial problems: too many producers and not enough production.

This highly unstable industrial structure has been implicitly engendered and financially sustained by techniques of military contracting and governmental policy towards the arms industry. The changing balance of the industry's investment priorities and military products in the 1950s and 1960s could have led to one of two patterns of industrial structure. Either a virtual bilateral monopoly could have developed, with the state procurement agencies dealing with one or two giant producers, or defence contracting would have to be inflated in price terms in order to maintain sufficient profitability for a larger group of contractors each receiving a smaller number of orders. The financial demands on military budgeting were likely to accelerate under either of these scenarios. But, in addition, an overall concentration in the population of contracting firms would probably have entailed the closing of existing production facilities and hence a militarily unpalatable risk of a reduction in the national emergency capacity for wartime production. The practice of state agencies and governmental decisions has been to promote a modified version of the second scenario.

The starkness of the choice was partially eased by circumstantial factors. The exogenous demand for larger volumes of standard aircraft hardware from the build-up of the South-East Asian war in the 1960s expanded the amount of distributable orders. Military procurement protocols also allow legitimate criteria for purchasing on qualitative rather than pure cost criteria.[18] There is an implicit state industrial policy in contractual and financial relations between the state and the aerospace firms which seems dedicated to maintaining a form of pseudo-competition amongst six or seven major firms but which does not threaten their existence, even though commercial logic is flouted by the persistence of excess capacity – estimated at around 45% of the industry's total.[19]

This industry structure is maintained by two tactics of Federal contracting known amongst defence critics as the 'follow-on' and 'bail-out' imperatives. Additionally there has been at least one instance when the commercial failure of a major firm has been averted by direct Federal financial support. So when Lockheed was faced with near-insolvency because the British engine producer, Rolls-Royce, was unable to meet its contractual obligation for the commercial L-1011 Tristar jet airliner, Congress voted $250 million under Emergency Loan Guarantee legislation to tide Lockheed over.[20] As of 1979, Lockheed had sold 160 L-1011s against an estimated break-even point (for recouping costs) of 300 aeroplanes.[21]

The logic of the 'follow-on imperative' is to maintain a particular supplier of one type of aircraft with a follow-on order for another, newer, model when the previous item is no longer required. Greater or lesser degrees of 'follow-on' have been observed for the seven elite airframe producers (those reaching annual sales of $1 billion) since 1960.[22] The 'bail-out imperative' suggests that a new development or production contract is awarded following emergence of a financial crisis affecting one firm in particular.

A competitive element is present when the Department of Defense invites tenders for the research and development phase of new or revised weapons. Tendering companies often spend several million dollars simply preparing the tests specifications and justifications for the development programme they have yet to commence formally.[23]

Commercial criteria persist in the financing of the development phase after the contract has been awarded but the further into the programme the supplier and the procuring agency go the more the supplier gets the upper hand and the less commercial principles govern the relationship. While the Defense Department normally finances outlays on a cost-plus basis (i.e. any provable unforeseen cost increases are allowable) there are deductions on the negotiated profit margin. But because some of the more expensive outlays are (because of the aforementioned changes in weapons technology) on the development side anyway, the contractor will not mind this. In addition snags, changes in weapon requirements and the incentive to make a project as specialised to their company as possible to secure the more lucrative production phase, all conspire to escalate costs (and the supply of working capital/revenues). Overheads, but few profits, are secured at this stage.

In the less complex production phase (assuming the development contractor receives that phase of the contract) technological uncertainty is reduced and continual 'follow-ons' may make the contractor more knowledgeable about likely costs on the production side. Longer production runs on the more well-proven production equipment allow standard cost reduction exercises and the production workers that a contractor has probably had to 'hoard' against this stage of the programme can be set to work in a more intensive fashion. Now the major (prime) contractor can act more like a monopsonist and political agent himself by imposing deadlines, prices and quality targets onto the many small sub-contractors, especially the makers of the more standard components.[24] While cost over-runs and negligible profit margins prevail in development contracts, cost under-runs and therefore respectable rates of profit predominate in the production phases.[25]

Britain

The industrial processes in American aerospace are then inextricably inter-twined with dominant cultural and political features of that society: its ideology of 'free enterprise' (which precludes direct state control), the postwar rise of the military establishment, and legal and administrative checks on business organisation and practice. The British industry shares several of its American counterpart's underlying economic pressures and problems which need not be repeated in detail now. The escalation of the research and development proportion of total costs and the accompanying shrinkage in the numbers of independently viable domestic contractors means that capital funds and economies of scale are similarly elusive in Britain. But, in addition, more fragmented systems for the organisation and management of production typical of British industries have confounded state-inspired attempts to control these problems. In spite of the intractability of these difficulties several British governments in the postwar period were encouraged by the political legitimacy of state intervention and control in industry to initiate attempts at the rationalisation of capacity and processes through directed mergers of the major producers and, later, their formal nationalisation.

Unlike the US, anti-monopoly legislation has not constituted an obstacle to state attempts at restructuring which have been guided less by ideologies of market competition and/or economic collectivisation than quasi-technocratic notions of micro-economic efficiency. Whereas the American companies have retained many of the characteristics of commercial marketing and internal management control that competition and the business culture have inculcated throughout the dominant corporate sector, British aerospace businesses have exhibited the delegated direction, localised controls, and incoherent marketing strategies typified by other UK industrial sectors. Finally, and most importantly, the political environment has been one in which despite its greater involvement in the structure of the industry the different state agencies lack the administrative resources for the kind of detailed scrutiny and regulation of contractors' affairs that is possessed by the US Department of Defense and presumed by Congress.

Although the British industry in the late 1950s faced similar problems of changing aircraft technology and weapons strategy, on the defence side there was the added handicap of a much smaller domestic airline market to use as a launching pad for overseas sales. National prestige would ensure that the major national airlines would buy British (so no effective difference from the US there) but the major carriers were owned by majority state share holdings and subject to episodic direction by government policy makers. Industrial policy was beginning to be influenced by the ethos of technocratic rationalisation which the subsequent Labour governments of 1964 to 1970 made into a near-official ethos.[26]

In 1958 there were 14 major airframe companies and five prominent aero-engine firms. The same forces that were leading to overcapacity in the USA, namely higher development and technology costs to be spread over smaller production runs, presented a much more serious problem for the relatively minor British 'market'. Accordingly ministers and civil servants developed a policy for 'rationalising' the industry to retain manufacturing capacity but fill it with fewer model types whose still magnified research and development costs could be met from the greater financial support resources of merged companies.[27] The *quid pro quo* for industry compliance was to be greater financial support of research and the award of military contracts to the properly re-organised successor firms. On several occasions the state's 'efficiency' criteria became the effective requirements for the bidders' success. In at least one case a specially formed contracting enterprise was rejected by the Ministry of Supply and a different enterprise formed which met the financial and technical resources criteria. Over the two years 1958 to 1960 the 19 engine and airframe companies were reduced to five major groups all formed in either direct or anticipated response to the state's procurement sanction. This was almost the directly opposite policy to the United States practice of using procurements to maintain the independent identity of the separate contracting companies there!

The subsequent phases of enterprise re-structuring arose because, like other company mergers in postwar Britain, the immediate financial gains and objectives were not accompanied by any systematic re-organisation of the overlapping production facilities nor the imposition of central controls over the subsidiaries' operational managements.[28] Overlap of design and production facilities, the lack of effective financial and planning controls were all associated with the 'hoarding' of labour. Hoarding was practised to keep plants in operation despite short production runs.

The latter were induced by the small size of the domestic market (compared to USA) but, as with the over-capacity problem mentioned above in the United States, the situation was exacerbated by the state procurement practices of 'sharing out' work which could (experts believed) be concentrated on a smaller number of sites and management and research facilities. Further re-organisation of the industry took place in the 1960s partly through internal re-structuring and divisionalisation (BAC in 1963–4, Hawker–Siddeley in 1965), and then by the demise of Handley Page and Beagle. Rolls-Royce took over the other engine manufacturer, Bristol Siddeley Engines; but this merged entity had to be nationalised in 1971 as a result of technical delays and financial miscalculations in the development of the RB 211 engine for the Lockheed L-1011. The reasons given were: safeguarding the nation's technological expertise, trading credibility, domestic airlines and defence requirements; and the 'solvency of many major firms' as suppliers to Rolls-Royce – involving, overall, 100,000 jobs.[29]

The Labour government of 1975–9 nationalised and merged Hawker–Siddeley and BAC into the British Aerospace Corporation (BAC). While the current government are presently returning share ownership in BAe to private capital the corporation remains a single entity. It has been argued that its new status is not free of government influence and commitment because of the ambiguous specification of financial accountability favoured by British governments and administrators.[30]

Indeed it is difficult to see how far the state can 'commercialise' BAe because its main domestic civil customer is the national airline (also currently in a state of public–private limbo). In addition, major overseas civil markets are now mainly devoted to the politically co-ordinated European consortium of Airbus Industrie. This latter has come to constitute the only effective means for the cost-sharing and volume production by which competition against the American majors (Boeing, McDonnell–Douglas and Lockheed) can be mounted.

This move to a renewed attempt at foreign sales is significant because it ultimately reflects back on developments in production methods and labour policies. Throughout the 1960s and 1970s research and development cost increases led to more pressure (often by government financial incentives) to seek out foreign sales. Civil aircraft had effectively lost out to American competition there by the late 1960s, although the airframe enterprises were able to continue successful overseas selling of some Royal Air Force models (cf. the Harrier jump-jet and the Tornado).

The American dominance in the engine market led to defence sales and the United Kingdom government 'launch aid' grants for the Rolls-Royce engines. But these were insufficient to finance the exponentially increasing costs of jet engine development (as the RB 211 fiasco shows).

The post-1970 trend to airline stipulation of engine–airframes combinations has led to increased commercial rivalry between the big three jet-engine manufacturers: Pratt and Whitney (the major profit earner for the United Technologies Corporation), the aero-engine division of General Electric, and Rolls-Royce. This competitive pressure (stemming from the limitations on product differentiation in jet engines and the volatility in demand amongst the world's airlines) has also promoted the influence of American production management strategies at Rolls-Royce while British Aerospace (with a different method, markets and products) seems to continue in a more sedate manner.[31]

Labour markets and production organisation

In both countries then there has been difficulty in establishing continuity and volumes in product orders. In the United States this has been partly because of the ideological and political pressures for the maintenance of an inflated number of independent firms. In the United Kingdom the difficulties have arisen from the limited size of the domestic market and (at least until recently) weaknesses in managerial organisation of product sites; despite integration of some top management functions via nationalisation. In addition, in both countries increasing technological sophistication in the military product side and, in the US, the peculiarities of the contracting system has pushed the major firms towards increasing the allocation of resources to development work and to proportionately less attention for final production processes. Labour markets also tend to reflect these emphases.

As a result of all of these factors, production organisation and labour utilisation patterns have failed to move in the direction of sites for mass manufacturing of standardised times by dedicated capital equipment and the sub-division of semi-skilled labour. Aerospace firms and their official paymasters have, of course, been concerned with the limited changes in labour productivity but the above constraints have led to more indirect tactics via technological aids to management and sub-contracting of production work rather than the techniques of Fordist manufacture.[32] The technologies the major firms apply to enhance overall productivity are the ones favoured by the military and are intrinsically linked to techniques of design, calculation, planning and project coordination, that is, those engendered by the preponderance of development work.

In the United States the larger scale and higher coordination levels of projects favours expenditure on 'managerial' technologies, for example, cost-monitoring and project coordination systems such as PERT (Performance Evaluation Review Technique).[33] However, the 'boom or bust' cycles lead to periodic purges of workers. In Britain on the other hand the capital and fixed overhead costs also have to go on equivalent research and development resources while managerial controls over the handling of labour costs has been of the localised and pragmatic kind typifying many other British manufactures for most of the postwar period.

Corporate production strategies are affected accordingly. Skilled labour remains a crucial asset. It is hoarded to deal with the frequent design modification necessary for defence programmes and to provide a substitute for seeking additional capital expenditure to overcome the long time lags that threaten to complicate contract specifications. But labour can also be shed quickly when the market or a defence contract cancellation threatens complete disaster. Boeing's employment figures crashed from 100,000 to 37,000 between 1970 and 1971.

Company–union lay-off provisions facilitate re-employment when business picks up, but in some districts (such as the engine-producing plants in New England and the southern California airframe establishments) competition then begins anew to hang on to skilled workers. The advantages of the union seniority policies favour employment stability for older workers. As a result the age profile is much higher than in other industries. This dependence on skilled labour is not alleviated by the nationwide shortage of skilled machinists. The public schemes are inadequate and the effective discrimination against younger workers (and companies' short-term investment attitudes toward labour) limits company training and apprenticeship intakes. A similar process has been developing nationally in Britain.[34]

Thus military aerospace product requirements are the principal contributors to the 'out of this world' economics of the American industry. Elements of price competition, over-capacity in production, high profit margins and low concentrations of production capital all co-exist amongst the major firms. But the inherent instability of finances and product markets persists and the resultant commercial pressures are deflected onto different categories of economic agent during different instances of the development and production process.

The limited degree of financial security provided to the major firms by the various forms of state support, together with the need for technically competent workers on limited-run 'quality' products suggests policies of job security and work-autonomy for many employees. On the other hand, the reverse, commercial, forces in the marketing of civil aircraft, together with the sub-contracting option and the incentives to cut operating costs in the production phases of military work, constitute pressures to vary employment costs to offset overheads and to limit workers' job autonomy in order to provide faster output.

The institutional regulation of workplace interests

Since, in peacetime, British and American aerospace companies have been treated as ordinary commercial employers their conduct of collective bargaining and employment rights is mainly influenced by the national institutions that prevail in most other industrial concerns. In the United States the impact of legal regulation has given rise to divergent interpretations.

Economic liberals have claimed that the same legal developments have been exploited by unions to restrict the areas of legitimate managerial decisions beyond the limits necessary for the effective exercise of capitalist economic efficiency. In this view, such central commercial practices as sub-contracting of work, manning levels, and trading links with other companies have been turned into areas of union control. Radical labour and legal historians, on the other hand, have seen in the later statutes and applications of labour relations law a 'judicial de-radicalisation of labour' (to use Klare's terminology). Broadly the combined actions of the National Labor Relations Board (the federal arbitration apparatus), the law courts and legally binding collective bargaining contracts of unions and managements have been interpreted as stifling an incipient pressure for shop floor actions against management authority.[35]

Clearly the different inferences drawn by these two perspectives depends in large measure upon the aspects of management or union practice which are deemed to be the most crucial for the enhancement of control by one side or the other. But the possibility then exists that both may have overlooked a more subtle reality.

Before assessing the role of legal regulation in the specific context of job controls in the aerospace industry we need a brief overview of the centrality of the law in American industrial relations more broadly, and the contrast (often explicitly or implicitly drawn by American commentators) with British experience.[36]

With the exception of the brief ineffectual 1971 Industrial Relations Act, civil law in Britain before the current round of Conservative legislation has been well-distanced from plant-level unionism, and state agencies (Department of Employment, ACAS, etc.) have acted largely in a 'firefighting' rather than a permanent regulatory role. Because the pattern of British bargaining has been two-tier with broad pay and conditions negotiated between national-level union officers and employers at the top, and negotiation of detailed pay and manpower arrangements by local managements and shop stewards' organisations at plant and company levels, workplace regulation has of necessity been highly decentralised.[37] Several industries have highly formalised procedures for the 'upward' referral of disputes and grievances arising at the workplace. But with particularly contentious or clumsily handled issues there was no formal sanction (apart from the uncertain and time-consuming applications to a civil court) to prevent unilateral action or resistance by one party or the other.

When this pattern is reinforced with the operation of 'custom and practice' safeguards against changes in working practices, job titles and manning arrangements, it is easy to accept that the possibility exists for successful resistance by plant-level unions to management attempts to save costs by new methods of raising output per worker. In aerospace and other metal-machining industries this capacity is illustrated in the arrangements for preserving numbers and control over jobs pursued by the Engineering Section of the Amalgamated Union of Engineering Workers (AUEW).

New layouts, machine tools and coordination and routing of tools and materials were taken on subject to acceptable pay rates for changes to working practices and the provisos that each operator would have responsibility for his machine and no more; and that apprentice-trained craftsmen would always have first call over these jobs, if their own were ever lost. This priority for tradesmen (or 'dilution' arrangements) and control over the tools are ancient protocols of craft unionism in Britain. When I observed these practices in a study of the introduction of Numerically Controlled (NC) machine tools it was clear (in the late 1970s) that the theoretical minimum manning arrangements had been successfully raised and the possible use of cheaper semi-skilled labour precluded. As will be explained in the next section, this is not to say that it is possible to work NC technology without machinists' skills (quite the reverse) only that management could not attempt to do this because of the strength of craft traditions and the capacity to realise them through plant and shop floor bargaining.[38]

On the face of things, unions in America are precluded from exercising such informal but effective controls over working methods and manning arrangements. Legally there is nothing to stop unions negotiating with management for the right to these kinds of controls in any particular shop or plant. But, naturally enough, unless these controls are already established and considered irreversible then employers are unwilling to accede formally to them. As contractual agreements became the norm in postwar American bargaining, so the contents, or the 'language' of the contract became issues of critical importance. Provable breakages of contract leave either of the parties open to litigation.

The problem from the union side is that employers have on the whole seemed to avoid getting in a position where they have to cede any union or workgroup autonomy in working practices. The British craft principle of the tradesmen's right to the control of his machine would not be countenanced in the American context, nor would any co-determination of manning be as admissible a legitimate principle. These restraints follow from two features of contractual bargaining.

In the first place, the contending parties are not free to determine what issues they will give primacy in bargaining. The provisions of the NLRA (as amended) have been interpreted by the courts as giving them the responsibility to ensure that certain aspects of conditions of employment are 'mandatory' subjects that have to be included in the bargaining process. This is because NLRB and its reviewers (the courts) also have a statutory duty (when approached) to direct that 'good faith' (i.e. genuine as opposed to phoney) bargaining takes place. Court decisions may therefore set the pattern for what aspects of work and employment the parties have to try to reach agreement on. Unions have largely been ineffective in getting work practices included as mandatory. Indeed it was deemed a minor juridical revolution when in 1964 the Fireboard Paper Products Corporation case led to sub-contracting out of work being judged a legitimately (i.e. mandatory) bargainable term of employment by a Supreme Court majority verdict.[39]

The second weakness stemming from the legislation from the unions' point of view is that the NLRA has been interpreted by the courts as removing certain subjects (which may have to be bargained about in good faith), that are mandatory, from the requirement of juridical definitions as to whether they are also definable in law as joint control issues. Since the courts cannot adjudicate on such issues, the status quo prevails in the sense that such issues remain tacitly within the separate spheres of management rights and union interests. The convention that there are some areas of decision-making that are necessarily part and parcel of managerial property is thus reinforced, even though they are mandatory and require 'good faith' bargaining.[40]

All of these restrictions on gaining formal recognition of unions' legitimacy in work-related decision-making are further entrenched by constraints on intra-contract strikes. The Taft–Hartley Act was specifically intended to replace arbitration and mediation for disruptions when implicit or explicit contracts broke down. The detailing of grievance procedures for individual workers' cases is minute. Supreme Court judgements have penalised unions who have struck on issues deemed to be arbitrable. Finally, employers have taken to securing 'no strike' clauses into contracts agreed with unions. The latter have been extended in some contracts agreed with unions to a requirement that the union officers explicitly repudiate 'unofficial' strikers and waive the rights of employment that the contract gives to employees.

The most obvious inference for the radical interpretation from these developments and evidence from adjudicated cases is aptly summed up by Brody:

> In England where union contracts did not penetrate down to the factory floor, the shop stewards carved out a bargaining realm quite independent of the union structure. In America, fractional bargaining [between the immediate work group and the line bosses] could not evolve into a comparable shop bargaining system. The work place rule of law effectively forestalled the institutionalisation of shop group activity.[41]

But the workgroup is not the only source of job controls and devolved craft unionism is not the only institution for contradicting managerial controls. Before returning to the case of work practices and job allocation in aerospace production work, we should bear in mind two features of the American legal-contractual process which make the direct management controls implied by the formal-contractual system problematic.

First, in the adjudication of mandatory issues the courts seem to have remained faithful to the original NLRA view of the rationale for unions, that is, that they represent the rights of the individual worker in a sphere where he or she might not otherwise gain protection or redress. Hence all manner of terms and conditions of employment concerning the individual's stake in his job are mandatory: promotion, discharge, lay-offs, etc. many of which are covered by the category of 'seniority': in other words movement into and out of jobs.[42] The compromise of spheres of decision-making mentioned above works out in this area to mean that the employer has the right to decide what work is to be done and by how many. But the union can complicate this by exercising its 'right' to set criteria as to who should, or should not do it.[43]

The second feature of the legal-contractual process which weakens its interpretation as a web of controls over workers' tactics of resistance is provided by the protracted contests which the General Electric corporation fought with its unions throughout much of the postwar period. The company tried to maintain a minimal involvement with the NLRA arrangements. The major involvement of the General Electric's engines division in the aerospace business also makes this reference of direct relevance to the present chapter.

General Electric chose to sit on the sidelines of NLRB activity because of the preference for a 'first and only offer' strategy. This approach, initiated by company vice-president Lemuel R. Boulware,

(and attempted recently by some British public enterprises such as
BL) preferred the risk of strike confrontations to arbitration, on the
principle that a final but fair offer stood more chance of avoiding
interminable negotiation and stoppages than the more conventional
bidding strategy. The Boulwarism of the 1950s and 1960s was
effective in some respects against a divided union opposition. But
after some nine years of litigation the courts eventually rejected
Boulwarism root and branch on the 'absence of good faith' provisions. In the meantime, of course, bargaining and conflict continued.
After the early management successes the unions became adept at
mobilising workgroups into guerilla-style strikes which evaded the
'no strike' provisions in the contracts. In particular plant level
representatives developed the tactic of striking against an issue that
was formally 'grievable' by the contract provisions but using the
resultant economic pressure to extract concessions on other issues
that the terms of the contract defined as outside the jurisdiction of
joint determination.[44]

Whether or not the GE saga is representative in any broader sense,
the conflicts there suggest strongly that the courts' writ over the
actual conduct of bargaining and tactics is limited and that judicial
interpretation, when applied, does not oppose management strategies of limited issue bargaining (of the kind practised currently by
some British public companies). Even more important for the question of circumscribed workplace militancy is the evidence that
contract provisions and no-strike clauses are inadequate to preclude
union–workgroup actions. Unions may thus attack the kind of
work-practice issues (such as 'who will perform what kind of work')
that 'management rights' clauses formally deny.

*Impact of administrative and regulatory conditions on job control
in aerospace*

Workers control jobs along two main axes. Directly, through the
exercise of skills, discretion and technical knowledge, individual
workers are able to limit management's capacity to monitor and
control the execution of tasks. Indirectly, workers' organisations can
create similar checks on management's interventions winning agree-
ments/acceptances of such factors as line speeds, manning levels per
job, output quotas, etc. Where direct individual controls are limited
by the technical nature of the production process (as with auto-

mobile assembly for example) then indirect collective controls become especially important. Where controls are effectively exercised along both axes, as with traditional craft workers' union-ism in British engineering and printing industries, then resistance to managerial direction of job content and work execution is (*ceteris paribus*) doubly reinforced.[45]

As the discussion in the preceding section showed, however, many radical analyses of American workplace unionism in the postwar period have concluded that it has been largely ineffectual as a source of job control. Because of emphasis upon centralised pay bargaining arrangements, and the force of deskilling and work-routinising technological change, it has been argued that job control has been pushed back to peripheral issues such as seniority guarantees in employment security and the representation of *individual* grievances over these and other terms of employment. But as we saw above, there is some evidence of these issues being pursued in a militant rather than simply formalistic fashion. Commentary sympathetic to management rights had also claimed several areas where unilateral management decision-making was checked by collective bargaining arrangements and precedents. The question that concerns us now is how do product markets and political conditions, interacting with the web of legal regulation, influence workers' control of aspects of their jobs in American aerospace?

The American case is analytically more important than the British because of the pressure of American management methods and objectives, because the institutions of labour law penetrate much more deeply than in Britain into plant level issues and because labour process and Marxist labour market theories, arose directly from the study of American developments. Existing evaluation of these theories through evidence from European cases must therefore be limited in scope.[46]

The state-administered commercial environment of the major US aerospace corporations creates various pressures on managements to influence more directly the detailed efficiency and character of the production organisation. As was noted in the first section of this chapter, development work though productive of high revenues is not necessarily the area where cost savings can show up in higher profit margins. Civil and defence production phases do have this clear characteristic. In addition, nearly all civil work is intensely competitive both for the airframe and engine producers. A particularly important feature of this market is ability to meet contract deadlines on time *and* within cost specifications. The RB 211 episode vividly illustrates the level of these pressures. A more recent development is the growing concern of government as an outside scrutineer (on defence and in the British nationalised firms) at low productivity levels on the production side. This has led the American defence agencies to add detailed work measurement criteria to the long list of quality and safety standards which are demanded of contractors. MIL Standard 1567 dated 30 June 1975 requires 'the application of a disciplined work measurement program as a management tool to improve productivity'.[47]

Conventional economic analysis might expect aerospace firms to replace scarce or unreliable inputs of skilled labour with more productive investment in the latest vintages of capital equipment. It would also expect that wages ought to be reduced in line with limited output levels by cutting rates, overtime and numbers employed through layoffs, redundancies, and cutbacks in hiring as appropriate.[48]

To the chagrin of market economists, of course, aerospace firms do not do this in any consistent fashion. Marxist conceptions of the labour process also suggest some of these changes but also predict they will be sought for power advantages. In addition to constant capital replacing variable (human) capital, labour of a specific type – more pliant, less skilled, but more interchangeable will be sought. Management and technological systems introduced will be specifically for this purpose and to enhance managerial control over all forms of labour employed. The limitations of this labour-process prediction are that any independent role for labour relations institutions is discounted while the market and organisational environments of the plant are taken for granted as necessarily conducive to the pursuit and success of these managerial strategies.[49]

Much of the labour allocation that takes place in aerospace plants is in accord with internal labour market concepts of bureaucratically administered hiring and firing and promotion processes. Seniority in employment does regulate promotions and discharges, and managements do as a result find themselves restricted in their capacity to regulate labour as a cost and output device.[50]

The industry's dependence on a mass of sub-contracting firms to accommodate the episodic surges and cutbacks in orders also suggests a classical dualisation of employment conditions and work roles; in this case, between a 'primary' labour force in the major corporations and 'prime' defence contractors on the one hand, and a secondary sector amongst the smaller sub-contractors.

But closer examination of Doeringer and Piore's seminal analysis of internal market processes suggests that the distinctions between individual and collective grievances and between work processes and employment terms may be far from watertight at crucial points along the frontier of control. Unions' pursuit of individual grievance cases to secure (formally or informally) redress on collective issues was pointed out in the discussion of legal constraints in the previous section. Doeringer and Piore noted a similar kind of check where management rearrangements of task specifications might trigger a blocking action by the unions. The formal-contractual grievances of individual workers whose seniority provisions were affected by the re-organisations of other jobs was taken as far as legal suits. It was also pointed out by these authors that bargaining to change the orderings of occupations for pay-rate purpose can feed back into the content of job re-design schemes which had originally given rise to the pay re-negotiation exercises.[51]

It should be recalled that the industry's product market instability and its over-commitment of capital and scientific manpower to research and development means that most work is in small batches of high quality components rather than longer runs of standardised items. This consideration accordingly limits the scope for production methods based on a routinised semi-skilled division of labour.

Managements seem to oscillate between different approaches to this skilled labour problem: hoarding it in their own plants when circumstances allow and sub-contracting to overcome shortages, while also sub-contracting to avoid extra recruitment and seeking some new production methods to allow capital substitution. In principle, automation of various small batch-production work tasks has been possible for several decades. The military have periodically tried to push the major corporations to develop and adopt different forms of this computerised equipment but the latter significantly, have often been unenthusiastic.[52]

The principal form of technological displacement of skill dependency is computerised design, planning and machinery. But the limitations of batch-size on scale-economies make conventional single purpose mechanical assembly and process technologies irrelevant. By displacing information processing and decision-making functions on multi-purpose machine tools from operators to computer programmers (and thence to computer records such as paper and magnetic tapes) it was anticipated that machine shop skill requirements would fall.[53]

Braverman, Edwards and Noble all describe the introduction of the pioneer technology in this category – numerical control of machine tools – as a means of simultaneously reducing the manual and calculational skills of machinists and putting more control over operations into the hands of planners and engineering managers. But against the 'deskilling strategy' interpretation is counter-evidence that the prime reason for introducing NC into the aircraft industries was the technical problems of machining in three or more axes in variable contours, a requirement set by the new metals and aerodynamic shapes of the jet planes that the military introduced after the Second World War. Whatever the intention there is a wide variety of evidence from America and Europe that the institutionalisation phase of NC usage has seen acknowledgments by managers of the need for the knowledge and experience of metal machining to be available when the NC machines are in operation.[54]

Heavy investment in automation machinery would anyway be inconsistent with the aerospace industry's circumspection over production capital. It is significant that NC was introduced (according to Noble's account) only because of the research patronage of the US Air Force (for the reasons just cited) and their direct financing of contractors' purchase cost. History is currently repeating itself with project ICAM (Integrated Computer Aided Manufacture). This scheme is promoted by the USAF to evolve and then disseminate a production system which links computer-aided design, computer-aided management (costing, planning and production scheduling) with Direct Numerical Control (centralised computing) of self-monitoring cells of NC machine tools (assisted by robots and automatic tool changing); this nourishes the technocratic vision of an unmanned factory.[55]

The future may therefore pose more fundamental problems requiring more radical union responses. But the recent past has shown that both informal and legal-contractual channels have helped to check the thrust of the 'technical controls' that managements have attempted. The focus of change remains in the last analysis not with corporate planners and (inter)national trade union officials but, as in Britain, down amongst the workshops and union locals. Some of the production constraints which confront managers on either the technical or manpower fronts work indirectly in unions' favour and, as suggested above, the labour relations' 'web of rules' sometimes can be manipulated to blunt changes.

The pressures mentioned above toward hoarding or recall arrangements of skilled labour maintain a constant core of experienced workers in the plants. Piore's evidence from several industrial processes in his 1960s studies showed how new work-techniques and equipment were accompanied by a maintenance of established wage rates rather than radically reduced ones. This was because older, more experienced, workers were allocated to the new tasks and equipment as a safety measure and in order to get the new processes operationalised as soon as possible.[56] Something similar seems to have happened with NC and the related technologies in aerospace machine shops. Less skilled labour was used and found wanting when it came to 'filling in' with metal machining savvy.[57]

Piore hints at the role of union policies in claiming new job responsibilities for established grades of labour. This is a long standing concern of unions in their attempts to combat the exercise of 'management rights' to determine new methods and uses of labour. Background documents going back to the early 1960s show how the electrical unions (paradoxically representing large numbers of machinists because of the single-union provisions of NLRA) fought in arbitration cases to get the then new NC operating jobs classified as at least equal in skill and responsibility to comparable conventional machining work. A review of current and recent IAM and United Auto Workers contract provisions also suggests the knock-on effects of the seniority strategy that was mentioned earlier.[58]

Bargaining contracts minutely list hundreds of job grades and often the duties associated with them. These listings are for the purpose of preserving rights to job security, promotion prospects and pay preservation. When 'new' jobs are instituted or old ones replaced as a result of technical or organisational changes, unions can exploit the mandatory and contract-guaranteed rights to individual job security and seniority by bargaining for the new job as the preserve of an existing grade – and of course one of at least equal pay. Since these will be claimed to concern skill levels, the more experienced worker may be retained. These notional skills may later be realised into practised skills as the worker engages in his own private battles to exercise them in a new context.[59] British machinists struggled for control of such jobs on the basis of devolved bargaining at shop level and through the exercise of craft principles of skilled job preservation and control over the tools. American unionists pursue a similar goal by a more formal, but indirect route; though legalistic and normative discourse presumes that workshop-level controls are outside their jurisdiction.

Finally let us briefly consider the sub-contracting strategy by which managers may seek to evade their own shortcomings in terms of either productive capacity or shortages of suitably skilled workers. The immediate advantages to the management of the large 'prime contractor' firms are profit-margin improvements. In theory the Department of Defense can regulate the financial relationships between different levels of contractor, and will certainly provide government inspectors to check on quality and technical specifications. But in practice the 'primes' can exercise dictatorial powers over the smaller sub-contractors.

Cost over-runs may not be accepted by the prime contractor though he will normally gain compensation from the defence agencies for his cost increases. Sub-contractors' delays may be penalised. Safe in the knowledge that the sub-contractor may have become over-dependent on the same type of orders from one prime, sub-standard work can be rejected and the prime can try to impose minor changes on the sub-contractor for no extra price increase. (Perhaps aware of the enjoyment of these kinds of benefits by their American competitors, Rolls-Royce has recently announced (seemingly with Parliamentary approval) that it will contract out as much as possible of its short-run machining requirements.)[60] When orders slump and trade is reduced the prime can maintain his own turnover by bringing back production to his own plants securing the jobs and future availability of core workers. But this exercise of naked market power, and the semi-political jurisdiction that goes with it because of the defence contract's delegation of powers to the prime contractor (e.g. perpetual access to jigs and fixtures that are loaned for the purpose of the sub-contract) can have, and has had, deteriorating effects upon the structure of the major firms' business environment.

Sub-contractors may get dependent on the primes but the latter may also get 'locked in' to a relationship with particular sub-contractors, especially in a slump with sub-contractors going out of business, and alternative candidates may not be available. Further, the quality priorities in defence work limit the number of suitable suppliers. The search costs of finding alternatives may be excessive in a contracting market and the 'education' of the sub-contract in desired levels of quality and precision may take an excessively long time. Finally, the main firm may neglect to inquire too carefully into the sub's methods of producing a certain part. The sub-contractor may deviate from the original plans in order to make a job economical, or in order to achieve a better resolution of a design specification. Cancelling the sub-contract will then leave the prime at the bottom of a long and inconvenient learning curve for reproducing the products' desired qualities.[61] It may therefore be misleading to characterise this segmentation of production in terms of a simplistic dualism.

Some sub-contracting takes place amongst and between plants of the major corporations in order to 'fill in' spare capacity, or because government contracts specify who the principal sub-contractors should be. Those arrangements place another limit on the concentration of production work in large plants and add to the heterogeneity or 'mish mash' character of work on the shop floor. However even many of the smaller sub-contractors are reliant upon sophisticated machine tools and are held to the ubiquitous quality requirements (Department of Defense 'registered' sub-contractors have Federal inspectors permanently assigned to their shop). These may pressure the shop owner/manager to train up his workforce to higher level of skills, while the recurrent tightening of the labour market for experienced workers maintains some pay rates, at, or about, union rates even amongst non-unionised sub-contractors.

Generalised sub-contracting can also turn out to have unfortunate implications for the primes' management's relations with their own workers. On the upswings of an aerospace demand cycle competition for labour gets acute. A main contractor may find himself in competition with his sub-contractor for scarce labour; perhaps defeating the very reason the job was sub-contracted in the first place (i.e. the sub's access to appropriate labour). Where sub-contractors are unionised then, as in other industries, strikes in the suppliers put the major contract at risk but more so because of 'over-run' penalties. Sub-contracting may antagonise the unions at the main plant who, though they may not be in a position to damage the practice, may look for an alternative issue as compensation.

More recently, and especially in the engine sector (with its large numbers of machined components), two alternative strategies to routine sub-contracting have been developed: overseas sub-contracts (to win favour in the eyes of foreign airline customers on some occasion) and 'parallel production' facilities, a replication or extension of the prime's own main establishments which has a related advantage as a hedge against labour conflicts amongst its own workforce (e.g. Pratt and Whitney with an old plant in Hartford, Connecticut and a new parallel facility in Maine).

Each of these strategies is inconsistent with conventional arguments for economic efficiencies through large-scale plant operation or comparative advantages in specialisation. The influences promoting them are in part a function of the politics of labour control. Managements are seeking to evade the strands of the 'web of rules' that may stick to them as well as to labour. At bottom however they (and the classic market conditions they engender in labour markets and sub-contract competition) are effects of the political strategies and administrative procedures by which the state's military and executive agents seek to engineer the semblance of a market-orientated industry. The resulting structure of enterprises suffers from over-capacity in its plants and under-capitalisation in its production processes. While it alternately clings on to its skilled workers and discharges them, labour markets remain volatile and the technological rationalisation of production is limited by the variability in volumes and products. The latter syndrome while stemming from the state-induced structure is complicated but not resolved by the resort to outside contracting. Last, but not least, state-sponsored labour-relations legislation which had a more general interest in view has created modes of bargaining and resistance whose effects upon work rationalisation schemes are as limiting (in their own way) as job-control based on shop floor bargaining.

Conclusion

The political and product market conditions of production organisation and job controls in aerospace cannot be claimed as universal. But some aspects of these conditions are present in several other industries. Objectives such as quality in short runs of components and the completion of final assembly operations to specific times may (perhaps increasingly in the advanced economies) reduce the importance of price considerations.[62] The state also plays a significant role in other industries; as a major purchaser and as a coordinator and/or administrator of enterprise structure, product characteristics and process innovations. The market economists' dream of an industrial world in which the state is permanently excluded from all of these activities would require a transformation that is more fantastic than the social changes envisaged by Marxists. In many respects the economic decisions of state agencies are as inseparable from those industrial market structures where politics are employed to maintain autonomous commercial processes as where they are used to directly administer or control business. This much is clear from the different patterns of industrial development in aerospace as between Britain and America.

The broader economic performance of an industry may be reduced by the workers' organised controls over employment and work practices. This question has been deliberately left open here. What the preceding analysis has tried to suggest is that the British institutions of shop floor bargaining and craft style union tactics may not be the only relevant source of these controls. The lesson for Britain seems to be that greater industrial efficiency, to the extent that it is related to such practices, may not follow from tighter legal specification of bargaining procedures and agreements, nor from related administrative regulation. This thesis might already have been verified in practice if the 1971 Industrial Relations Act had ever been put into full operation.

The crucial factors affecting the influence of legal regulation on job control in America are: the tactics and strategies of unions which often span different industries, the philosophies and decisions of legal practitioners and the structure and processes of the arbitrating institutions. While the precise influence of all of these factors taken together varies according to the particular industrial environment at any specific time, there is no reason to suppose that job control is drastically higher or lower in aerospace than in other cases since their presence is general throughout most of the economy.

The more general lesson therefore seems to be that the pressure from workers for job control is ubiquitous and will find some expression whatever the form of the institutions for regulating its pursuit between managements and unions. What is more the combined influence of the state in the spheres of legal regulation of bargaining and administration of business and product market structures may influence the processes by which wage-labour is divided and controlled at work in ways which are, as yet, imperfectly understood even by the most critical theories.

The state's effects in both the legal regulation of collective bargaining and in the administration of the economic environment may be both unanticipated and equivocal in relation to the interests of labour and capital. This conclusion suggests that political evaluation of the state's involvement in either of these spheres as necessarily either unwarranted or partisan ought to be held in check. A more equitable and productive exercise of power by the contestants in the workplace might follow if all of the potential consequences of state involvement were first of all clarified and acknowledged.

NOTES

1 This article derives from fieldwork conducted in the USA thanks to financing from the Nuffield Foundation, and in Britain on the basis of a Social Science Research Council grant. I also wish to thank Steve Early, Frank Emspak, Charles Ferguson, Maryellen Kelly, Henry Knorr, Charles Sabel, Paul Schrade and officers and numerous local representatives of the United Automobile Workers and International Association of Machinists for help at various stages of the American fieldwork. Steve Tolliday and Jonathan Zeitlin gave valuable help in the revision of the original paper.

2 The impact of current economic and industrial relations changes on the 'frontier' of job control in British industry and its significance for relevant theories is discussed in M. J. Rose and B. Jones, 'Management Strategy and Trade Union Response in Plant-level Work Re-organisation Schemes' in D. Knight and H. Wilmott (eds.), *Job Re-Design* (London, forthcoming).

3 For the view from the right, see F. A. Hayek, *1980s Unemployment and The Unions* (London, Institute for Economic Affairs, Hobart Paper 87, 1980); and from the left, see R. Hyman and T. Elger, 'Job Controls, the Employers' Offensive and Alternative Strategies', *Capital and Class*, 15 (1981), pp. 115–49.

4 Cf. H. Beynon, *Working for Ford* (London, 1973), especially ch. 8; also R. Hyman, *Marxism and The Sociology of Trade Unions* (London, 1971), p. 32; and *idem, Industrial Relations: A Marxist Introduction* (London, 1975), ch. 6.

5 The Institute for Economic Affairs constitutes the major source and forum for these ideas in Britain. Cf. *inter alia*, A. Seldon, *Corrigible Capitalism, Incorrigible Socialism* (London, 1980) and S. C. Littlechild, *et al., The Taming of Government* (London, IEA Readings 21, 1979).

6 See, for example, J. Holloway and S. Picciotto, 'Capital, Crisis and the

State', *Capital and Class*, 2 (1973), pp. 76–79; and I. Gough, 'State Expenditure in Advanced Capitalism', *New Left Review*, 92 (1975), pp. 80–92.

7 From a Marxist perspective, see D. Strinati, 'Capitalism, The State and Industrial Relations' in C. Crouch (ed.), *State and Economy in Contemporary Capitalism* (London, 1979); and for a pluralist view, A. Flanders, *Collective Bargaining: Prescription For Change* (London, 1967), pp. 34–50.

8 H. Braverman, *Labor and Monopoly Capital* (New York, 1974); A Zimbalist (ed.), *Case Studies in the Labor Process* (New York, 1979); R. C. Edwards, *Contested Terrain: The Transformation of the Work Place in the Twentieth Century* (New York, 1979); and D. M. Gordon, R. C. Edwards and M. Reich, *Segmented Work, Divided Workers* (Cambridge, 1982).

9 Amongst the many criticisms of the claims arising from the labour process conception of work organisation, see S. Wood (ed.), *The Degradation of Work? Skill, Deskilling and the Labour Process* (London, 1982); and C. Sabel, *Work and Politics* (Cambridge, 1982), pp. 37–70. For the 'functional' view of the state cf. Braverman, *Labor and Monopoly Capital*, pp. 284, *et seq.*

10 For a discussion of the limitations of neo-classical concepts for analysis of production see J. Elster, *Explaining Technical Change* (Cambridge, 1983), ch. 4.

11 See the essay by Howell Harris in this volume.

12 K. Hartley, 'The Mergers in the UK Aerospace Industry 1951–1960', *Journal of the Royal Aeronautical Society* 69, (1965), p. 851. G. R. Simonsen (ed.), *The History of the American Aircraft Industry* (Cambridge, Mass., 1968), ch. 9.

13 Corporate composition compiled from H. L. Butler, G. J. Podrasky and J. Devon Allen, 'The Aerospace Industry Revisted', *Financial Analysis Journal*, (August, 1977), pp. 22–67. Employment figures from B. Bluestone, P. Jordan and M. Sullivan, *Aircraft Industry Dynamics: An Analysis of Competition, Capital, and Labor* (Boston, Mass., 1981), pp. 34, 42.

14 J. B. Rae, *Climb to Greatness: The American Aircraft Industry 1920–1960* (Cambridge, Mass., 1968), pp. 39–57. J. S. Gansler, *The Defense Industry* (Cambridge, Mass., 1980).

15 Bluestone *et al.*, *Aircraft Industry Dynamics*, pp. 21–2, 40–1.

16 D. C. Mowery and J. Rosenberg, 'The Commercial Aircraft Industry' in R. R. Nelson (ed.), *Government and Technical Progress* (New York, 1982), pp. 140–4.

17 Gansler, *The Defense Industry*, pp. 103, 136, claims that vertical integration has increased in recent years. But this concentration appears to be mainly due to the need for access to the new avionics technology and to the demise of many of the sub-contracting firms.

18 *Ibid.*, p. 75.

19 *Ibid.*, pp. 84, 172–3.

20 UK Government, Department of Trade and Industry, *Rolls-Royce and*

the RB 211 Aero Engine (London, HMSO, Cmnd. 4860, 1972), p. 19.
21 Bluestone *et al.*, *Aircraft Industry Dynamics*, p. 9.
22 J. R. Kurth, 'Aerospace Production Lines and American Defense Spending', in R. G. Head and E. J. Rokke (eds.), *American Defense Policy* (Baltimore/London, 1973); US Congress Joint Committee on American Defense Production, *Testimony on American Defense Production*, (Washington DC, 1972), pp. 63–90.
23 F. M. Scherer, 'The Aerospace Industry', in W. Adams (ed.), *The Structure of American Industry* (New York/London, 1971), p. 364; Gansler, *The Defense Industry*, p. 74.
24 Gansler, *The Defense Industry*, ch. 6.
25 Scherer, 'The Aerospace Industry', pp. 367–8.
26 S. Young with A. V. Lowe, *Intervention in the Mixed Economy* (London, 1974).
27 Hartley, 'The Mergers in the UK Aerospace Industry', p. 846.
28 *Ibid.*; UK Government, Committee of Inquiry into the Aircraft Industry (Plowden) *Report* (London, HMSO, Cmnd. 2843, 1965), pp. 75–9; D. F. Channon, *The Strategy and Structure of British Enterprise* (London, 1973), p. 113; R. Loveridge, 'Business Strategy and Community Culture: Manpower Policy as a Structured Accommodation to Conflict', in D. Dunkerley and G. Salaman (eds.), *International Yearbook of Organisational Studies* (London, 1982).
29 UK Government, *Rolls-Royce*, p. 20.
30 M. R. Garner, 'British Airways and British Aerospace: Limbo for Two Enterprises', *Public Administration* 58 (Spring, 1980), pp. 13–24.
31 For Rolls-Royce, cf. *Business Week*, 31 August 1981, p. 62, *Financial Times*, 23 June 1982, p. 12, *ibid.*, 7 May 1982, p. 113, and 19 April 1983, p. 25. The more general pressures of the recession are however now forcing British Aerospace into plant rationalisations: cf. *Financial Times*, 26 May 1982.
32 *Aviation Week and Space Technology*, 26 January 1981, pp. 65–6; J. G. Milliken and E. J. Morrison, 'Management Methods from Aerospace', *Harvard Business Review* (March/April, 1973) pp. 6–10, 14–16, 19–22, 158–63; K. B. Zandin, 'Productivity Cost Effectiveness and Compliance: Three Keys to Success for Aerospace Companies', *Institute of Industrial Engineers Annual Conference Proceedings* (Fall, 1980), pp. 470–4; R. J. Thayer, 'Organisational Structures used in Software Development by the US Aerospace Industry', *Journal of Systems and Software*, 4 (1980), pp. 283–97.
33 See Milliken and Morrison, 'Management Methods'.
34 See S. Qualtrough and J. Jablonowski, 'Filling the Need for Skilled Workers', *American Machinist* (Special Report), 712 (June, 1979), pp. 131–46, for USA. For UK see: Engineering Industry Training Board, *The Craftsman in Engineering: an Interim Report* (Watford, Herts., 1975) and National Economic Development Office, *Engineering Craftsmen, Shortages and Related Problems* (London, 1977).
35 K. Klare, 'Judicial De-radicalization of the Wagner Act and the Origins of Modern Legal Consciousness, 1937–44', *Minnesota Law Review* 62

(1978), pp. 265–339. For assessments which suggest various degrees of union restrictions of 'management rights' and the commercial authenticity of the latter see *inter alia*, F. Meyers, *The Ownership of Jobs: A Comparative Study* (University of California, Los Angeles, Institute of Industrial Relations, Monograph No. 11, (1964); D. Lewin, 'The Impact of Unionism on American Business. Evidence of An Assessment', *Columbia Journal of World Business* (Winter, 1978), pp. 89–103; D. E. Cullen and M. L. Greenbaum, *Management Rights and Collective Bargaining. Can Both Survive?* (Cornell University, New York State School for Industrial and Labour Relations, Bulletin 58, 1966); M. K. Chandler, *Management Rights and Union Interests* (New York, 1964).

36 For a review and critique of this literature see S. Tolliday and J. Zeitlin, 'Shop Floor Bargaining, Contract Unionism and Job Control: An Anglo–American Comparison', in N. Lichtenstein and S. Meyer (eds.), *The American Automobile Industry: A Social History* (Champaign–Urbana, Illinois, forthcoming, 1985).

37 The structure of bargaining up to the 1960s is described in the Report of the Royal Commission on Trade Unions and Employers Associations 1965–1968 Cmnd. 3623 (London: HMSO, 1968), pp. 12–37; for recent developments see W. Brown (ed.), *The Changing Contours of British Industrial Relations. A Survey of Manufacturing Industry* (Oxford: 1981).

38 See B. Jones, 'Destruction or Redistribution of Engineering Skills? The Case of Numerical Control', in S. Wood (ed.), *The Degradation of Work?* pp. 196–200; and 'The Definition and Control of Occupational Tasks in The Process of Technological Change', *Final Report to Social Science Research Council*, (Boston Spa, Lincs., 1979) pp. 29–33.

39 H. H. Wellington, *Labor and The Legal Process* (New Haven, Conn., 1968), pp. 68–71, 73–6.

40 *Ibid.*, pp. 62–5.

41 D. Brody, *Workers in Industrial America* (New York, 1980), p. 206.

42 Wellington, *Labor and The Legal Process*, pp. 62–5.

43 Meyers, *The Ownership of Jobs*, pp. 10–11.

44 See J. W. Kuhn, 'Electrical Products', in G. G. Somers (ed.) *Collective Bargaining: Contemporary American Experience* (Madison, Wisconsin, 1979); for evidence of similar tactics by the steel and automobile unions cf R. Herding, *Job Control and Union Structure* (Rotterdam, 1972), pp. 185–6. A 1975 strike at General Electric over machinists' work assignments was entirely within the 'legal' provisions of the contract: see F. Kashner, 'A Rank and File Strike at G.E.', *Radical America*, 12 (November, 1978), pp. 43–60.

45 For a historical analysis of job control in the British engineering and printing industries see J. Zeitlin, 'Craft Control and The Division of Labour: Engineers and Compositors in Britain 1890–1930', *Cambridge Journal of Economics*, 3, 3 (1979) pp. 263–74.

46 Amongst British critiques of Braverman, see S. Wood (ed.), *The Degradation of Work?*

47 Cited in Zandin, 'Productivity, Cost Effectiveness and Compliance'.

48 See, for example, K. Hartley and P. A. Watt, 'Profit, Regulations and the U.K. Aerospace Industry', *Journal of Industrial Economics* 29, 4 (June 1981), pp. 413–28; and Gansler, *The Defence Industry.*

49 See S. Wood (ed.), *The Degradation of Work?* 'Introduction'; also W. Lazonick, 'Industrial Relations and Technical Change: The Case of the Self-Acting Mule', *Cambridge Journal of Economics*, 3, 3 (1979) pp. 231–62.

50 P. B. Doeringer and M. Piore, *Internal Labor Markets and Manpower Analysis* (Lexington, Mass., 1971) chs. 2–3; Edwards, Reich and Gordon, *Segmented Work*, pp. xii–xvii, 5–7; C. Kerr, *Labor Markets and Wage Determination. The Balkanisation of Labor Markets and Other Essays* (Berkeley, Ca., 1977), pp. 21–37 and on the early development of internal labour markets in the West Coast airframe industry in the 1940s, pp. 53–86.

51 Doeringer and Piore, *Internal Labour Markets*, pp. 100, 126.

52 See references in note 32 above; *Business Week*, 3 August, 1981, p. 61.

53 For the earlier NC developments, see D. F. Noble, 'Social Choice in Machine Design. The Case of Automatically Controlled Machine Tools, and a Challenge for Labor', *Politics and Society*, 8 (1978) pp. 331–2.

54 See Braverman, *Labor and Monopoly Capital*; Edwards, *Contested Terrain*, pp. 123–5. Noble, 'Social Choice in Machine Design'. For counter-argument and evidence, see Sabel, *Work and Politics*, pp. 63–70, and Jones, 'De-skilling or Redistribution of Skills?'.

55 N. E. Nilson, 'Integrating CAD and CAM – Future Directions', *Society of Mechanical Engineers*, Technical Paper, MS. 77–962 (1977), pp. 12, 17.

56 M. J. Piore, 'The Impact of the Labour Market upon the Design and Selection of Productive Techniques within the Plant', *Quarterly Journal of Economics*, 82, 4 (1968) pp. 435–49; Doeringer and Piore, *Internal Labor Markets*, pp. 126–8.

57 Interviews with various union representatives and production engineers and shop managers in West Coast airframe plants (B. Jones, 'Different National Constraints Upon New Production Technology', Report to Nuffield Foundation, University of Bath, 1982).

58 Contract provision linking technical change to seniority and job classification agreements can be found in recent major UAW and IAM agreements with McDonnell–Douglas, Lockheed and Pratt and Whitney, 1977–80.

59 M. Burawoy, *Manufacturing Consent* (Chicago/London, 1979).

60 *Financial Times*, 23 June, 1982, p. 12.

61 Interviews with sub-contractors and prime contractor managements 1981. C. Sabel and S. Brusco, 'Artisan Production and Economic Growth', in F. Wilkinson (ed.), *The Dynamics of Labour Market Segmentation* (New York, 1981).

62 C. Sabel, *Work and Politics*, ch. 5.

Index